LEADERS and PERSONALITIES of the Third Reich:

THEIR BIOGRAPHIES, PORTRAITS, AND AUTOGRAPHS

by
CHARLES HAMILTON

1st Edition

Copyright **1984**
by
CHARLES HAMILTON

ISBN No. 0-912138-27-0

Printed in the United States of America

Designed
by
Roger James Bender

Type Set
by
Clyborne Typographics

R. JAMES BENDER PUBLISHING
P.O. Box 23456, San Jose, Calif. 95153 (408) 225-5777

TABLE OF CONTENTS

To my daughter
CAROLYN BROOKS HAMILTON
who has the instincts of a true
chronicler and is fascinated by the
history of the Third Reich.

INTRODUCTION

Hitler was a Teutonic god run amuck. No man was ever more worshipped or more hated. He was the flawless nihilist. His philosophy was to conquer and destroy, then rebuild. His soldiers were men of Krupp steel. Hard, bold, loyal. Not even the Spartans, not even the ancient Romans were their fighting equals. The Nazis were almost, but not quite, invincible. Almost, but not quite, the Master Race.

The ancient world that Alexander the Great conquered could be swallowed up unnoticed in the vastness of the Fuehrer's mighty domain. The nations Hitler could not seduce with clever lies he battered into submission with *Panzers* and *Stukas*. His armies rumbled over Europe, knocking out kingdoms and devouring republics.

Some of Hitler's cohorts were henchmen without morals. They drenched the paths of glory with blood. They dotted Germany and Poland with labor camps and death camps and turned the swastika into a symbol of horror. They are the tyrants we will not and dare not forget.

Hitler commanded the world's mightiest legions. His warriors held great nocturnal rallies lit up by flaming torches. They unfurled huge swastika banners. They swore eternal allegiance to a Fuehrer who promised them a brave new world ruled by Nazi supermen. A Reich that would last a thousand years.

The flames that Hitler lit got out of control. They swept back upon him and decimated his armies. They burned his great cities. In the end Hitler was destroyed by his insane belief that the Germanic race was superior to all others. His twelve years of glory and conquest crumbled away in the smoking rubble of Berlin.

Today, four decades later, nearly all traces of Hitler's Europe are vanished. But in the history books his goose-stepping troops continue to march. There is no era in man's vainglorious past that is more intriguing--and more frightening--than Hitler's dozen years of power. He and the men who fought with him and against him spellbind each new generation.

Here in this volume I have gathered the signatures and scripts of nearly three hundred leaders of the Third Reich. The pages devoted to Hitler alone constitute a complete monograph on his handwriting and on his career as an artist. The chirography of other leaders is enlivened with hundreds of rare photographs, many never before published. A running text illumines the life of each personality.

This book will, I hope, provide a feast of information and a reservoir of aid for historians, scholars, collectors, students, and for all who are fascinated by the most flamboyant, mysterious and fearsome empire in history.

BOOKS BY CHARLES HAMILTON

Cry of the Thunderbird (1950)
Men of the Underworld (1952)
Braddock's Defeat (1959)
Collecting Autographs and Manuscripts (1961)
Lincoln in Photographs (with Lloyd Ostendorf, 1963)
The Robot That Helped to Make a President (1965)
Scribblers and Scoundrels (1968)
Big Name Hunting (with Diane Hamilton, 1973)
The Book of Autographs (1978)
The Signature of America (1979)
Great Forgers and Famous Fakes (1980)
Auction Madness (1981)
American Autographs (1983)
Leaders of the Third Reich (1984)

The first 500 copies of the First Edition are serial numbered. This collector's volume is No. _45_ .

Photograph of Hitler, inscribed and signed, Munich, February 24, 1939.

Hitler's Handwriting

ADOLF HITLER (1889-1945)

It was the summer of 1936 and the shadow of the swastika was spreading over Europe. I sat in my living room with a young lady friend, a very pretty Jewish girl who spoke German fluently. We listened as the radio carried Hitler's latest harangue around the world.

The anger and force in Hitler's voice finally reached a frenetic climax. I watched a look of horror creep over the face of my companion. Her lips parted slightly and her blue eyes opened wide in fear as she listened raptly to the Fuehrer's concluding words. Suddenly she turned to me, grasped my arm and whispered: "My God! He almost makes me hate the Jews!"

Hitler was perhaps the greatest orator of all time. Unlike Demosthenes and Cicero, who made their appeals from a tiny stage to small audiences, mostly legislators, or Patrick Henry, who addressed his immortal words about liberty to the tiny Virginia House of Burgesses, Hitler molded the opinions of a mighty nation and led its people into a maelstrom of folly and destruction.

Hitler's voice was ringing and clear, his sentences brief and very vigorous. He often spoke entirely without notes, drawing his power from spontaneous inspiration. His eyes had a fierce, hypnotic quality. Those who met him face to face were captivated by his gaze. My friend, the late George Sylvester Viereck, a poet and author who knew Hitler and was illegally imprisoned as a Nazi agent during World War II, told me: "Hitler's eyes were dark and penetrating, truly gripping, but his thoughts were not lucid." Albert Speer, the architect, described the Fuehrer as "hypnotic, pedantic, petty, illogical and irrational." Mussolini, who knew Hitler well and feared him, was no doubt motivated by envy when he observed privately: "He's quite mad. A silly little clown."

Hitler was born in Braunau, Upper Austria, on April 20, 1889. At nine he became a choir boy in the Catholic church at Lambach. Years later he claimed that he developed his great vocal power while singing hymns. Hitler was a brilliant but lazy and rebellious student. Because of his talent at drawing, he decided on a career in art. But he did not overlook his oratorical rehearsals. His close boyhood friend, August Kubizek, recalled young Adolf practicing elocution in an open field.

In 1907 Hitler moved to Vienna with the hope of getting into the Academy of Arts or the School of Architecture. His failure in the entrance examinations changed the course of history.

During World War I Hitler served as a dispatch carrier. He was twice wounded and once gassed. In 1914 he won the Iron Cross (Second Class) and in 1918, the coveted Iron Cross (First Class), an unusually high award for an enlisted man. The act of heroism for which he received this medal is not known, but apparently he captured an enemy officer and about a dozen soldiers. This second award, with his wound badge and Nazi Party badge, were the only medals he ever wore, a stark contrast to Hermann Goering, whose massive chest almost collapsed under the weight of bejewelled decorations.

In 1919 Hitler joined the German Workers' Party, which he soon took over. Hitler rose to power in the beaten and hungry Germany of the postwar years. In 1922 he got the support of General Ludendorff. In 1923 he was arrested and imprisoned for nine months after the unsuccessful Beer-Hall Putsch in Munich. While in prison he dictated *Mein Kampf* to his secretary, Rudolf Hess. In 1932 Hitler was defeated by Hindenburg in the presidential election, but in the following year he was named chancellor by Hindenburg. On the death of Hindenburg in 1934 Hitler merged the powers of president and chancellor and took the title of "Der Fuehrer."

In quick succession the new Fuehrer put into effect a ruthless anti-Semitic policy, broke the Treaty of Versailles, rearmed Germany, and inaugurated a series of bloodless conquests. His invasion of Poland in 1939 touched off a world war that ended in May 1945, a week after Hitler, his armies totally defeated and his country in ruins, shot himself in a Berlin bunker.

If Plutarch were alive today and writing his parallel lives, would he write parallel lives of Hitler and Attila or perhaps Hitler and Genghis Khan? I think not. Attila and Genghis Khan were, it is true, ruthless conquerors, but there the similarity ends, for these early scourges were tactical geniuses and Hitler was not. He was an intuitive strategist who succeeded - and failed - with nothing more than mere "hunches."

I believe that Plutarch's choice for a parallel life would be Nero, the most notorious tyrant of antiquity. Nero rose to power by treachery and murder. Like Hitler, Nero was politically astute and vulgarly cultured. Nero wrote bad poetry by the quire and painted mediocre portraits. Hitler was an artist and an architect. Both dictators set great and infamous fires; Nero, the city of Rome and Hitler, the Reichstag, then put the blame on their enemies. Like Hitler, Nero corrupted those around him and murdered or forced the suicide or exile of those he could not debase.

Both men began their rules with popular reforms and with the building of beautiful edifices, but soon sank into degeneracy. Nero persecuted Jews and Christians alike, but virtually all the Christians he executed were converted Jews.

After his former counselor, Seneca, took part in a plot to slay him, Nero ordered Seneca to commit suicide. After the failure of the bomb plot on July 20, 1944 to murder him, Hitler forced Field Marshal Erwin Rommel to take poison.

When his army was in revolt and his empire finally collapsed around him, Nero took his own life. Hitler also killed himself under similar circumstances.

So striking is the similarity between the careers of these two tyrants that, if you believe in reincarnation, you can have little doubt that Nero returned to life after nearly twenty centuries minus his effeminate curled hair but with many of his effete mannerisms to which he added an insolent little moustache.

Such is the mystique surrounding Hitler that his personal relics and autographs are eagerly sought and fetch enormous prices.

THE DEVELOPMENT OF HITLER'S HANDWRITING

The S.S. Lejeune pitched and rolled on its homeward voyage from Brest, France, to the United States early in October 1945. The ship carried a cargo of war veterans slated for discharge. I stood at the rail chatting with an infantry corporal.

"Are you taking home any souvenirs, sergeant?" he asked.

"Not a one," I said. "I'm grateful to have my own whole skin to take home."

"I've got a dufflebag full. Helmets, insignia, daggers. You name it, I've got it."

"Any signed documents?"

"Funny you should ask. I had a whole packet of letters written by Hitler in 1919 to a friend, some innkeeper who put Hitler up when he was broke. The

These dramatic photographs of Hitler in action, taken by F. Bauer of Munich and personally signed in pencil by the photographer, are from the private collection of Heinrich Himmler and are believed to be unpublished.

Hitler's oratorical gestures were the result of careful practice in front of the mirror. The Fuehrer studied for years to create the impression of spontaneity.

guy was scared to keep them so he gave them to me. But it was the helmets or Hitler, so I pitched the letters in a garbage can."

The wanton destruction of historic documents always infuriates me. I walked away from the corporal after dropping the brusque comment: "You threw out a fortune. Your Hitler letters were worth thousands of dollars."

Early letters of Hitler are very rare. Penned in a clear, readable script, with occasional misspellings and grammatical errors, they recount his early struggles and triumphs. Relatively abundant, but still of great scarcity, are letters from the years of his rise to power, 1924 to 1932. Anything handwritten after 1933 while Hitler was Fuehrer is almost impossible to find, since even his most intimate correspondence was usually dictated to a secretary.

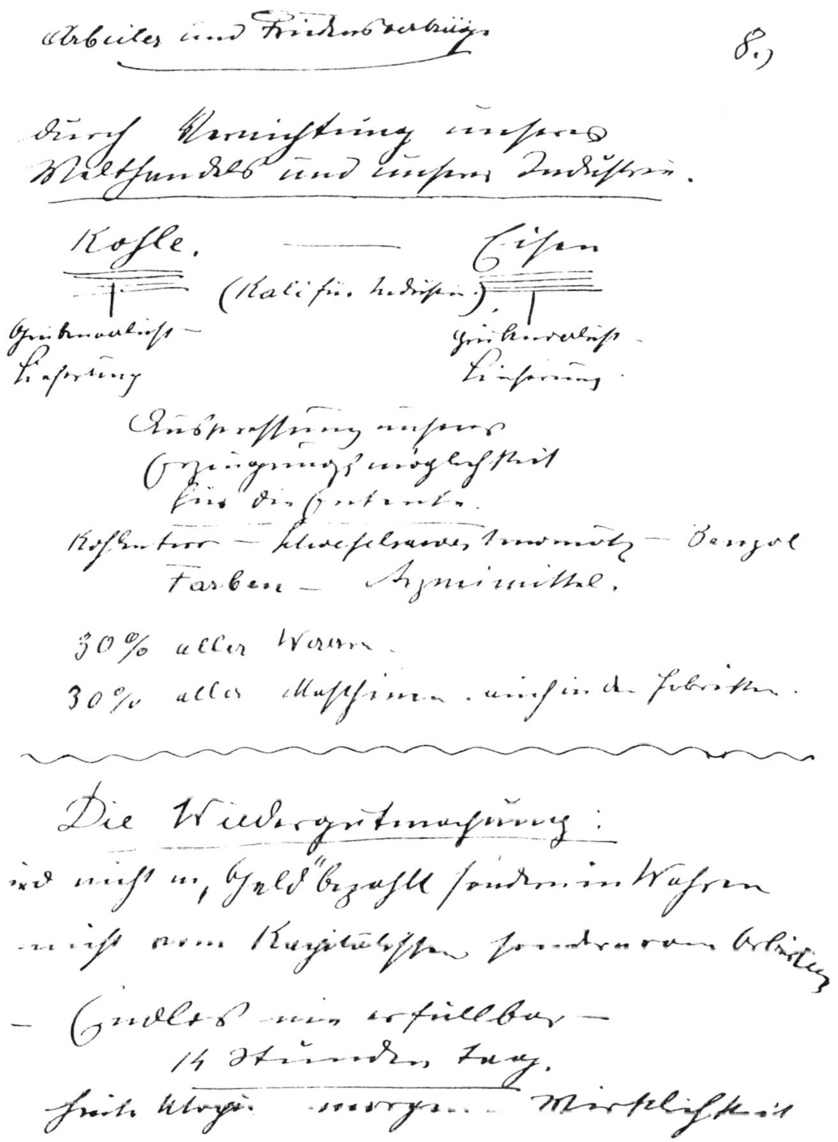

Arbeiter und Frontkrieger 8.)

2.) durch Vernichtung unseres Welthandels und unserer Industrie.

Kohle. —— Eisen

(Kali für Industrie).

Ausschaltung unserer Erzeugungsmöglichkeit für die Entente.

Kohlenteer — Schwefelsaures Ammoniak — Benzol

Farben — Arzneimittel.

30% aller Waren.

30% aller Maschinen ... in den Fabriken.

Die Wiedergutmachung:

wird nicht in „Geld" bezahlt sondern in Waren

nicht vom Kapitalisten sondern vom Arbeiter

— Endlos unerfüllbar —

14 Stunden Tag.

heute Utopie morgen Wirklichkeit

Holograph notes for a speech. Hitler condemns the Treaty of Versailles and the international attacks on Germany. The Fuehrer's handwriting is swift and tumultuous. The inspired madness tumbles out in such profusion that Hitler can hardly record his angry accusations. But there is not a word blotted out. Not a single correction. The torrent of wild emotion is interruped only by savage underscorings.

The world-famous graphologist, Marie Bernard, says of Hitler's handwriting: "These notes of a speech reflect in irridescent colors Hitler's oratory performance. The enormous intensity is recognizable in the lyrical d's, the refined strokes with the needle-like sharpness changing abruptly to a pastose [heavy] pressure stroke. The writing seems hectic, constantly wavering, changing its musical rising from crescendo to decrescendo, from loud to gentle, embedded in a passionate current of emotions, fits of fury and despair, cunning knowledge of the human mind, interwoven with violent outbursts of moods. A spiritual enthusiasm seems to have seized the script, thrown on the paper impatiently, driven by irrational powers."

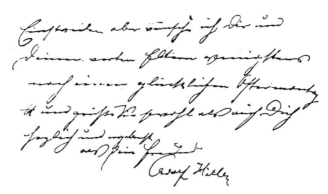

Hitler, age 19 (April 1908), sending his regrets to a friend.

As a soldier (1915), Hitler writes a neat hand and reveals the philosophy of his maturity: "Victory is not as important as it is to get rid of internationalism."

[handwritten letter in German script]

Hitler, age 19, the conclusion of a friendly letter.

Hitler in 1916, during his recuperation in a field hospital in Beelitz after being wounded by shrapnel.

Hitler sends birthday flowers from Bayreuth (1925) to a lady friend. Signed in full on the front of the card with a lengthy greeting on verso (pictured at bottom), bearing his nickname "Wolf."

16

A friendly note from Landsburg Prison (April 10, 1924) where Hitler was incarcerated after the unsuccessful Beer-Hall Putsch.

Last page of a letter written in 1925, noting that "our fight must continue."   17

Herrn

Hermann Fobke

In Erinnerung an die gemeinsame

Festungshaft

herzlichst zugeeignet

Adolf Hitler

München, Weihnachten 1925

18/Jan. 1929.

AH

Lieber Vater Fegg!

Soeben erfahre und lese ich
vom Tode Ihrer lieben Frau. Außer-
dem erzählt mir Hanke. Schaub
daß Sie auch Ihr Tochter verloren
haben. Zu diesem großen Unglück
lieber Fegg nehmen Sie auch meine
allerherzlichste und aufrichtige
Beileidsbezeugung entgegen.
Ich fühle mit Ihnen.

In aufrichtigem
Mitleid

Ihr

Adolf Hitler

18

Inscription in a first edition of *Mein Kampf*, Munich, 1925, to Hermann Fobke, a member of "Stosstrupp Hitler" who was in prison at Landsberg am Lech with Hitler. He was deputy Gauleiter of Hannover-South from 1925 to 1928.

Hitler sends his housekeeper her salary, February 2, 1932.

A brief note to Alfred Rosenberg, refusing to accept his resignation as foreign policy expert.

A letter of condolence to an old friend, January 18, 1929.

Adolf Hitler   Berlin, den 20.2.1933.

Lieber Weiss Jackl !

        Herzlichen Dank für Deinen Glück-
wunsch. Ich freue mich besonders über die
Anteilnahme meiner alten Kameraden.

                In alter Erinnerung

Herrn Jakob Weiss,
Abens/Hallertau.

                    _____

Der Führer und Reichskanzler   Berlin, den 30. Juni 1937.

                Sehr geehrter Herr Professor!

        Durch Vermittlung des Herrn Ministerialrats
Karl Hagmüller in Wien erhielt ich heute Ihr Schreiben
vom 4.Juni mit Ihrem Lichtbild aus dem Jahre 1900, also
aus der Zeit, da Sie mein Lehrer waren. Ich habe mich
über Ihre Zeilen wie über die wohlgelungene Photographie
aufrichtig gefreut und sage Ihnen in Erinnerung an diese
Jahre herzlichen Dank dafür. Ich freue mich zu hören,
dass Sie trotz hohen Alters gesund und rüstig sind, und
wünsche, dass Ihnen diese gute Gesundheit auch fernerhin
erhalten bleibe.

        Mit freundlichen Grüssen verbleibe ich
            Ihr ergebener

Letter of thanks to an old comrade, Berlin, February 20, 1933.

Concluding page of the last will and testament of Hitler, Berlin, May 2, 1938. Compare the bold signature on this document with the cramped, furtive signature on the will dictated only a few hours before his suicide (April 29, 1945).

The busy dictator thanks his former history teacher, Professor Dr. Leopold Poetsch, for sending him a photograph, Berlin, June 30, 1937.

der 2. und 4. Armee als Aussenstelle OKH/ Gen.Qu.
Meldungen sind durch die Aussenstelle wie bisher
von der Heeresgruppe an OKH/Gen.Qu zu geben.
Zuweisungen an die Armeen befiehlt OKH/Gen.Qu.
Die Verteilung im einzelnen nimmt nach diesen
Weisungen Aussenstelle OKH/Gen.Qu. vor.

Personelle Verringerung der bisherigen
O.Qu. Abteilung der Heeresgruppe auf das unbedingt nötige Mindestmaß ist erforderlich. Die
Vorschläge sind durch Obkdo. Heeresgruppe um-
gehend vorzulegen.

Der F ü h r e r

OKH/GenStdH/Op Abt (roem.1a)
   Nr.   /45 g.Kdos.Chefs.
      31.3.45

Last page of a military directive issued by Hitler from his Berlin bunker, March 31, 1945, signed in blue pencil. His signature is much deteriorated.

After the July 20 bomb plot, Hitler's signature started to deteriorate and his physical appearance and health changed markedly. He became, in fact, an old man.

Vor allem verpflichte ich die Führung der
Nation und die Gefolgschaft zur peinlichen Ein-
haltung der Rassegesetze und zum unbarmherzigen
Widerstand gegen den Weltvergifter aller Völker,
das internationale Judentum.

Gegeben zu Berlin, den 29. April 1945, 4.00 Uhr.

Last page of Hitler's political testament, signed only a few hours before his
suicide, in which he urges that the fight against the Jews continue "without
mercy," Berlin, April 29, 1945. Also signed in the lower left as witnesses by Dr.
Joseph Goebbels and Martin Bormann, and in the lower right by Generals
Wilhelm Burgdorf and Hans Krebs.

Belgium Army Museum

Willi Johannmeyer, who was attached
to the office of the Wehrmacht's adjutant to the Fuehrer from November
1944 and was Hitler's army adjutant
from April 2, 1945, left the Fuehrer
bunker on April 29, 1945 carrying a
copy of Hitler's political testament addressed to Field Marshal Schoerner.
Johannmeyer was not able to reach him,
however, and buried the document in
the back garden of his family home in
Iserlohn. He died on April 14, 1970 in
Frankfurt am Main.

23

Der Oberbürgermeister
der Reichshauptstadt

Vor dem Oberbürgermeister der Reichshauptstadt Berlin als
Standesbeamten von Berlin oder vor dem *Walter Wagner*

als Standesbeamten der Reichshauptstadt, vom Oberbürgermeister
beauftragt - sind zum Zwecke der sofortigen Eheschließung erschie-
nen

1. *Adolf Hitler*
geb. 20.
wohnhaft: *Berlin, Reichskanzlei*
Vater:
Mutter:
Eheschließung der Eltern:
ausgewiesen durch:

2. *Fräulein Eva Braun*
geb.   in
wohnhaft:
Vater:
Mutter:
Eheschließung der Eltern:
ausgewiesen durch:

3.
als Zeuge: *Goebbels, Joseph*
geb.
wohnhaft: *Göringerstr. 20*
ausgewiesen durch:

4.
als Zeuge: *Martin Bormann*
geb. 17.6.00   in *Halberstadt*
wohnhaft: *Heiligberg*
ausgewiesen durch:

The original marriage contract between Adolf Hitler and Eva Braun, April 29, 1945. The bride and groom both declared that they were of pure Aryan descent and that there were no hereditary impediments to their marriage. Both signed at the conclusion of this extraordinary, much blotted document. Their smudged signatures were witnessed by Dr. Joseph Goebbels and Martin Bormann, as well as an amazed municipal councilor, one Walter Wagner, who had been recruited by Goebbels from a nearby fighting unit to perform the ceremony.

Die Erschienenen zu 1 und 2 erklären, daß sie rein
arischer Abstammung und mit keiner die Eheschließung aus-
schließenden Erbkrankheiten befallen sind. Sie beantragen
mit Rücksicht auf die Kriegsereignisse wegen außerordentlicher
Umstände die Kriegstrauung und beantragen weiter das Aufgebot
mündlich entgegenzunehmen und von sämtlichen Fristen Abstand
zu nehmen.

Den Anträgen wird stattgegeben. Das mündlich abgegebene
Aufgebot ist geprüft und für ordnungsgemäß befunden worden.

Ich komme nunmehr zum feierlichen Akt der Eheschließung.
In Gegenwart der obengenannten Zeugen zu 3 und 4 frage ich Sie,
ob Sie gewillt sind, die Ehe mit
einzugehen. In diesem Falle bitte ich Sie, mit "ja" zu antworten.

ob Sie gewillt sind, die Ehe mit
einzugehen. In diesem Falle bitte ich auch Sie mit "ja" zu
antworten.

Nachdem nunmehr beide Verlobte die Erklärung abgegeben
haben die Ehe einzugehen, erkläre ich die Ehe vor dem Gesetz
rechtmäßig für geschlossen.

Berlin, am 29 April 1945

Vorgelesen und unterschrieben:

1.) Ehemann:
2.) Ehefrau:
3.) Zeuge zu 1:
4.) Zeuge zu 2:
5.)

als Standesbeamter

Eva Braun was so excited that she almost forgot that she'd become Frau Hitler. She started to sign as *Braun* and then crossed out the *B*, but she did add *geb.* (born) *Braun* after *Hitler*. This amazing contract contains not one word about love or fidelity. It was, in fact, little more than a pathetic troth between two corpses. Hitler and Eva had already agreed to a suicide pact and were as good as dead. They had less than a day to live.

arbeiterinnen, an der Spitze meinen alten Sekretären, Sekretärinnen, Frau Winter, usw., die mich jahrelang durch ihre Arbeit unterstützten.

Ich selbst und meine Gattin wählen, um der Schande des Absetzens oder der Kapitulation zu entgehen, den Tod. Es ist unser Wille, sofort an der Stelle verbrannt zu werden, an der ich den grössten Teil meiner täglichen Arbeit im Laufe eines zwölfjährigen Dienstes an meinem Volke geleistet habe.

Gegeben zu Berlin, den 29. April 1945, 4.00 Uhr

Last page of Hitler's last will and testament, signed in the Berlin bunker on April 29, 1945. Witnessed in the lower left by Martin Bormann and Dr. Joseph Goebbels and in the lower right by Nicolaus von Below. Setting a weird, erratic signature to the document, Hitler proclaims that he prefers death to the dishonor of surrender. He orders that his body and that of his wife, Eva Braun, be burned.

THE DEVELOPMENT OF HITLER'S SIGNATURE

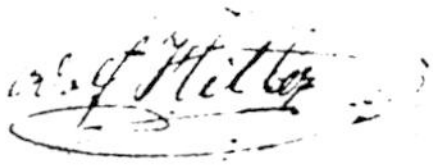

[signature]

May, 1906, age 17

[signature]

1908, age 19

Die   Nationalregierung :

[signature]

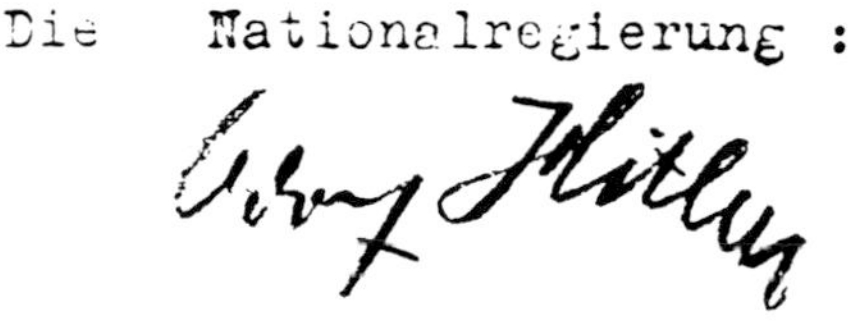

November, 1923, age 34

**Hitler in 1923,
age 34.**

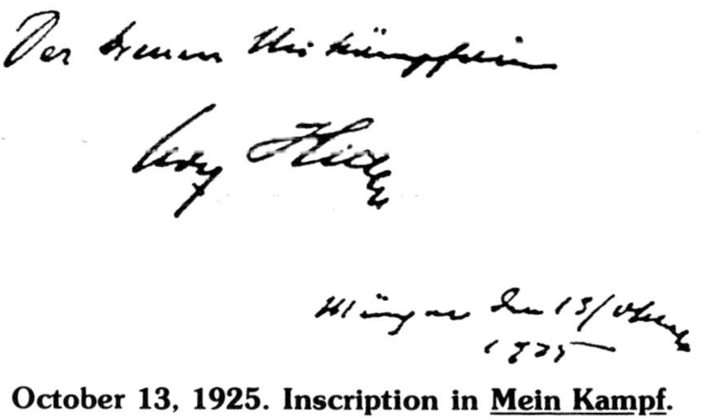

[signature]

October 13, 1925. Inscription in <u>Mein Kampf</u>.

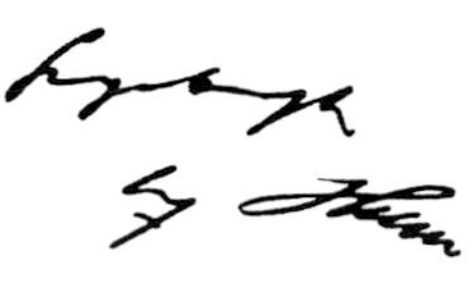

[signature]

November, 1932, age 41

March 5, 1933. Also signed by Major Walter Buch, Martin Bormann's father-in-law.

July 24, 1936, age 47

1936, age 47

Hitler in 1933, age 44, as chancellor of Germany.

January 30, 1937

November 28, 1938

Der Führer und Reichskanzler

Der Oberbefehlshaber des Heeres

1939, Also signed by Field Marshal von Brauchitsch

May 13, 1939, age 50

The Fuehrer on his 50th birthday (April 20, 1939).

July 19, 1940

November 29, 1941, age 52

King Boris of Bulgaria visiting Hitler at Obersalzberg on June 7, 1941.

Führerhauptquartier, den 17. Mai 1941.

Der Führer

May 17, 1941, age 52

January 11, 1944.

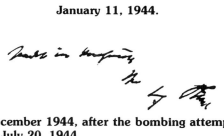

December 1944, after the bombing attempt
of July 20, 1944.

Hitler in 1944, shortly after the bomb attempt on his life (July 20)
which temporarily crippled him.

March 15, 1945. Six weeks before his suicide at age 56.

HITLER'S AWARDS AND APPOINTMENTS

The Nazi era in Europe was one of splendor and horror. Hitler erected magnificent buildings of marble and granite in which he sometimes committed his legal murders. His soldiers marched in resplendent uniforms, bedecked with glittering braid and medals. They wore handsome ornamental daggers, wrought with Teutonic cunning.

In the age of Nazi flamboyance, nothing created by the Fuehrer was more striking than the official documents awarding medals and promotions. Most of these award documents, printed in black and gold with a blind-stamped Nazi seal, bore the Fuehrer's signature, sometimes in facsimile but often authentically signed in brilliant blue or black ink.

Apparently Hitler liked to put his signature on these beautiful documents, for he personally signed thousands of them. The more important awards were handsomely bound in rich maroon imitation leather or creamy vellum, stamped in gold on the cover with the Nazi eagle and swastika. Of the countless military documents that have passed through my hands during my half century as a philographer, none has equalled in appearance the beauty of the coveted Knight's Cross of the Iron Cross.

If nothing but the military awards signed by Hitler and Goering and Himmler survive ten thousand years hence, historians could certainly reconstruct from them the story of the world's greatest conflict. The first documents of the Nazi regime, boldly signed by President Hindenburg and countersigned by Adolf Hitler bear the traditional Prussian eagle. After Hindenburg's death in 1934, Hitler was the principal signer. The Nazi swastika replaced the Prussian emblem. Documents became more and more florid, audacious in their ornamentation, and Hitler's signature grew larger.

When the Fuehrer's fortunes changed, his signature began to shrink. During the sweep of the Allies through Europe, the Nazis were often forced to issue military awards and promotions on cheap, makeshift paper. It must have grieved the Fuehrer to sign these unimpressive scraps. The signature he set upon them was weird and cramped, eloquently telling of his dramatic fall from power.

Appointment of Dr. Hans Lammers as deputy secretary in the chancellery. Signed by President Paul von Hindenburg and Adolf Hitler. The embossed Prussian eagle in the lower left was soon to give way to the Nazi insignia.

The new chancellor, Adolf Hitler, curtails the powers of the Reichstag. Also signed by Hindenburg and Wilhelm Frick.

Im Namen des Reichs

Der Generalmajor H i e l s c h e r , Kommandeur der Reichs
wehrzentralwerbestelle Dresden, scheidet mit dem 31.Oktobe
1934 unter Bewilligung der gesetzlichen Versorgung und der
Berechtigung zum Tragen seiner bisherigen Uniform aus dem
Heeresdienste aus. Er erhält für die dreimonatige Entlas-
sungsfrist und zwar vom 1.November 1934 bis 31.Januar 1935
die zuletzt bezogenen Gebührnisse aus Kapitel VIII A 2
Titel 1 a des Heereshaushalts.

Berlin, den 20.Oktober 1934.
Der Führer und Reichskanzler

Der Reichswehrminister   Der Chef der Heeresleitung

Für das Reichswehrministerium.

Nr. 2893/34 P A (1).

**Authorization for a retired officer to wear his uniform, October 20, 1934. Also
signed by von Blomberg, Minister of War, and von Fritsch, C-in-C Army.**

Mit Zustimmung des Führers und Reichskanzlers

Adolf Hitler

verleihe ich als Zeichen der Dankbarkeit
und in Anerkennung für besondere Dienste

Herrn Reichsminister Dr. Frick

den Stern und die Erste Klasse
des Ehrenzeichens des Deutschen Roten Kreuzes

Berlin, den
18 Aug 1938

Herzog von Sachsen-Coburg und Gotha
Präsident des Deutschen Roten Kreuzes

Red Cross award issued in Hitler's name by the president of the Red Cross to
Wilhelm Frick, 1938.

Der Führer und Oberste Befehlshaber
der Wehrmacht

Berlin, den 29.11.1939

Ich genehmige ausnahmsweise die Wiedereinstellung

der Leutnante a.D.

Joachim R o h r   und

Heinz   R o h r .

Recall of two officers, Berlin, November 29, 1939.

**Hitler declares war on Poland during his speech in the Reichstag on
September 1, 1939. Dr. Lammers is on his right and Dr. Dietrich is on
his left.**

Jm Namen des Deutschen Volkes !

Es erhält ein Rangdienstalter seines Dienstgrades

Name   Truppenteil   Rangdienstalter
(Wehrbez.Kdo.)

                    der Oberst z.V.

Brinckmann   Oberkommando der Wehrmacht
(Berlin VI)   (Ausl)   1.Juli 1941.

                Führerhauptquartier, den 14.Juni 1941.
                        Der Führer

Der Oberbefehlshaber des Heeres   Der Chef des Oberkommandos der Wehrmacht

Für das Oberkommando des Heeres.
Nr.3050/41 PA/Ag P1/1.Abt.(c).

Military field promotion, issued on ordinary paper, signed by Hitler, von Brauchitsch, and Wilhelm Keitel.

IM NAMEN
DES DEUTSCHEN VOLKES
VERLEIHE ICH
DEM OBERST

KARL BECKER

DAS RITTERKREUZ
DES EISERNEN KREUZES

FÜHRERHAUPTQUARTIER
DEN 29. OKTOBER 1942

DER FÜHRER
UND OBERSTE BEFEHLSHABER
DER WEHRMACHT

Award of the Knight's Cross of the Iron Cross to Karl Becker, October 29, 1942. Such awards were usually bound in parchment or imitation full maroon leather.

Im Namen des Deutschen Volkes!

Mit dem 31.Oktober 1943 werden unter Verleihung des Rechts
zum Tragen der bisherigen Uniform aus dem aktiven Wehrdienst
entlassen:
                der General der Infanterie
O t t o (Paul) in der Führerreserve des Oberkommandos des
       Heeres (Fr.D.St.:b.d.Offz.z.Vfg.d.Ob.d.H.(Sonst.Offz.))
       (R.D.A.: 1.12.40(8));

              der Generalmajor
v o n P l e h w e in der Führerreserve des Wehrkreiskomman-
       dos XX (Fr.D.St.:Kdr.d.Wehrbez.Bromberg) (R.D.A.:
       1.10.43(36)).

           Führerhauptquartier,den *22* .Oktober 1943
            Der Führer

                              Oberkommando des Heeres
                                  I.A.

                            Generalleutnant und Chef des
Für das Oberkommando des Heeres   Heerespersonalamts
Nr. 7400 /43 g.Ag P 1/Chefabt./Ref.9

Retirement of two officers with permission to wear their uniforms, October 22, 1943, signed by Hitler with a diminutive, almost invisible signature. Also signed by Hitler's Wehrmacht (combined army forces) adjutant, Major General Rudolf Schmundt.

Major General Schmundt, as Chief of the Army Personnel Office in 1943.

THE DECLINE AND FALL OF TWO DICTATORS
TRACED IN THEIR SIGNATURES

Adolf Hitler. In the earliest signature (November, 1923) there is almost a poetic rhythm, an expansive feeling as the future dictator grasps the implications of his rising position in the world. Ten years later, as the new chancellor, his signature has grown in size and power. The *Af.* (for Adolf) resembles the Nazi symbol, soon to be dreaded throughout the world. The *f*, taken alone, looks like a naked sword raised in defiance.

November 1923, age 34

March 5, 1933, age 43

December 1934

June 1936

January 1937

May 1939, age 50

July 19, 1940

For the next eight years, Hitler's signature changes little, except to grow in vigor and sharpness. But by 1942, as the Russian disasters piled up and the United States entered the war, the *itler* has become more illegible, sometimes almost blotting itself out. It plunges downward in a dangerous spiral, reflecting the increased depression of the writer. By August 2, 1944, the Fuehrer's signature has turned into a spastic scrawl and the expansive exuberant second loop in the capital *H* has vanished. Hitler is a beaten man. The effect of the bomb blast (July 20, 1944) has transformed a once huge and defiant scrawl into an aimless, insensitive, tremulous series of breaking waves.

April 20, 1942, his 53rd birthday

July 12, 1942

August 2, 1944

March 15, 1945

The final two signatures, signed on the last full day of Hitler's life, are little more than blots. The swastika-like *AF* looks like a self-destructive lightning bolt. Even the hysteria has disappeared from the wild strokes. All that remains is the final eradication.

April 29, 1945, the last full day of Hitler's life

April 29, 1945

Il Duce, von Ribbentrop, Hitler, Count Ciano, Dr. Goebbels, King Victor Emmanuel III, and Hess reviewing Italian troops in Rome, May 1938.

Benito Mussolini. The signature of Mussolini (1931) is that of a "sawdust Caesar" trying to look important. It is designed to impress. It is a swelling of the chest in pen and ink. Earlier, in 1920, we perceive in his script a man of the arts, a writer. The clarity of his political essays is reflected in his clear, simple signature. By August 1922, Mussolini was the most powerful man in Italy, soon to seize control of the government in a dramatic march on Rome.

1920, age 37

August 1922, age 39

In 1931 Mussolini affects an imperial signature, dropping his first name. Why portray the whole tiger when a single claw, razor-sharp, will terrify all enemies?

Here, at the peak of his power, there is a certain ferocity in the way Mussolini writes, pushing the pen up and down as if it were a plunging dagger. In 1937 all pretense of statesmanship disappears and Mussolini assumes the character of a tough soldier. The sharp angles of his name look like a row of bayonets.

June 1931, age 48

1937, age 54

The final signature (January 14, 1945), reveals an annihilated man, defeated at every turn. The bayonets, the power he counted upon, are gone. In about three months, on April 28, 1945, Mussolini will be shot by Italian partisans and strung up by the heels in Milan.

**January 14, 1945, age 62, about three months
before his execution on April 28, 1945**

FACSIMILE SIGNATURES OF HITLER

Hitler personally signed enormous numbers of documents and letters. Those he could not sign himself because of time or place limitations bear his printed signature, often with counter-signatures, sometimes authentic but more often printed, of his trusted lieutenants Frick, Meissner, Goering, Ribbentrop, Himmler, and others.

Among the most frequently encountered documents and letters that bear printed signatures of Hitler are:

1. Awards such as the Iron Cross and the German Mother's Cross
2. Commissions for lower ranking officers
3. Civil commendations or appointments made en masse
4. Christmas or New Year's greetings on correspondence cards adorned with his name and the Nazi insignia in gold
5. Routine letters on "Privatkanzlei" (Berlin) stationery.

The enormous number and variety of printed signatures of the Fuehrer and their striking similarity to authentic signatures makes it impractical to illustrate more than a few examples. With a few exceptions (such as the Privatkanzlei letters) facsimile signatures are printed in blue ink with wide pen strokes. Printed signatures of Hitler are usually large and bold.

The best way to determine authenticity is to examine the suspected signature under magnification. A printed signature may reveal tiny air bubbles in the ink, bubbles that do not occur in pen strokes where the flow of ink is even. The most conspicuous tell-tale sign of a printed signature, however, is the utter lack of cross-overs which occurs when one stroke of the pen goes over another. Write your own signature and then examine it under magnification. Notice how you can see where the ink of one stroke lies on top of another. In Hitler's signature there are two very distinct and obvious crossovers; the bar-crossing of the f in Af. and the bar-crossing of the capital H. If the signature is printed, these crossings will have the same consistency, often with very tiny air bubbles visible, as the rest of the signature. If hand-penned by Hitler, the stroke will lie heavily upon, and plow through, the underlying strokes.

The enlargement of Hitler's signature above clearly shows the two crossovers on the "f" in "Af" and the bar crossing on the "H."

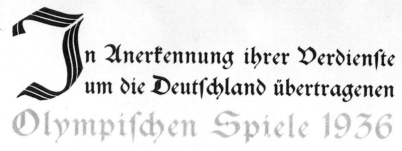

In Anerkennung ihrer Verdienste
um die Deutschland übertragenen

Olympischen Spiele 1936

verleihe ich

der

Frau Marie Provaczikova

das

Deutsche Olympia-Ehrenzeichen
zweiter Klasse.

Berlin, den *7. April* 1937

Der Deutsche Reichskanzler

Award of second-class honors at the Olympic games, 1936, signed with a printed signature.

DER FÜHRER

Hitler's printed signature on a Mother's Cross document, 3rd Class.

DER FÜHRER UND REICHSKANZLER

Aus Anlaß der Vollendung Ihrer

50

jährigen Dienstzeit spreche ich Ihnen meine herzlichsten Glückwünsche sowie meine besondere Anerkennung für die treuen Dienste aus, die Sie in ununterbrochener und hingebender Arbeit geleistet haben.

Certificate of congratulations on fifty years of service, signed with a printed signature.

ADOLF HITLER

BERLIN, im April 1943

Für die mir anläßlich meines Geburtstages übermittelten Glückwünsche spreche ich Ihnen meinen aufrichtigen Dank aus.

Sie haben mir damit eine große Freude bereitet.

Correspondence card, engraved with Hitler's name and the Nazi insignia in gold, sending thanks for birthday greetings, 1943. Hitler used similar cards, nearly all signed with lithographed blue signatures, to convey his personal greetings at Christmas and on New Year's.

ADOLF HITLER
PRIVATKANZLEI

BERLIN W 35
FRIEDRICH-WILHELMSTR.13
FERNRUF: 12 76 01

DEN 9.Mai.1937

TAGEBUCH-Nr. AZD/378
BEI RÜCKFRAGEN UNBEDINGT ANZUGEBEN

Doktor Hugo Eckener !

Die Art der Geschehniße in den letzten zwei Tagen macht es unumgänglich, daß Sie sofort nach Berlin kommen.

Ihre Anwesenheit ist erforderlich bei der Besprechung einer gründlichen Untersuchung, die anlässlich der Explosion des Luftschiffs Hindenburg eingelitet werden soll.

Es handelt sich um den Tod, den Ihr Nachfolger, Kapitän Ernst Lehmann, in diesem unerklärlichen, tragischen Unglück gefunden hat.

Der Führer und Reichskanzler

Letter signed with Hitler's printed signature in black, matching the ink of the letterhead. The signature is identical with the preceding facsimile. (Slightly reduced.) I have seen two different copies of this important letter to Eckener, asking that Eckener conduct an inquiry into the Hindenburg disaster. The only difference in the last two letters is that the word *gefunden* in the last paragraph is hyphenated in a different place. It is possible that a forger may have reproduced the letterhead and signature (using the facsimile on Hitler's correspondence card) and then typed in the message. The fact that two different copies of the letter to Eckener have turned up indicates that there may be more. In fact, any letter of Hitler (but not the correspondence cards) that bears this facsimile signature must be regarded as extremely suspect, possibly the work of the notorious New Jersey forger.

BESITZ-URKUNDE
Dem Parteigenoſſen

Dr. Wilhelm Frick
verleihe ich hiermit

dieDienſtauszeichnung
derNSDAP in GOLD
für 25 jährige aktive
Dienſtzeit in derNSDAP

MÜNCHEN,
den 30. Januar 1942

NATIONALSOZIALISTISCHE DEUTSCHE ARBEITERPARTEI

Award of the Nazi party 25-year service cross to Wilhelm Frick, bearing a printed signature.

FÜHRER-HAUPTQUARTIER. DEN 28. OKTOBER 1942
DER FÜHRER

Berlin, den 28. Januar 1941
Der Führer

Two remarkable printed signatures of Hitler's. The originals are counter-signed by Himmler and Frick. So artfully are these identical facsimiles printed that they reveal no air bubbles and appear to be written by Hitler in pen and ink. However, when held up one over the other to a bright light they superimpose, the unmistakable mark of facsimile signatures.

Many identical facsimiles have in the past masqueraded as originals. This is certainly the most deceptive and hard-to-spot of all Hitler's facsimile signatures.

Actual size of above facsimiles.

How Historians "Improve" on Historic Nazi Documents

At top: Last paragraph, with date line, of the original manuscript of Hitler's political testament. The two other copies on this page were both "improved" by forgery. The center example is from Trevor-Roper's *The Last Days of Hitler* and the bottom example is from Robert Payne's *Life and Death of Adolf Hitler*. The signatures vary greatly on the three documents. For example, notice the signature of General Hans Krebs at the lower right in the original testament. The capital *K* is almost illegible. Trevor-Roper made the *K* clearer (center) but Payne turned it into a plain, unmistakable *K* (bottom). Even Hitler's signature was faked. Examine each signature carefully and you will detect numerous deviations from the original in the "reproductions" supplied by Trevor-Roper and Payne.

Robert Payne, who was not familiar with the handwriting of the leading Nazis, did not recognize Goebbels' signature and even invented a character whom he averred signed Goebbels' name: "Dr. Joseph Fuhr, attached to Goebbels' secretariat." (There are other bizarre errors in Payne's book, including a reproduction of a snapshot of Hitler in death (April 30, 1945) that I consider highly suspect.)

48

Gegeben zu Berlin, den 29. April 1945, 4.00 Uhr.

Als Zeuge:

Dr. Joseph Goebbels.   Wilhelm Burgdorf
Martin Bormann.   Hans Krebs.

Gegeben zu Berlin, den 29. April 1945, 4.00 Uhr.

Als Zeuge:

Dr. Joseph Goebbels.   Wilhelm Burgdorf
Martin Bormann.   Hans Krebs.

Gegeben zu Berlin, den 29. April 1945, 4.00 Uhr.

Als Zeuge:

Dr. Joseph Goebbels.   Wilhelm Burgdorf
Martin Bormann.   Hans Krebs

49

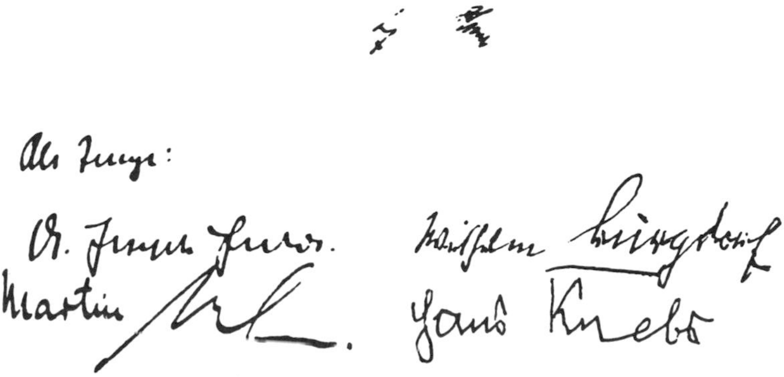

DAS VERDIENSTKREUZ
DES ORDENS VOM DEUTSCHEN
ADLER
DRITTER STUFE

BERLIN·DEN
DER DEUTSCHE REICHSKANZLER

DER CHEF DER ORDENSKANZLEI

DAS VERDIENSTKREUZ
DES ORDENS VOM DEUTSCHEN
ADLER
ZWEITER STUFE
MIT SCHWERTERN

BERLIN·DEN
DER DEUTSCHE REICHSKANZLER

DER CHEF DER ORDENSKANZLEI

Two distinctly different lithographed Hitler signatures in blue on unissued Order of the German Eagle documents.

FORGERIES OF HITLER'S AUTOGRAPHS

For nearly four years I pursued an elusive purveyor of Nazi forgeries, Wilhelm Reich of New Jersey. Whenever a fresh fabrication of Hitler or Goebbels turned up, I invariably traced it back to Reich, a specialist in German philography. Gradually I gathered a damning dossier on the man and his activities. My intention was to turn the entire file over to the United States postal authorities and assist them in the arrest and conviction of Reich.

One afternoon early in 1978 a man whom I'd never met dropped into my gallery. "I'm interested in Nazi autographs," he said. There was a slight trace of a German accent in his voice. He seemed to know a great deal about the Nazis and for a minute I had an uneasy feeling that I was chatting with a former party member. Our talk came to Hitler and Goebbels.

"There are some very clever forgeries coming out of New Jersey," I warned him. "Especially signed souvenir items of Hitler and photographs of Goebbels. Never buy any philatelic items signed by Hitler without consulting me. Keep away from signed photographs of Goebbels that are in any way discolored or stained, as if baked in an oven. Refuse any signed photographs of Hitler that do not bear the imprint of his photographer, Heinrich Hoffmann, or that were removed from pictorial biographies of the Fuehrer."

"Are these forgeries being done in New Jersey?" "In my opinion, yes. They are all the work of one man - Wilhelm Reich." My visitor fixed upon me a look of mingled dismay and astonishment..

He said: "I am Wilhelm Reich." For a brief moment, only a second or two, I was as amazed and flustered as Reich. Then I told him precisely why the finger of guilt pointed straight at him.

"I admit I sold the forgeries," said Reich, "but I didn't know they were fakes. I got them in response to advertisements I ran in German newspapers. When I found out they weren't genuine, I quit selling them. I haven't sold a forgery for about two years."

"I will accept your explanation," I told Reich, "but if you have any doubt in the future about authentication, I suggest you bring the suspect documents to me."

Reich has brought a number of Nazi documents to me since then, and I have written a pencilled O.K. and my initials on the verso of those that were genuine.

Hitler's is the most forged autograph of modern times. Despite the challenge of what Mark Twain called "that awful German language," there are more forgeries of Hitler than Napoleon on the market.

Fortunately for historians and philographers, most forgeries of Hitler are as obvious as his moustache. I was once offered a complete collection of signatures of the war criminals at Nuremberg, all crudely faked. When I told the vendor they were forgeries, he tore them up in my presence.

Many owners of forgeries are not so affable. On March 22, 1978, I was visited by an enormous man with an enormous moustache and an enormous voice.

"I am Heinrich von Papen-Manstein," he announced, in a thick German accent.

When I remained unimpressed by all this, he puffed his body up like a blowfish and added menacingly: "Remember zot name!"

From a briefcase he extracted several letters written in ink on large sheets of expensive paper and illustrated in pencil with drawings of soldiers. They were signed Adolf Hitler but looked unlike other early letters of the future dictator.

"What are these?" I asked.

"Letters of Hitler, orichinal letters, written durink Vorld Var Vun."
Usually when I spot a forgery I try to let the owner down gently, but von Papen-Manstein's abrupt and patronizing manner irritated me. I decided his fat, Goering-like derrière could withstand a good thump.

"These are fakes," I said. "Blatant fakes. The ink is 'wrong.' And where do you imagine Lance Corporal Hitler would get such elegant paper? Furthermore, these letters were never even folded to go through the mails." "Hitler zent dem flat." "From the front? Quite impossible. And look at the handwriting. It's not even a good imitation of Hitler's youthful script." My visitor was unconvinced. No doubt he'd put hundreds, perhaps thousands, of dollars into these elaborate forgeries. As I prepared to leave my gallery for another appointment, he began an angry monologue on my ignorance. No sooner had I closed the door behind me than he turned to my secretary and curled his lip in scorn: "So zat ees Charles Hamilton!"

The next day von Papen-Manstein attended my auction at the Waldorf-Astoria and bought the jacket and cap of what must have been an obese Nazi officer.

Of the many forgeries of Hitler that have crossed my desk, by far the most skillful were those of Arthur Sutton. His imitations, perfect copies of Hitler's scrawl, can be detected only because he used the wrong paper and ink. In 1976, with the cooperation of the postal authorities, I exposed the activities of Sutton, a twenty-six-year-old unemployed grocery clerk, who was then arrested, indicted, and given a suspended sentence.

Still, for every Sutton who is eliminated, there is some new and unidentified forger to add piquancy and excitement to the chase after rare documents and relics of the Third Reich.

Postcard photograph of Hitler bearing a forged signature. Hitler usually signed only very fine photographs of himself by the party photographer, Heinrich Hoffmann.

Postcard of philatelic interest, with authentic cancelled stamps portraying Hindenburg, bearing a forged signature of Hitler. Notice the very regular strokes of the *itler* in Hitler, not characteristic of the Fuehrer's genuine signature. Hitler very rarely signed souvenir items of this type. This and the preceding forgery both surfaced in New Jersey.

Drawing of a tank, bearing forged signatures of Hitler (upper right) and Rommel (lower right). The original drawing, on a large sheet of heavy paper, is handsomely colored and very attractive. Some years ago I was shown an entire file of these forgeries, most of them signed by Hitler and Rommel but a few signed only with Rommel's name.

Official printed signature of Hitler

Forged signature executed by Arthur Sutton and based on the official, printed example above. This is an extremely skillful freehand forgery.

Hitler's bookplate. There is considerable doubt that Hitler actually used this bookplate. Any books bearing this ownership plate should be viewed with suspicion.

Two forgeries of inscriptions in *Mein Kampf*. The imitation of Hitler's handwriting is inept, lacking the force and vitality of the Fuehrer's script.

Authentic inscription in a first edition (1925) of *Mein Kampf*. Hitler thanks Philipp Bouhler (business manager of the Nazi Party) for his work and extends Christmas greetings, December 24, 1925.

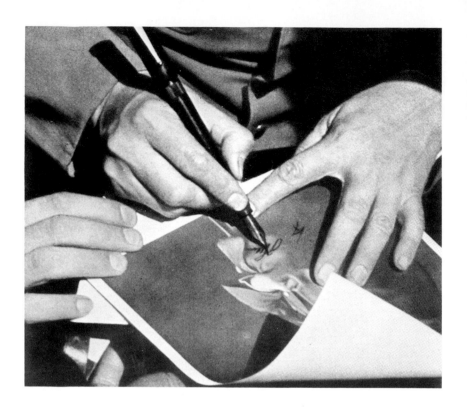

Postcard photograph of Hitler bearing a forged signature. Aside from the fact that Hitler rarely signed photographs of this type, the tremulous strokes (as in the lower bar of the f), heavy nib of the pen (unlike Hitler's own pen), and the incorrect formation of some of the letters, notably the H, betray this excellent forgery. The stroke that begins the capital H is poorly executed (curved instead of straight) and the lower loop of the H does not extend far below the rest of the surname as it does in genuine signatures of the Fuehrer.

These photos show Hitler signing photos for two of his devoted admirers.

THE BOGUS HITLER DIARIES

Possibly the crudest forgeries that ever fooled anybody were the notorious Hitler diaries. From the day they were "discovered" every expert on the payroll of *Stern*, who owned the diaries, or Rupert Murdoch, who bought the publication rights, instantly condemned them as naive fabrications. Scholars familiar with Hitler's life and habits knew he could not have written them. The thoughts in them were not those of the great dictator. The handwriting was totally different from Hitler's. Every page of the diaries was scribbled neatly, in a tripping script utterly unlike the powerful, dagger-like pen strokes of the Fuehrer. When the diaries first showed up, I saw two xerox pages and said of them: "They wouldn't fool an intelligent ten-year-old." Weeks later, after the diaries were condemned by a scientific test of ink and paper, even those who were reaping huge sums from their publication admitted the fraud. And the forger, Konrad Kujau, also known as Konrad Fischer, who had been aided by Gerd Heidemann, the reporter who "discovered" the forgeries, confessed to the sordid imposition.

57

Consisting of 62 cheap volumes, each stitched into a cover of imitation leather, the diaries contained about 50,000 words, long enough to impress amateur sleuths but by comparison with other notorious fakes not a particularly lengthy manuscript. The leaves were secured by threads, so that the forger could jettison any pages on which he made mistakes. The pages were also lined, a help to the forger in keeping his script straight. Many forgeries are instantly betrayed because the lines weave, like the path of a drunk making his way down the street, because the forger must concentrate on penning individual letters in the words rather than on aligning the writing. The first diary volume bore two brass letters in Gothic script (FH) that the publisher insisted were AH, Hitler's initials, with a slightly defective A. In a debate with stone-faced Peter Koch, the editor of *Stern* (subsequently fired), I pointed out that the letters FH stood for *Fuehrerhauptquartier*, or Fuehrer's headquarters.

Aside from the fact that the notebooks were cheap dime-store products that Hitler would never have used, there were also red wax seals on each cover. These seals bore the Nazi insignia but were not Hitler's personal seals, for they lacked the initials of the Fuehrer. The seals struck me as a ludicrous gilding of the fakes. The writing itself was very strange. The letters trembled, indicating that they were drawn, not written. Some of the words, it is true, did look like Hitler's words, but the pen strokes lacked the force and impetuosity of the Fuehrer's handwriting. The forger had not varied the letters, but had learned how to form each separate letter, say the capital H, and had stuck grimly to the pattern. In the actual writing of Hitler there is considerable variation in the forming of letters. The forger had failed, also, to capture the plunging character of Hitler's lines, with the final word of every line making a sharp descent. In the forger's pedestrian, methodical scrawl there is a certain feminine daintiness. But in Hitler's rapidly penned writing the torrent of words sweeps across the page like a breaking wave.

Hitler used many different inks in the course of the twelve years covered by the diaries (November 1932 until April 1945), and one would expect to see in the diaries examples of his brilliant blue and jet black inks, with occasional entries of grey. But the forger was negligent in this respect. Except for a few pencilled entries, the entire manuscript is in black ink. Many of the pages, too, were signed, unlike the usual diary in which the writer presumes his ownership and often does not bother to sign even the first page. The plethora of bogus signatures, not one of which actually resembles the authentic scrawl of Hitler, is one of the most obvious features by which the diaries can instantly be condemned as fakes. The signatures in the diary, too, are placed far beneath the last lines of text in many cases, whereas had Hitler penned the diaries he would never have left room for someone to add additional and perhaps spurious comments about his written name.

That the diaries were forged by a neo-Nazi is obvious, for Hitler comes off as "Mr. Nice Guy." According to the diaries, Hitler sponsored Hess's strange peace flight to England, constantly sought peace, and most amazing of all, knew very little about the Holocaust. It is significant, perhaps, that the forger, Konrad Kujau, liked to dress up in a Nazi uniform and solicit salutes from the patrons of the bars where he hung out.

At top: Authentic handwriting of Hitler's. The lines move like a cataract across the page and the pen strokes are swift and decisive, varying in intensity. The words are close together and at the end of each line the final word collapses. *At bottom:* Forged lines from the bogus Hitler diaries. The lines are methodical and fastidious, regulated and carefully penned. The words are too far apart. There is very little similarity to the spontaneous, explosive script of Hitler's.

Authentic handwritten line by Hitler, with his signature. The script is sharp and stabs its way across the page. The signature is rapidly penned, with five points on the *itler*, each point representing a letter in his last name.

Two forged lines and a forged signature from the Hitler diaries. The words are too far apart and the script moves laboriously and monotonously, without vitality. The *Af* (for Adolf) of the signature bears a curved bar (instead of straight) forming the first line of the *A* and a curved bar (instead of straight) forming the *f*. The bottom stroke of the *H* is labored and awkward, without the swift, rhythmic power of the original. There are six points on the *itler*, since the forger evidently was unable to count.

59

Front cover of the issue of *Stern* that contained the fake Hitler diaries. The initials FH (Fuehrerhauptquartier) are clearly visible on the cover of the first volume of the diaries. These initials would certainly not have been used by Hitler on any volumes that were his personal property.

At top: Bogus signature of Hitler's from the April 16, 1945 entry (the last one) in the diaries. At this time Hitler was actually crippled with Parkinson's disease, or a similar ailment. He could barely sign his name and could not eat without spilling food all over his shirt. However, the forger was so delighted and exuberant at completing his task that he put a large, triumphant signature at the end of the diaries' final entry. *At bottom:* Authentic signature of Hitler (April 29, 1945), enlarged four times for comparison with the faked signature. The tiny, original signature of Hitler looks like a crushed insect, every letter of it unrecognizable.

The Molders of Hitler's Mind

To a considerable degree, Hitler was influenced by the great thinkers, statesmen, and soldiers who preceded him. The Fuehrer worked out elaborate and unusual combinations of their ideas and theories to produce his own formula for Germany. In addition to the world-famous figures whose biographies and handwriting appear in this chapter, there were a number of propagandists who influenced Hitler and would now be forgotten if they had not. These include three rabidly anti-Semitic authors, Theodor Fritsch (1852-1934), Georg Lanz von Liebenfels (1872-1954), and Guido von List (1865-1919).

OTTO VON BISMARCK (1815-1898). First chancellor of the German empire. The founder of the Second Reich (1871-1918), Prince Bismarck epitomized for Hitler the man of strength and inflexible will who could and did rule with brutality. Bismarck's own career, in many ways, foreshadowed Hitler's. After a series of struggles for power, Bismarck eventually reorganized the German Bund as the North German Confederation, excluding Austria, under the leadership of Prussia. Like Bismarck, the Fuehrer detested Austria and mistrusted Austrians. Hitler felt secure only after he wiped out Austria with the *Anschluss* of 1938. Bismarck believed in the triumph of the will and advocated a policy of "blood and iron" as the solution to Germany's problems. Hitler followed the same course and even aped Bismarck in his successful invasion of France, the traditional enemy of Germany. The savagery of "the Iron Chancellor," as Bismarck was dubbed, inspired Hitler in his subjugation of foreign peoples. Bismarck was certainly one of Hitler's idols, but Hitler felt that Bismarck had failed in not recognizing the "menace" of the Jews. Although Hitler accepted Bismarck as a mentor, he was never able to understand or emulate the "Iron Chancellor's" occasional moderation and liberality. Hitler's failure to yield or retreat when advisable led to his ultimate destruction, just as Bismarck's willingness to concede a loss or fall back when necessary resulted in his enormous success in establishing a great nation.

Signature of Bismarck

Caricature of Otto von Bismarck, depicting him as a gouty, overblown imperialist. After his victory in the Franco-Prussian War (1870), Bismarck won the enthusiastic support of German nationalists, like Richard Wagner, but he turned many of his supporters against him when, as head of the German Reichstag, he granted equality of citizenship to the Jews.

Handwritten letter signed by Otto von Bismarck, 1873. The boldness with which Bismarck assaulted the paper with his pen resulted in an arrogant smudge on his signature.

Otto von Bismarck

HOUSTON STEWART CHAMBERLAIN (1855-1927). Anglo-German author; influenced Hitler's *Mein Kampf*. Born in Southsea, Hampshire, England on September 9, 1855, Chamberlain studied aesthetics and philosophy at Dresden. He quickly became an enthusiastic student of Wagner, joined the anti-Semitic circle of the famed composer, and married his daughter, Eva. A prolific author, Chamberlain wrote *The Foundations of the Nineteenth Century* (Munich, 1910) in which he foreshadowed all the major theories in *Mein Kampf*. Labelled in England "a turn-coat of a Briton" and "a renegade Englishman," Chamberlain espoused the thesis of the Germans as a master race with a mission to rule the world. He praised the Teutons as the creators and sustainers of civilization and attacked the Jews as "disruptive and degenerate."

Chamberlain's *Foundations*, unreadable today, became an instant best seller when Kaiser Wilhelm II praised it as a work of great importance. Hitler probably never read it, but he eagerly absorbed its ideas. In England Chamberlain's book was excoriated as "the crapulous eructations of a drunken cobbler," but the Germans hailed the author as a great Nordic prophet. Wilhelm II wrote to Chamberlain: "It was God who sent your book to the German people."

Chamberlain immediately recognized the rising Hitler (1923) as the long-awaited messiah who would build a great new Reich. Although old and paralyzed, he met and was spellbound by the future Fuehrer. "It is as if your eyes were equipped with hands," he wrote to Hitler, "for they grip a man and hold him fast. . . .At one stroke you have transformed the state of my soul."

In *Mein Kampf* Hitler drew deeply from the metaphysics of Chamberlain, transforming his philosophic terms into simple German. *Mein Kampf* expresses virtually all the Aryan ideals of the Anglo-German philosopher.

Houston Stewart Chamberlain

Signature of Houston Stewart Chamberlain

KARL VON CLAUSEWITZ (1780-1831). Prussian general and military authority. The author of the classic *On War* (3 volumes, 1833), von Clausewitz provided the philosophy of strategy that produced the great German victories in the Franco-Prussian War of 1870 and the initial victories of Hitler over the French and British in World War II. Clausewitz, an artillery officer who fought with the Russians against Napoleon and was a general in the Waterloo campaign at Ligny, was the military mentor of Hitler. After an intensive study of Frederick the Great's campaigns and the books of von Clausewitz and his more modern exponent, Heinrich von Treitschke (1834-1896), Hitler envisioned himself a brilliant strategist competent to guide or overrule his generals. His intuitive genius, evident in the early years of World War II, convinced the Fuehrer that his study of von Clausewitz had transformed him into a great military leader and led him to violate von Clausewitz's warnings about the danger of invading Russia. Hitler's belief in his own military talents led to the eventual defeat of the German armies.

Variant signatures of von Clausewitz

**General Karl
von Clausewitz**

CHARLES DARWIN (1809-1882). English naturalist. The great botanist who upset the entire basis of Christian theology with his theories on human evolution had a powerful indirect influence on the thinking of Hitler. Although educated for the ministry, Darwin used his family connections to get a job as ship's naturalist on the exploratory voyage of the *Beagle* (1831-1836), during which he gathered data on "natural selection," subsequently published in his *Voyage of the Beagle* (1840) and *Origin of Species* (1859). Darwin's startling theories shook the world. He not only upset the whole premise of Christianity with an oblique refutation of the Biblical version of man's origin, but he paved the way for Nietzsche's superman by his expostulation of "the struggle for existence" and "survival of the fittest." The fittest humans, of course, were a variety of supermen. Hitler's plan to eliminate the mentally unfit and to exterminate the Jews was inspired by a desire to "purify" the Teutonic race and create a Nordic superman. The Fuehrer was probably not cerebral enough to wade through the massive amount of data presented in the *Origin of Species*, but the impact of Darwin's theories was visible in many of the racist, political, and military ideas he implemented in the Third Reich.

Complimentary close of a letter with signature by Charles Darwin

Charles Darwin

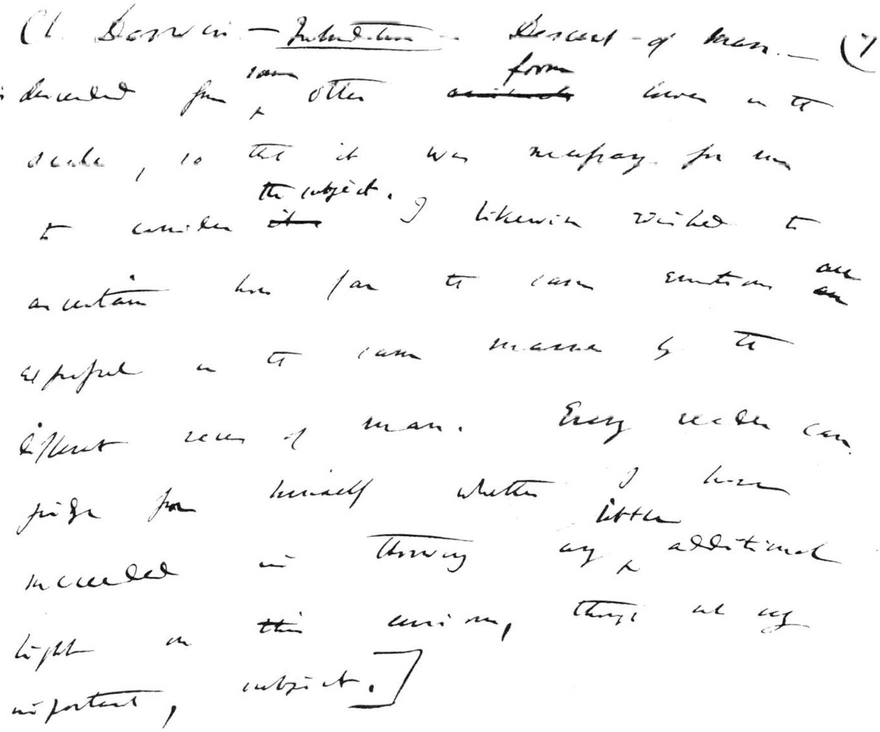

Ch. Darwin — Descent of Man — (7

is descended from some other form lower in the scale, so that it was necessary for me to consider the subject. I likewise wished to ascertain how far the same emotions are expressed in the same manner by the different races of man. Every reader can judge for himself whether I have succeeded in throwing any little additional light on this curious, though not very important, subject.

Handwritten manuscript page from Darwin's *Descent of Man* (1871)

DIETRICH ECKART (1868-1923). Hitler's mentor and the spiritual god-father of Nazism. Born on March 23, 1868 in Neumarkt, Upper Palatinate, Eckart began his career as a journalist and poet. He blamed his early lack of success on the Jews and Marxists. Later he blamed the Jewish socialists for Germany's defeat in World War I. In 1918, after the abortive "Jewish inspired" revolution which he despised, Eckart entered politics. He created in one of his poems the battle cry, "Germany awake!" (*Deutschland Erwache!*) Eckart was an early member of the German Workers Party out of which developed the Nazi party. He began a close friendship with Hitler and introduced the awkward young politician to all the "right" people in Munich. He also encouraged Hitler in his anti-Semitic ideas and nationalist aspirations.

Eckart's *Storm Song* was the oldest national hymn of the Nazis. In a pamphlet published shortly before his death, Eckart hailed Hitler as the first man to reveal that the Jews had undertaken a mass migration from Egypt after they had made a murderous, but unsuccessful, attack on the Egyptian ruling class. Moses was the first Bolshevist, said Eckart.

For many years Eckart was an alcoholic and drug addict. He was once confined to an institution for the mentally deranged. Weakened by his dissolute habits, and suffering from his incarceration after the Beer-Hall Putsch, he died of a heart attack on December 26, 1923 in Berchtesgaden. Hitler called Eckart his "North Star" and praised him lavishly in *Mein Kampf.*

Handwritten poem signed by Dietrich Eckart

Signed portrait of Dietrich Eckart

JOHANN GOTTLIEB FICHTE (1762-1814). German philosopher. It is doubtful that Hitler ever got through the diffuse and elusive concepts of Fichte's books, *An Essay towards a Critique of All Revelation* and *Science of Knowledge*, but the ideas of Fichte had an immense impact on the Fuehrer's thinking. When I was a student at U.C.L.A. I took an entire course devoted to Fichte's philosophy. Little recollection remains of this tedious intellectual adventure except that I got an "A" in a final examination devoted to an elucidation of Fichte's "transcendental subjective idealism" Fichte taught at Jena on the vocation of the scholar, but when it was discovered by pedagogues in authority that he looked upon God as the moral order of the universe, he was fired. Subsequently Fichte was a professor in Berlin where his vision of a German state built upon socialism with a league of peoples united in moral endeavor and true culture won wide acclaim and cheers from his audiences. Fichte proclaimed the "joy and grief of life" and looked upon life itself as an exercise in moral duty. This was precisely the philosophy that motivated Hitler and the Nazi party. The Fuehrer put into effect all the romantic ideals of Fichte: a socialistic state with a Teutonic messiah for the "primal people" (the Germans) and a self-sufficient Germany with a state-controlled economy that would provide "living space" for the "Volk." A pupil of Kant, Fichte also advocated a pragmatic approach to life that inspired Hitler in his opportunism in war and politics.

Conclusion of a handwritten letter signed in full by Fichte in Gothic script

Conclusion of a handwritten note signed by Fichte

Johann Gottlieb Fichte

FREDERICK II (1712-1786). King of Prussia; known as Frederick the Great. The hero of the Seven Years' War (1756-1763), Frederick was also the great hero of Adolf Hitler, who modeled his life, even his body, after the famous Prussian sovereign. Frederick was, when a youth, like Hitler, constantly beaten and abused by his father. Frederick was even arrested and tried as a deserter. Later he displayed great perseverance and courage in the face of fearful odds and won many battles, but he also suffered some awesome defeats. His body was slight, his eyes a penetrating blue, and these details struck Hitler so forcibly that he often stood in front of his favorite portrait of "Old Fritz" and commented on "how alike we are, the old king and I." In advancing age Frederick, like Hitler, was crippled with arthritis and his fingers were bent and shook constantly. This detail was also not lost on Hitler when, in the Bunker, he continued to liken himself to Frederick. One of Hitler's favorite books was Carlyle's *History of Frederick the Great.* The Fuehrer studied Frederick's campaigns assiduously and much of his knowledge of military strategy was derived from Frederick's great battles. Frederick was, like Hitler, a patron of the arts and very fond of music, poetry, and painting. He was also, or so Hitler convinced himself, anti-Semitic. Years ago I owned a superb handwritten letter by Frederick in which he composed a lengthy poem on his own inebriation. The letter was beautifully bound and bore an obsequious presentation inscription from Rudolf Hess to Hitler on the Fuehrer's 50th birthday. I've often wondered what Hitler thought about his hero writing a paean to drunkenness.

In the Bunker, Hitler turned more and more to his long dead hero for solace. As the end of the Third Reich approached, Hitler quoted Frederick's remark, penned during a moment of crisis and defeat: "If everything collapses, I shall calmly bury myself beneath the ruins." And when everything did collapse, Hitler prepared for suicide and ordered all his personal possessions destroyed, except the beloved portrait of Old Fritz that had accompanied him throughout his travels.

Conclusion of a handwritten letter by Frederick the Great, September 20, 1769, about furniture and furnishings. Frederick had small grasp of the German language and preferred to write and speak in French. His handwritten letters are nearly all in French and are invariably penned in a simple, clear script, and signed "Federic."

**Frederick
the Great**

Handwritten note signed in Gothic script. The signature "Fried" is an abbreviation of "Friedrich," the king's German signature, usually used only on official documents.

Variant German signatures of Frederick the Great. At the top left is Frederick's rare full signature in Gothic script. At the top right is an abbreviated form of his full signature. At the bottom are the signatures that appear frequently on commissions, military awards, and routine military letters dictated in German to his secretaries.

STEFAN GEORGE (1868-1933). German nationalist poet. Known as "the embodiment of Roman culture on Rhenish soil," George regarded himself as a priest and prophet. He adopted the nationalistic ideals of Nietzsche, especially the image of the superman. George called for a revival of ancient Teutonic customs and looked forward to the coming of a new Teutonic hero who would lead Germany into greatness. Attired in somber, black garments, George preached his gospel of ruthless power and the superman in city after city to all who would listen.

Handwritten letter by Stefan George in his informal script, signed with his French nickname, "Etienne."

Und wie schreitet es mit Jhren arbeiten vorwärts? Jn der erwartung auf diesem weg wieder eine nachricht von Jhnen zu haben freundlich

Jhr Stefan George

Handwritten verses by Stefan George

George established a cult called the Cosmics or George-Circle. One of his disciples, Alfred Schuler, was the first to use the swastika as a symbol. Schuler also began to give the George-Circle an anti-Semitic tone. Hitler's thinking was profoundly influenced in 1923 by the nationalistic ideals of Stefan George and the virulent anti-Semitic lectures of Schuler in Munich.

Indem ich zuerst Ihre freundliche Zustimmung erwarte bleibe ich in ausgezeichneter künstlerischer hochachtung

Stefan George.

Handwritten note by Stefan George (1896)

Hochachtend Ihr
St. George

Conclusion of a handwritten letter by Stefan George (1898)

GEORG WILHELM FRIEDRICH HEGEL (1770-1831). German political philosopher. A mystic whose writings are at times as obfuscated with sesquipedalian metaphysical meanderings as Kant's, Hegel saw in the State the embodiment of mind and spirit, the "movement of God through history."

Conclusion of a letter signed by Hegel

Georg Hegel

Hitler accepted this view of politics and molded it to suit his purposes. Bismarck also adopted Hegel's view of the State and even Marx and Lenin found in Hegel a doctrine to justify the dictatorship of the proletariat. Hegel looked upon the State as "divine will," incomprehensible to the people. This was precisely the view that enabled Hitler to justify his actions in building a greater Germany through brute force. Hegel regarded war as a "purifier," as did Hitler. Hegel wrote that the State "has the supreme right against the individual, whose supreme duty is to be a member of the State." Hegel predicted that Germany's hour would come and a great hero would revive the nation's ancient glory. Hitler, of course, believed himself to be the messiah who would regenerate the world through the genius of Germany.

Handwritten note signed by Hegel

Full signature of Hegel, with his title as professor of philosophy at the University of Berlin (1820).

ALOIS HITLER (1837-1903). Father of Adolf Hitler. Alois Schicklgruber was born in Strones, Lower Austria, on June 7, 1837, the illegitimate son of Georg Heidler, an itinerant miller, and Anna Maria Schicklgruber, a peasant girl. Five years later the parents married, but Alois was not legitimized and continued to use his mother's name until he was almost forty. Alois was raised by his father's brother, Johann Nepomuk Heidler. Johann eventually had Alois legitimized and in 1877, 12 years before Hitler's birth, Alois changed his name to Hitler.

At 18 Alois joined the Customs Service and spent most of his remaining life as a customs official, a highly respected, impeccably dressed officer many social notches higher than the wandering miller and peasant girl who were his parents. After two marriages with women who died young, Alois Hitler married, on January 7, 1885, his second cousin, Klara Poelzl, who became the mother of Adolf Hitler.

Alois retired from the Customs Service at 58. He dabbled in bee keeping and buying and selling farms, but spent most of his time quaffing beer in village inns. After a few drinks Alois would frequently explode into bursts of anger and flog his son Adolf with a belt or cane. Alois was horrified when young Adolf expressed his ambition to carve out a career in the arts. Alois died suddenly of a lung hemorrhage on January 3, 1903, leaving his widow with a small pension and Adolf free to seek his fortune in Vienna.

Adolf Hitler, contrary to popular belief, never used his grandmother's name Schicklgruber. Nor is there, as some historians have averred, any evidence that Hitler's grandfather, Georg Heidler, was Jewish.

Alois Schicklgruber Hitler, about 1895

O. Spronk

Signature of Alois Hitler

Early signature of Adolf Hitler. There is a remarkable family resemblance in their writing, perhaps a subconscious effort on Adolf's part to imitate his father's script.

Tombstone of
Alois Hitler

Adolf Hitler placing flowers on his father's grave

IMMANUEL KANT (1724-1804). German philosopher and metaphysician. A brilliant thinker who cloaked many of his profoundest ideas in verbal obscurity, Kant wrote the most influential philosophical work of his age - *The Critique of Pure Reason.* While professor of logic at Koenigsberg, Kant tried to determine the laws and limitations of man's knowledge.

Although Hitler was not an abstract thinker and probably never read a line of Kant's (except for some convenient quotations to justify the ethics of Nazism), he was deeply influenced by Kant's political thinking. Kant occasionally flirted with the idea of political freedom, but he abhorred democracy and advocated a dictatorial government. Out of Kant's political ideas grew the intense nationalism that inspired Hegel, Nietzsche, Bismarck, and eventually Hitler.

Autograph quotation signed by Immanuel Kant, in Latin and Roman script, 1783. "Auditari suo honoratissimi."

Immanuel Kant, with facsimile signature under his portrait.

Handwritten letter signed by Kant to his publisher (De La Garde) in Berlin. Writing in Gothic script, from Koenigsberg, December 21, 1792, Kant sends thanks for the great care his publisher took in all details in publishing Kant's *Critique of Judgment.*

LUDWIG III (1845-1921). King of Bavaria. An active militarist, Ludwig succeeded to the throne of Bavaria on November 5, 1913 on the death of his father. To Adolf Hitler, a 25-year-old aspiring artist, the new king represented the masculine virtues of a triumphant Germany. Hitler had little respect for the Hapsburg emperor of Austria, the antediluvian Franz Josef, whom he looked upon as the relic of a decaying dynasty. On the outbreak of war, Hitler, then living in Munich where King Ludwig also resided, dispatched a petition (August 3, 1914) to the king, requesting that as an Austrian subject he be permitted to join a Bavarian regiment. According to Hitler's own account, Ludwig III granted his request the following day.

On August 16 an exuberant Hitler was enrolled in the 1st Company of the 16th Bavarian Reserve Infantry, known as the List Regiment after the name of its original commander, Colonel List. Hitler then underwent a period of intense military training. On October 8 Ludwig III personally witnessed the solemn ceremony by which Hitler and a few other Austrian recruits swore allegiance to him, as well as to Wilhelm II of Germany, and the Emperor Franz Josef. Hitler always remembered the occasion because he got a double ration and a noon meal of roast pork and potato salad.

At the end of World War I King Ludwig was forced to abdicate. He lived first in Berchtesgaden, then in a castle assigned to him on the shores of the Chiemsee. On November 13, 1918 he formally signed his abdication and released all Bavarian troops, including Hitler, from their oath of allegiance. Ludwig III died in Sárvár, Hungary on October 18, 1921.

Adolf Hitler in the cheering crowds outside the Feldherrnhalle in Munich at the outbreak of World War I on August 1, 1914. On August 3, Hitler sent a petition to King Ludwig III of Bavaria requesting permission to enlist in a Bavarian regiment. On August 4, 1914 Hitler was granted authorization to enroll in the 16th Bavarian Reserve Infantry Regiment.

Karl
May

KARL MAY (1842-1912). German author of stories about American Indians. May was the favorite author of young Adolf Hitler and had a profound influence on the future dictator. Although May never visited America and knew very little about the Western frontier, his books inspired millions of young Germans with the pioneer virtues of stoicism and courage. As a boy Hitler led his playmates, sometimes even recruiting girls, in acting out the plots of May's novels. May's leading hero, Old Shatterhand, was a Teutonic frontiersman whose bizarre oaths - "Hang it all, fellows" [Zum Henker, Kerle!] and "Pshaw and damnation, sir!" - delighted young Adolf. Hitler decided to follow the Indian method of accepting torture or punishment without emotion. Once his father Alois, possibly in a drunken fury, beat him with a cane and Hitler proudly counted 230 blows during which he refused to cry out. Years later, when chancellor, Hitler took great pride in his set of May's works, all specially bound in vellum, occupying a place of honor in his library. They were the Fuehrer's main source of information about Americans. During the Russian campaign Hitler ordered his officers to study Karl May's books about Indian fighting. "That's the way Russians fight," he said. "Hidden like Indians behind trees and bridges, they jump out for the kill."

Not long ago I spent an entire evening chatting with a former Nazi officer, now a prominent New York art dealer. After dinner we talked of the war and then of art, and graphology, and of the great lyric poet Rainer Maria Rilke on whom the art dealer had written a monograph. Then I browsed through his library. As I exclaimed over the beauty and rarity of many of his sumptuously bound art books, he interrupted and pointed to a row of tatterdemalion old volumes. "These are my greatest treasures," he said. "The books of Karl May I read and re-read when I was a boy." Then he blushed and added: "I still look into them now and then."

Handwritten paragraph of Karl May explaining his philosophy of authorship. "I don't write anything for children, but for grownups. . . .My books and my work are for comprehension."

BENITO MUSSOLINI (1883-1945). Italian dictator. The ersatz Caesar in Rome, an ex-soldier like Hitler, played an important role in Hitler's approach to psychological politics. As Hitler began his rise, he sedulously aped Mussolini. The Italian dictator had made a famous march on Rome. Hitler decided that he, too, would make a famous march. (It fizzled out in the Beer-Hall Putsch.) The flamboyant uniforms of the Italian Fascists, their striking insignia which featured spread-winged eagles, their great parades and rallies--all were slavishly imitated by Hitler. Mussolini strutted his role to perfection with gestures and shouts from a great podium. Hitler played follow the leader. The Fuehrer cribbed Mussolini's idea of a personal oath to "the leader." His German troops mimicked the Italian stiff, outstretched arm salute. Hitler copied the ceremonial consecration of battle or memorial flags and Il Duce's organization of secret police.

Mussolini allocated for himself the grandiose title of "Il Duce" (the leader). Hitler called himself "Der Fuehrer" (the leader). But there was, as it turned out, a huge difference between the Italian showman and his German pupil. Hitler possessed a genius far superior to that of Mussolini and in the end it was the student who led the teacher.

This remarkable photograph, taken at the first meeting between Mussolini and Hitler in the spring of 1934, shows a disgruntled and unhappy Fuehrer standing humbly behind a triumphant Mussolini. Hitler had been upstaged by Il Duce. He had arrived at the airport in Rome wearing an old trench coat and battered fedora. The Italian leader met him. Mussolini was dressed like a Ritz Hotel doorman, his puffed-out chest resplendent with gold braid and medals, an ornamental dagger at his hip, his black boots polished, his uniform neatly pressed. The encounter was an emotional and diplomatic triumph for Mussolini, but it was the last time that he, or any other foreign leader, would ever win such an advantage over the Fuehrer.

Signature of Benito Mussolini, Rome, August 29, 1931

Rare signed photograph of Mussolini yachting in civilian attire, September 10, 1931. When not signing a photograph of himself in military regalia and weighed down with medals, Mussolini's signature actually shrank.

Mussolini's mistress, Clara Petacci, frolicking at sea. Clara was later shot and strung up by her heels to the roof of a garage in the Piazzale Loreto with *Il Duce*.

Handwritten love letter signed "Ben" by Mussolini. Writing to Claretta Petacci, probably about Clara's miscarriage of Mussolini's baby. ". . . .I feel that the days of summer are near, no matter if it is September. . . . .I will see you. . . blooming like a flower. The days of anguish are also the days of great love. I love you, my little one. . . ."

FRIEDRICH NIETZSCHE (1844-1900). German philosopher. Nietzsche wrote eloquently of a superman, an individual of brute power, fierce and without conscience. Nietzsche divided the world into masters and slaves. He foresaw the coming of a great leader who would destroy the decadent old order and build a brave, new world of *Übermenschen* (Overmen or Supermen). That Nietzsche never envisioned a demagogue like Hitler establishing the New Order, or that he was an admirer of the Jews and hated Wagner's Jew-baiting, were facts that the Nazis brushed aside in their zeal to adapt Nietzsche's ideas to their own political and moral credos.

A professor of classical philology at Basel, Nietzsche denounced all religion and championed "the doctrine of perfectibility of man through forcible self-assertion and glorification of the superman." He suffered a mental breakdown and died insane.

When I was a senior in high school, I first read Nietzsche's *Thus Spake Zarathustra* and was caught up in a wild cataract of emotions. I recall discussing the book with my best friend. I said: "I don't know whether it's poetry or philosophy but it's full of glorious dreams and hopes, none of which can ever come true. It's pure romance. There can never be a superman. There can never be a super race." I must now confess that I hadn't the remotest inkling that in ten years I would be a soldier fighting against a man who was actually trying to implement Nietzsche's ideas of a master race.

I once owned a copy of Nietzsche's *Man and Superman* that had belonged to Mussolini. In the margins the Italian dictator had penned his ideas for transforming Italy into a land of supermen. Obviously Nietzsche's writings immensely influenced Il Duce, as they did Hitler. It would almost be correct to say that the bible of the Nazis was not *Mein Kampf* but *Thus Spake Zarathustra*.

Friedrich Nietzsche in 1868, the year he met Wagner

Nietzsche's signature, 1868

Handwritten title page of Nietzsche's
Thus Spake Zarathustra **(1886)**

Signature of Nietzsche, 1872

Torino,
3. Mai 1888

**Handwritten conclusion of a letter by
Nietzsche, May 3, 1888**

Nietzsche and his mother, about 1872. Two decades later, when Nietzsche succumbed to mental illness, his mother took care of him.

Singe mir ein neues Lied; die Welt ist verklärt und alle Himmel freuen sich.

The startling change in Nietzsche's handwriting after he lost his reason. *At top,* **Nietzsche's writing in 1889, when he was still sane.** *At bottom,* **Nietzsche's script and signature two years later in 1891 during his madness.**

Hitler contemplating a bust of Nietzsche, about 1933

ARTHUR SCHOPENHAUER (1788-1860). German philosopher. In his celebrated treatise, *The World as Will and Idea* (1818). Schopenhauer identifies the *will* with *force*. This was precisely the construction that Hitler put upon the word *will*. In the Fuehrer's mind, the *will* was perhaps the most important of all moral weapons. When Leni Riefenstahl created a classic film that depicted the splendor and pageantry of the Nazis, it was entitled *The Triumph of the Will.*

In his approach to morality and war, Hitler emphasized Schopenhauer's ideas of the power of the will. To Hitler, as to Schopenhauer, there was "no other being except *will. Wollen ist Ursein--*"*will* is primal being."

Schopenhauer as a young man

Page 449 of the original manuscript of Schopenhauer's classic work, *The World As Will and Idea* (1818).

Schopenhauer in old age

Handwritten letter signed by Schopenhauer to a bookseller, July 27, 1844. The philosopher sends a list of books he wants to buy-Burns, Shelley, Lessing, Walter Scott, and Calderon.

FRANZ VON STUCK (1863-1928). Allegorical artist. The wild, impassioned paintings of this noted German artist fascinated Hitler. The Fuehrer detected in the tormented violence of von Stuck fragments of his own rampant imagination. He was inspired afresh by every viewing of von Stuck's creations. In one portrait of Medusa, her hair a mass of writhing serpents, Hitler perceived the eyes of his mother, whose hypnotic gaze he had inherited. The Fuehrer told his friend Putzi Hanfstaengl that von Stuck and Wagner were the creative artists who had most profoundly influenced his life. In his brilliant study, *The Psychopathic God: Adolf Hitler*, Robert G.L. Waite suggests that the Fuehrer pictured himself as von Stuck's celebrated Wotan in "The Wild Chase," and even modeled his personal appearance after the fierce galloping figure in the painting. Of "The Wild Chase," painted in 1889, the year of Hitler's birth, Waite writes: "The huntsman in von Stuck's picture bears an uncanny likeness to Adolf Hitler. There is the dark brown hair with the famous forelock over the left temple, the brooding eyes, the large nose, the memorable little mustache. A blood-red cape swirls in the wind, and he brandishes a

Signature of Franz von Stuck

Note:
The "von" in his name was added in 1906 indicating that the signature was written prior to that date.

bloody sword. Hitler's favorite images are also pictured: decapitation, wolves and death. . .ravished women and corpses are left in the path of the galloping horseman."

"The Wild Chase" by Franz von Stuck. Although painted in 1889, the year Hitler was born, the painting appears to embody a portrait of Hitler.

"Pursuit" by Franz von Stuck. The eerie paintings of von Stuck often contain fierce masculine figures that suggest Hitler himself in their appearance and intensity.

RICHARD WAGNER (1813-1883). German composer. The tumultuous, almost orgasmic music of Wagner's operas had an immense influence on Hitler. The soaring chords bound him body and soul to the composer. The Fuehrer and Wagner held the same views and sought the same goals. Both were vegetarians; both were loners, without close friends, almost solipsistic; both were nationalists who extolled the great past of Germany and longed for a master race; both believed in Aryan superiority; and, above all, both had a fierce and abiding hatred for the Jews. In his notorious essay on "Judaism and Music," Wagner revealed himself as a rabid anti-Semite. He condemned the Jews as "the most heartless of human beings" and yearned for the day when "there will be no longer any Jews." He urged a war upon this "enemy of mankind."

Hitler was inspired as a youth by Wagner's music and it was while he was entranced by it that he conceived his great plans for the future of Germany. He said years later: "For me, Wagner is someone godly and his music is my religion. I go to concerts as others go to church."

Hitler considered marrying Winifred Wagner, the composer's daughter-in-law, and he treated Wagner's grandsons like his own children. Hitler, as historians know, had a prodigious memory and he knew by heart the words to many of Wagner's operas. The Fuehrer identified with the romantic heroes of the composer, especially *Tannhäuser*. No doubt in his mind's eye he perceived himself as a knight in shining armor.

Youthful portrait of Richard Wagner by Jager

Early signature of Wagner with his title as *Kappellmeister* to the king of Bavaria

Handwritten letter signed by Wagner, Bayreuth, 1872

90 **Handwritten music signed by Wagner, 1865**

Richard Wagner, about 1875

Title-page of the first edition of the libretto *Tannhauser* (Munich, 1850), depicting Tannhauser as a gallant knight in armor holding a banner.

Official portrait of Hitler, 1938, depicting him as a Wagnerian hero, no doubt Tannhauser.

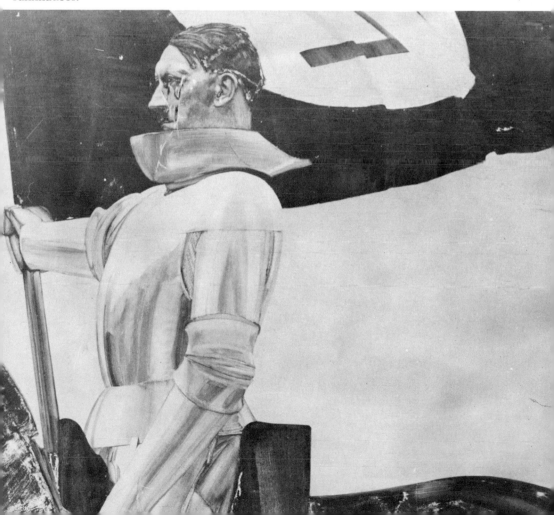

Hitler and Bormann exam‑
ing photos of the French Ca‑
paign (June 17, 1940).

The Fuehrer's
"Inner Circle"

MARTIN BORMANN (1900-1945). Hitler's "right-hand" man during the war. A shadowy figure who moved darkly in the background of Nazi intrigue, Bormann was born on June 17, 1900 in Halberstadt, joined the party on February 17, 1927, and became chief of staff to Rudolf Hess on July 1, 1933. He was made a Reichsleiter on October 10, 1933, appointed leader of the party chancellery on May 29, 1941, and Hitler's personal secretary on April 12, 1943. A political murderer, Bormann had served a year in prison for the crime. His ruthless and crafty mind appealed to Hitler, and during the war he became an almost invisible man who wielded enormous power.

Faithful to Hitler to the very end, Bormann remained in the Berlin bunker until after the Fuehrer shot himself, then disappeared in the same mysterious way he had lived. Last seen following a tank into combat, Bormann committed suicide on May 2, 1945, although his whereabouts are constantly reported in South America, and energetic avengers still pursue him.

At Nuremberg in 1946 Bormann was tried as a war criminal and sentenced to death in absentia.

Bormann's signature

Handwritten New Year's greetings signed in full by Martin Bormann.

Early signature of Bormann, 1935, age 35.

Bormann's signature, Munich, 1938, age 38. This is the characteristic signature that appears on most of his letters.

Martin Bormann in uniform. Bormann was camera shy and was rarely photographed. Few Germans even recognized him.

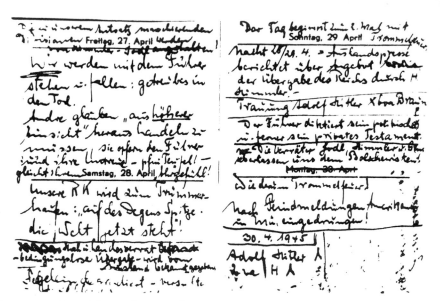

Two pages from Martin Bormann's diary. Here Bormann records the last days in the bunker, April 27 to April 30, 1945.

DR. PAUL JOSEPH GOEBBELS (1897-1945). Nazi Minister of Propaganda. Superbly educated in philosophy, Greek, and Latin, Goebbels was a ferret-faced, slight man with a withered left leg. As a frustrated author whose writings remained unpublished, he discovered in the Nazi party a perfect vehicle for his adroit mind and clever oratory. He greatly admired Hitler and rose from Gauleiter of Berlin and Nazi propaganda leader (1930) to Minister for Propaganda and National Enlightenment (1933-1945).

Dr. Goebbels speaking at a rally, about 1934.

Goebbels was a skilled myth-maker and spread the Nazi doctrines with great ability. During the course of his career he had the books of many great authors, including Einstein, Freud, Zola, Jack London and Helen Keller, burned. He forced the arts and letters of Germany into a constricting mold, utterly suppressing freedom of speech and the press. He was also a noted anti-Semite; he once said, "I treasure an ordinary prostitute above a married Jewess." In the Fuehrer's Berlin bunker on May 1, 1945, the day after Hitler's suicide, Goebbels committed suicide, along with his wife. (He shot himself; she took poison.) An SS orderly then gave them the *coup de grace*, to make sure no life remained. Frau Goebbels also poisoned her six children.

Signed photograph of Goebbels

Ich wünsche diesem Kurse Glück und Segen.

18. Oktober 1935.

Dr. Goebbels.

Handwritten greetings signed by Goebbels, October 18, 1935.

*und meinem herzlichsten Glück-
wünschen für Mutter und Kind.
Heil Hitler
Ihre Dr. Goebbels und Frau.*

Handwritten greetings to mother and child, signed by Goebbels: "Heil Hitler, Your Dr. Goebbels and wife."

Mit Hitler Heil!

Jhr

1935, age 38   1938, age 41

Forgery of a signed photograph of Goebbels, with a burn-like stain in the margin, characteristic of the Goebbels forgeries which first surfaced in New Jersey.   99

MAGDA GOEBBELS (1901-1945) Wife of Joseph Goebbels and close friend of Hitler. Magda's second marriage, to the Nazi propaganda minister, was successful in spite of the constant infidelities of her husband. Goebbels once wrote: "Every woman inflames my very blood. I pace back and forth like a wolf." Once, when Joseph had a passionate fling with a beautiful Czech actress, Magda demanded a divorce. Hitler intervened and put an end to the affair. Hitler often admitted that he was "attracted" to Magda and compared her to his beloved niece, Geli Raubal. The Fuehrer, it was said, persuaded Goebbels to marry Magda so she would always be near him. Magda once confided to Frau Otto Meissner that Hitler had sired her son Helmuth during a Baltic vacation in 1934. (Helmuth's blood group A matched Hitler's.) Magda had six children by Goebbels, all of them favorites with "Uncle Adi," the Fuehrer.

Magda and Joseph Goebbels remained in the bunker with Hitler as the Russian army closed in on Berlin. During Hanna Reitsch's last visit to Hitler, Magda hugged her and burst into tears. "My dear Hanna," she said, "you must help me to help the children out of this life. They belong to the Third Reich and the Fuehrer, and if these two things cease to exist, there will be no place for them." Magda wrote to her son by a previous marriage, then a prisoner in an Allied camp, and told him that a world without Hitler and Nazism was not worth living in. She murdered her six children with vials of potassium cyanide. Then, on the evening of May 1, 1945, arm in arm with her husband, she climbed a steep stairway to the Chancellery garden where she ended her life.

Note:
Magda married Joseph Goebbels on December 12, 1931.

Hitler, Magda Goebbels and her husband, Joseph, in the mid-1930s.

July 1935 signature of Magda Goebbels.

HERMANN GOERING (1893-1946), Reich Marshal and Commander-in-Chief of the Luftwaffe. Goering began his career as a fighter pilot in World War I; he scored 22 victories, received the Pour le Mérite, and was the last commander of Richthofen's squadron. In 1922 he joined the Nazi party and in 1923 was wounded in the unsuccessful Beer-Hall Putsch. After three years of exile in Sweden (Goering was later to talk Hitler out of invading this nation which gave him sanctuary), he returned to Germany and was one of the first Nazis elected to the Reichstag. On August 30, 1932 he became president of the Reichstag.

Goering's career, launched in an aura of idealism, now disintegrated into gangsterism as he helped to build up the Nazi police-state, established the first concentration camps, and made Himmler chief of the Gestapo. By 1933, Goering was the second man in Nazi Germany, and in 1935 was appointed by Hitler to command the Luftwaffe.

Early signature of Hermann Goering, 1918, as a World War I ace.

Photograph of Goering, about 1923.

During World War II, Goering's vaunted air force at first enjoyed great success, but when he failed to win the Battle of Britain by attacking industrial targets, he authorized terror bombings on civilians, wasting not only the power of the Luftwaffe but rousing the ire of the whole civilized world.

The subsequent failure of the Luftwaffe at Stalingrad cost Goering his standing with Hitler and for the final two years of the war he lived in semiretirement, hunting, collecting stolen art, and designing fancy uniforms and new and elaborate medals.

By 1944, Goering was almost a forgotten man and his obesity, lacquered fingernails, and rouged face were subjects for national ridicule.

Shortly before his suicide in April 1945, Hitler sacked Goering and placed him under house arrest. The Luftwaffe chieftain was captured and tried at Nuremberg. The judges found that "his guilt is unique in its enormity." Sentenced to be hanged, Goering swallowed a cyanide capsule on the morning set for his execution (October 15, 1945).

Goering as Reichsmarschall, 1940.

Last page of an early handwritten letter signed by Goering, September 19, 1924, to Leo Negrelli. "Italy must seek to find strong allies. One such ally would be a National Socialist Germany under Hitler's leadership."

1928, age 35

Heil Hitler?

Signature of Goering on a visiting card, 1935.

1935, age 42

Handwritten note by Goering, sending good wishes to a friend.

Berlin, im April 1937

Der Präsident

Generaloberst, Reichsminister der Luftfahrt
und Oberbefehlshaber der Luftwaffe

April 1937, from a citation for contributions to aviation

VERLEIHUNGS-URKUNDE

ICH VERLEIHE
SEINER EXCELLENZ
DEM HERRN
CAVALIERE

BENITO MUSSOLINI

CHEF DER KÖNIGLICHEN UND
KAISERLICHEN REGIERUNG
ROM
DAS GOLDENE
FLUGZEUGFÜHRER-UND
BEOBACHTER-ABZEICHEN

BERLIN/APRIL 1937
DER REICHSMINISTER DER LUFTFAHRT
UND OBERBEFEHLSHABER DER LUFTWAFFE

Göring

GENERALOBERST

Award of the Pilot-Observer Badge with Diamonds to Benito Mussolini, signed by Goering, April 1937.

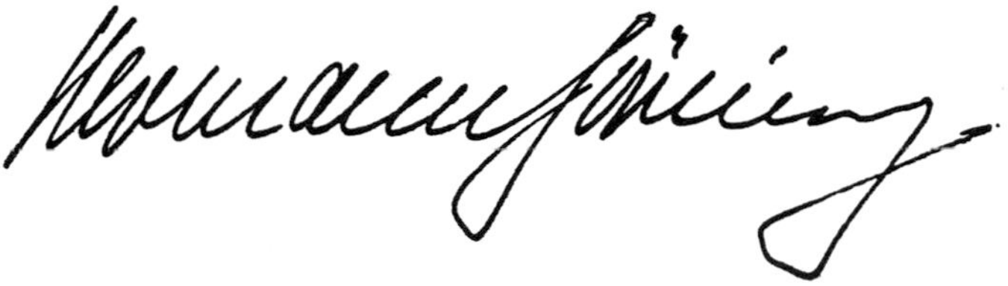

About 1940

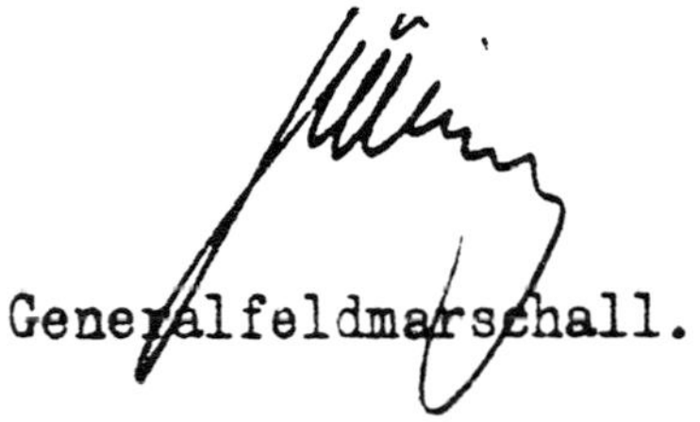
Generalfeldmarschall.

1940, age 47

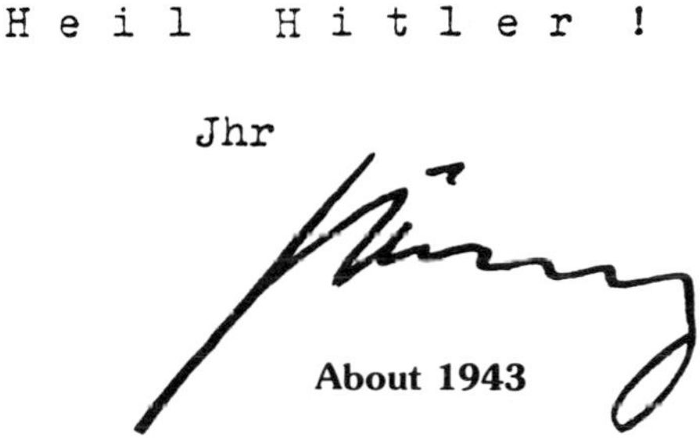
Heil Hitler !
Jhr

About 1943

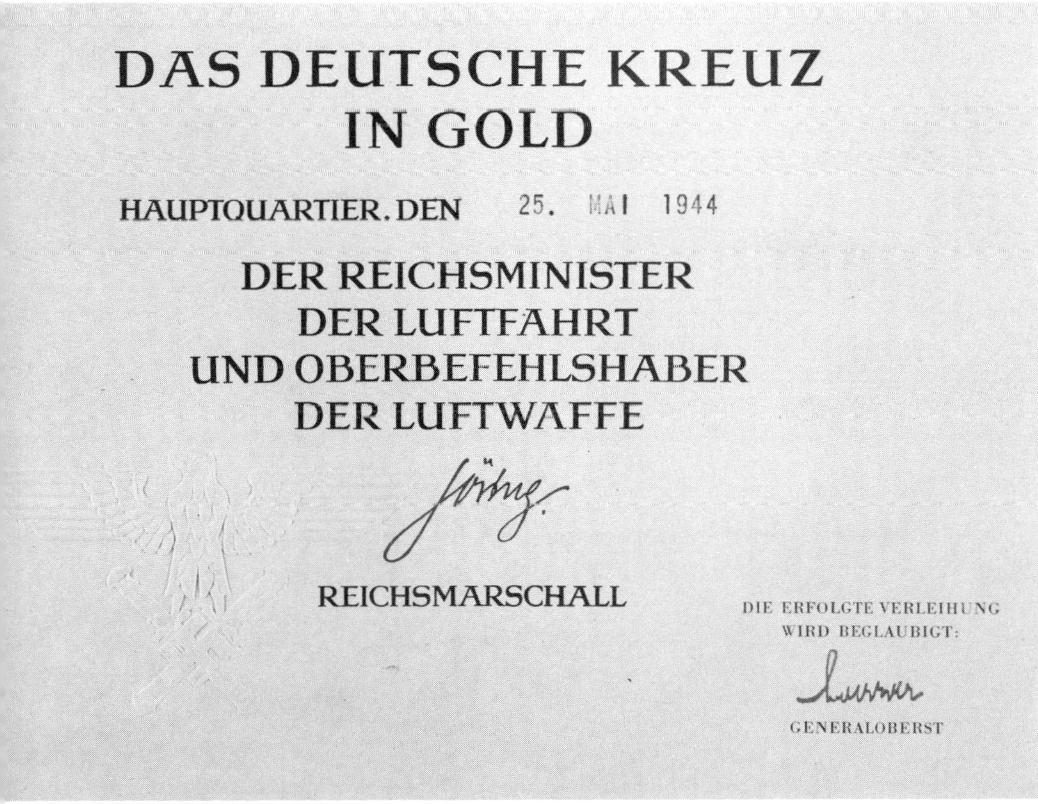

DAS DEUTSCHE KREUZ
IN GOLD

HAUPTQUARTIER, DEN 25. MAI 1944

DER REICHSMINISTER
DER LUFTFAHRT
UND OBERBEFEHLSHABER
DER LUFTWAFFE

Göring

REICHSMARSCHALL

DIE ERFOLGTE VERLEIHUNG
WIRD BEGLAUBIGT:

Loerzer

GENERALOBERST

Award of the German Cross in Gold signed by Goering and World War I ace, General Bruno Loerzer, May 25, 1944.

Hermann Göring [signature]

October 1945, as prisoner of war

Goering arrives at a detention camp on May 7, 1945, shortly after surrendering to U.S. Seventh Army forces.

Caricature of Goering by Peis at Nuremberg, about 1946.

[handwritten letter]

L. GOERING (H) INTERNAL SECURITY DET.
C. I. S. C. C. P. A. C. APO 403 U.S. ARMY.

Handwritten letter signed by Goering as prisoner of war, about 1946. Goering has also printed his name and address at the bottom of the card. "I don't know where Emmy [his wife] and Edda are. . .I beg you to tell me their addresses. . .we must endure great suffering. . ."

Goering reading a book in his prison cell. Note the few personal items allowed on the small wooden table next to his cot.

EMMY SONNEMANN GOERING (1893-1973). Actress; second wife of Hermann Goering. In her youth, Emmy was a provincial actress but she developed into a beautiful and gracious lady who caught the eye of Hermann Goering. Widowed since the death of his first wife Carin in 1931, Goering married Emmy on April 10, 1935, a union that met with Hitler's approval. The splendiferous wedding rivaled any Hollywood spectacular. The bride and groom were showered with precious gifts, including jewels, oriental rugs, and two paintings by Cranach. Their lavish marriage ceremony was reported live on radio in all its riotous details. The couple left the church while an enormous band played the celebrated march from *Lohengrin*.

Emmy soon became a favorite with the unmarried Fuehrer. Before long she was the unofficial first lady of the Third Reich. She presided eloquently over social affairs among the Nazi leaders. In the months before and after the suicide of Goering on October 15, 1946, Frau Goering endeared herself to American officers by presenting them with swords and daggers from the enormous collection that her husband had gathered. Emmy was subsequently convicted of being a Nazi and was barred from the stage for five years. Deprived of any way to make a living, Emmy spent her last years with her daughter Edda in a tiny apartment in Munich. She died on June 8, 1973.

Phot. Rosemarie Clausen

Emmy Göring

Signed portrait of Emmy Goering to Wilhelm Brueckner

A. Southard

Verso of above photo thanking Brueckner for his Christmas wishes and basket of flowers.

RUDOLF HESS (1894-   ), Deputy Fuehrer and second in command only to Goering in line of succession to Hitler. Born in Alexandria, Egypt, and educated in Switzerland and Hamburg, Hess was a strange man, with deep-set eyes and gaunt, bony features. He served in World War I and was twice wounded, winding up as a lieutenant in the air force. Seduced by the oratory of Hitler, he joined the Nazi party in 1920 and after the Beer-Hall Putsch (1923) was sent to Landsberg prison, where he set down *Mein Kampf* at Hitler's dictation.

A dedicated follower of the Fuehrer, Hess became a member of Hitler's cabinet council in 1933 and helped to plan the invasions of Austria and Czechoslovakia. On May 10, 1941, a distraught Hess flew to Scotland in his Messerschmitt-110 fighter aircraft, and parachuted out near the Duke of Hamilton's estate under the impression that the Duke, whom he had met at the 1936 Olympic games in Berlin, would assist him in presenting peace proposals to the British government. Hess sincerely wanted peace, but, as it turned out, he wanted a peace favorable only to Germany. His unauthorized flight shocked Hitler, and, in fact, the entire world, and Hess was imprisoned by the British.

At Nuremberg, despite his paranoia and intermittent amnesia, he was judged sane, found guilty of aiding in a conspiracy to wage a war of aggression and sentenced to life imprisonment. Now the sole prisoner of Spandau jail, this befuddled old man occupies himself by reading and strolling in his little garden.

Rudolf Hess, about 1935

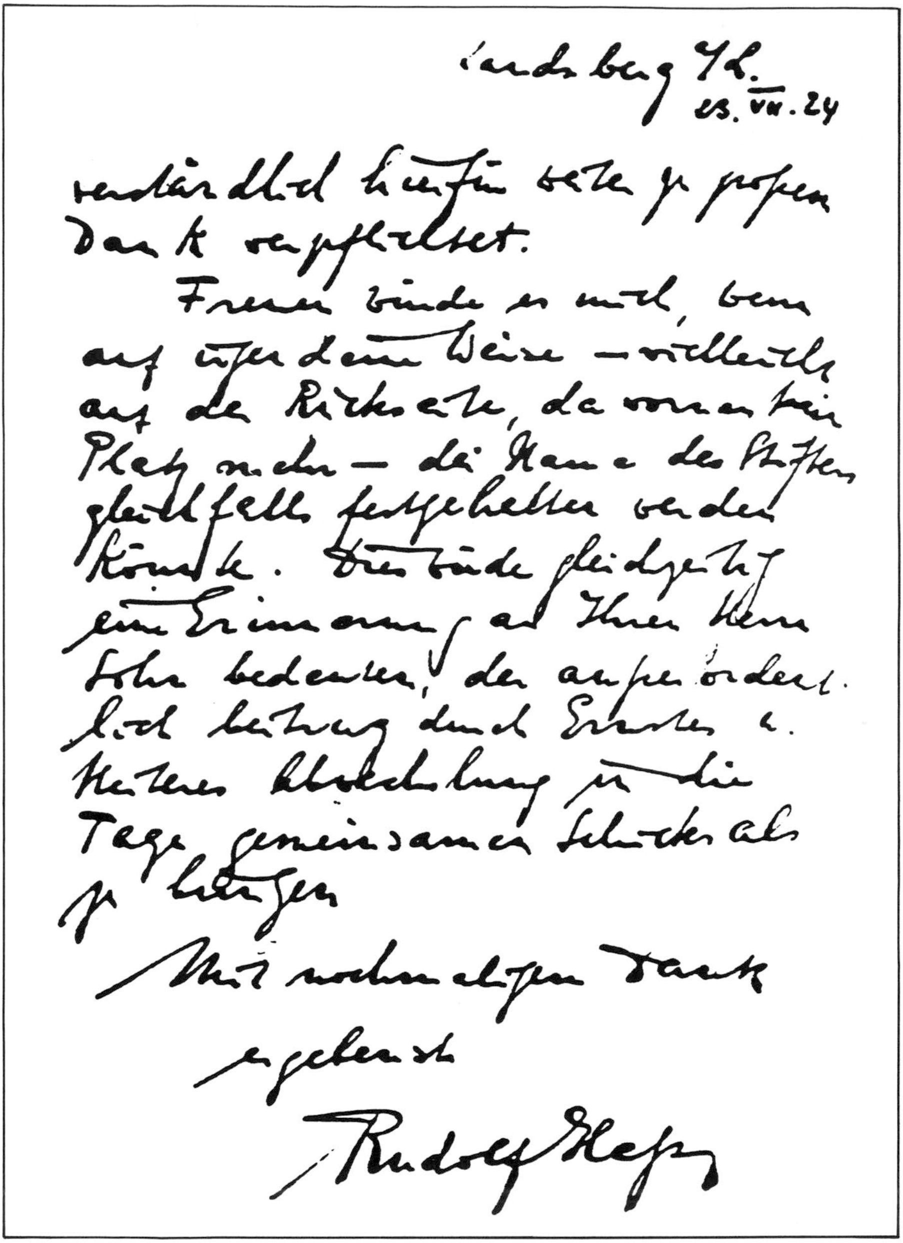

Landsberg/L.
23.VII.24

verständlich hierfür bitte zu großem
Dank verpflichtet.
Freuen würde es mich, wenn
auf irgendeine Weise — vielleicht
auf der Rückseite, da vorne kein
Platz mehr — die Namen des Stifters
gleichfalls festgehalten werden
könnte. Dies würde gleichzeitig
eine Erinnerung an Ihren Herrn
Sohn bedeuten, der außerordent-
lich beitrug durch Erzählen u.
Weiteres Abwechslung in die
Tage gemeinsamer Schicksals
zu bringen.
Mit nochmaligem Dank
ergebenst
Rudolf Hess

Early handwritten document signed by Rudolf Hess, Landsberg Prison, July 23, 1924.

Mit deutschem Gruss

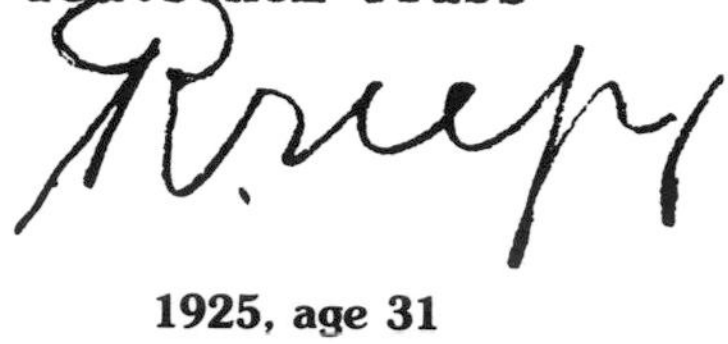

1925, age 31

Full signature   1939, age 45

Herr General feldmarschall
                von Rundstedt
in Erinnerung an das Zusammen -
treffen in großen Tagen der deutschen
Geschichte.
                        Weihnachten 1940

                Rudolfhess.

Photograph of Hess (second from right) inscribed to Field Marshal von Rundstedt (far right), 1940.

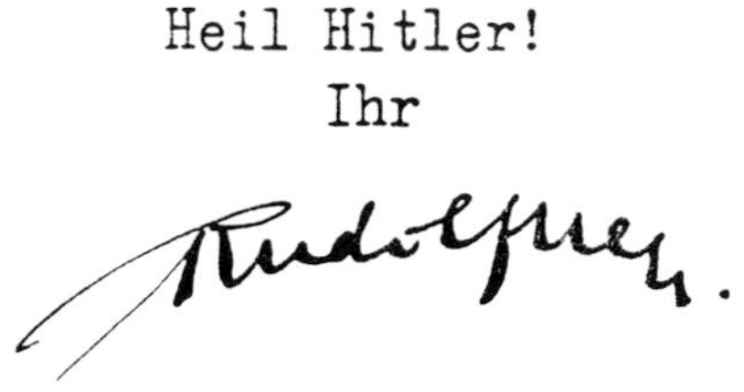

Heil Hitler!
Ihr
Rudolf Hess.

Conclusion of a typed letter signed, 1940, age 46

Hess at Nuremberg, about 1946

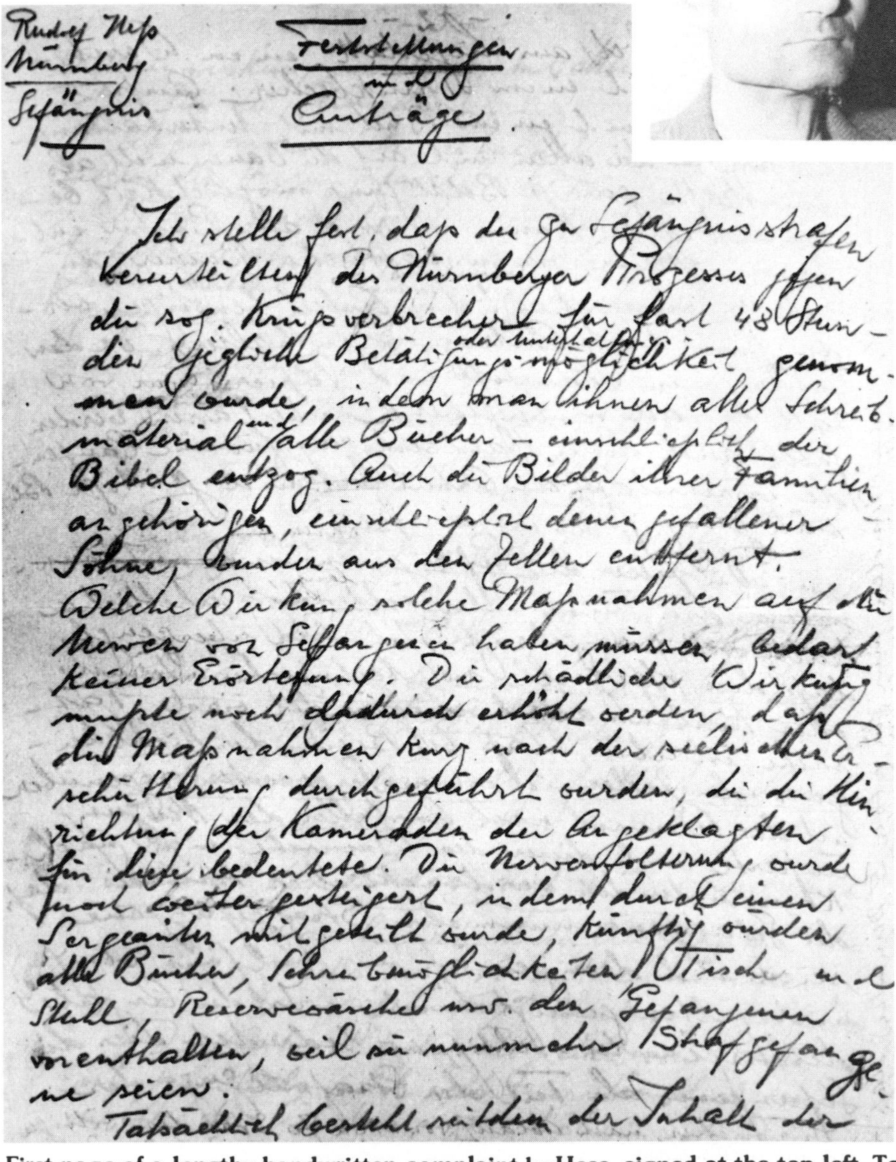

Rudolf Hess
Nürnberg
Gefängnis

Feststellungen und Anträge.

Ich stelle fest, daß den zu Gefängnisstrafen Verurteilten des Nürnberger Prozesses gegen die sog. Kriegsverbrecher für fast 48 Stunden jegliche Betätigungs- oder Unterhaltungsmöglichkeit genommen wurde, indem man ihnen alles Schreibmaterial und alle Bücher – einschließlich der Bibel entzog. Auch die Bilder ihrer Familienangehörigen, einschließlich denen gefallener Söhne, wurden aus den Zellen entfernt. Welche Wirkung solche Maßnahmen auf die Nerven von Gefangenen haben müssen, bedarf keiner Erörterung. Die schädliche Wirkung mußte noch dadurch erhöht werden, daß die Maßnahmen kurz nach der seelischen Erschütterung durchgeführt wurden, die die Hinrichtung der Kameraden der Angeklagten für diese bedeutete. Die Nervenfolterung wurde noch weiter gesteigert, indem durch einen Sergeanten mitgeteilt wurde, künftig würden alle Bücher, Schreibmöglichkeiten, Tische und Stühle, Reservewäsche usw. den Gefangenen vorenthalten, weil sie nunmehr Strafgefangene seien.

Tatsächlich besteht seitdem der Inhalt der

First page of a lengthy handwritten complaint by Hess, signed at the top left. To his jailers at Nuremberg: "My soul is troubled and my nerves are tortured. . ."

Rudolf Hess' handwriting changed very little during his lifetime. There is a curious book, published in 1979, entitled *The Murder of Rudolf Hess*, in which the author contends that Hess is not the man now imprisoned at Spandau. He writes: "As for the prisoner's handwriting, Frau Hess insists not only that it is the same as her husband's but that it has never varied since he was a young man. . .This is a striking fact, but not, in my view, a conclusive one. Given practice, it is relatively simple to imitate someone else's hand."

After some fifty years of experience in the autograph field, and after having instigated the arrest and conviction of half a dozen forgers, I can unequivocally state that it is absolutely impossible to counterfeit handwriting without detection. In my opinion the man in Spandau is definitely Rudolf Hess.

HEINRICH HIMMLER (1900-1945). Himmler joined the Nazi party in 1923 and took over the S.S. (Schutzstaffel) in 1929 when it numbered about two hundred men. In 1934 he became chief of the Gestapo (Secret State Police) and speedily built it into one of the most feared organizations in world history. Himmler controlled a virtual private empire by the time the war broke out. In 1943, he became Minister of the Interior as well.

Once, when Reichsfuehrer Himmler personally witnessed the execution of about one hundred Jews, he became so ill at the sight that he nearly fainted. His squeamish stomach was, however, not upset by the establishment of extermination camps where millions of Jews were gassed or starved to death.

Tom Poole

Himmler's identify card while a member of Freikorps "Oberland."

In 1944 Himmler was appointed chief of the home army, and in April 1945, a week before Hitler's suicide, he made an effort to negotiate the surrender of Germany. When the attempt failed and Berlin fell, Himmler tried to escape into his native Bavaria by shaving off his moustache, dressing as an army private, and putting a black patch over his left eye. The disguise did not fool the British. Himmler was captured and on May 23, 1945, he killed himself by biting on a phial of potassium cyanide hidden in his mouth.

Tom Pooler

Himmler's identity card for the Reichs-Kriegsflagge Veterans' organization.

Heinrich Himmler, age 30

Cats drawn by Himmler. From a school notebook, age about nine.

Christmas list of Himmler at about age ten or eleven, requesting a tie, formal gloves, a gun, 25 play grenades, a military book, and a wallet.

1939

Der Reichsführer-SS   Berlin, den 9. November 1938.

SS-Sturmbannführer

S c h u l z Erwin , SS-Nr. 1o7 484 .

Ich verleihe Ihnen den Degen der SS

Ziehen Sie ihn niemals ohne Not!
Stecken Sie ihn niemals ein ohne Ehre!

Wahren Sie Ihre eigene Ehre ebenso bedingungslos, wie Sie die Ehre
anderer zu achten und für Schutzlose ritterlich einzutreten haben!

Dieser Degen soll in Ihrer Sippe Besitz verbleiben, wenn Sie ihn ein Leben
lang untadelig getragen haben. Scheiden Sie vorher aus der SS aus, so
fällt er zurück an den Reichsführer-SS.

Vergessen Sie keinen Augenblick, welch großes Vertrauen die Schutzstaffel
Adolf Hitlers Ihnen durch Verleihung dieser Waffe geschenkt hat.
Bleiben Sie in guten und schlechten Tagen immer der gleiche!

Führen Sie den Degen in Ehren!

H. Himmler

Award of an SS dagger, signed by Himmler. "Never draw it without reason! Never sheath it without honor!"

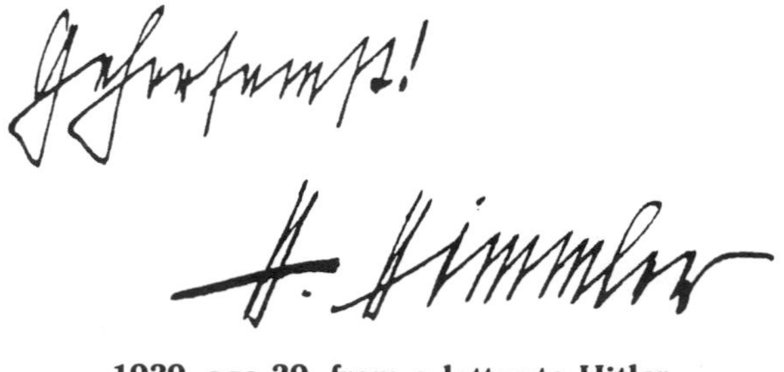

Gehorsamst!

H. Himmler

1939, age 39, from a letter to Hitler.

Autograph note signed on verso of his visiting card, December 21, 1939, sending a Christmas present.

Complimentary close from a typed letter, 1939.

Schenk

Himmler as Reichsfuehrer-SS

Für Ihre Wünsche zum Weihnachtsfest und für das Jahr 1937 sage ich Ihnen meinen besten Dank. Ich wünsche Ihnen und uns allen, daß wir im neuen Jahre mit immer gleichem Pflichtbewußtsein – jeder freudig an seiner Stelle – für den Führer und Deutschland arbeiten und kämpfen können.

Heil Hitler!

Reichsführer-SS
und
Chef der Deutschen Polizei
im Reichsministerium des Innern

Gmund, im Januar 1937

Christmas greetings for 1937.

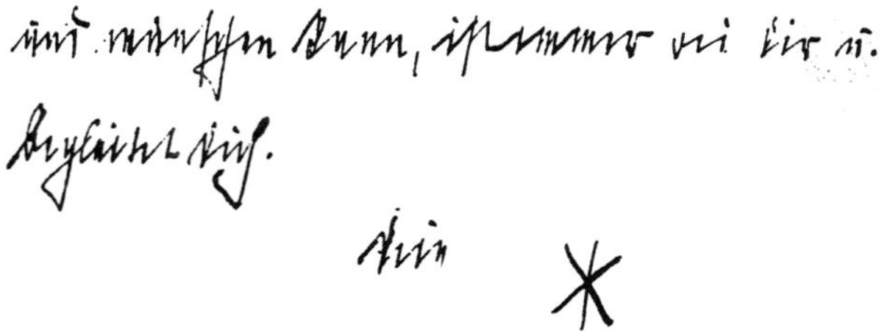

Conclusion of a handwritten letter by Himmler to his mistress, Maria Podherzer, 1940, signed with a star or asterisk.

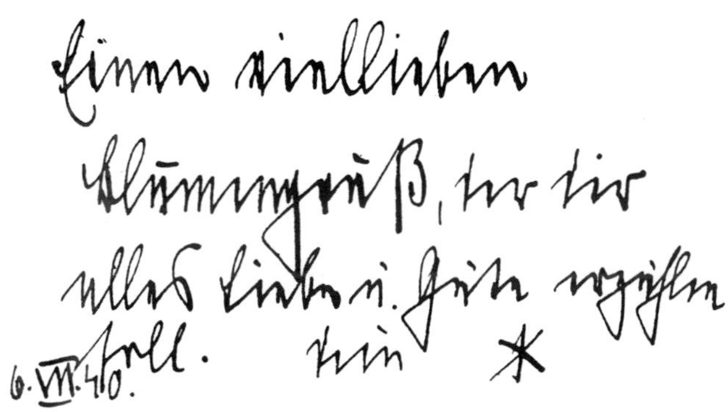

Handwritten note to his mistress, July 6, 1940, sending flowers. Signed with a star.

etwas auszuruhen. Jedenfalls bleibe ich zwar
hier, nehme aber dann die Arbeit in vollem
Umfang wieder auf.

Marga war mit Püppi 14 Tage an der
Ostsee, was beiden sehr gut getan hat.
Beide grüssen Dich sehr herzlich u. schicken
Dir viel gute Wünsche.

Und nun mit einem herzlichen Gedenken:
Dank u. Heil Hitler
Dein getreuer
H. Himmler

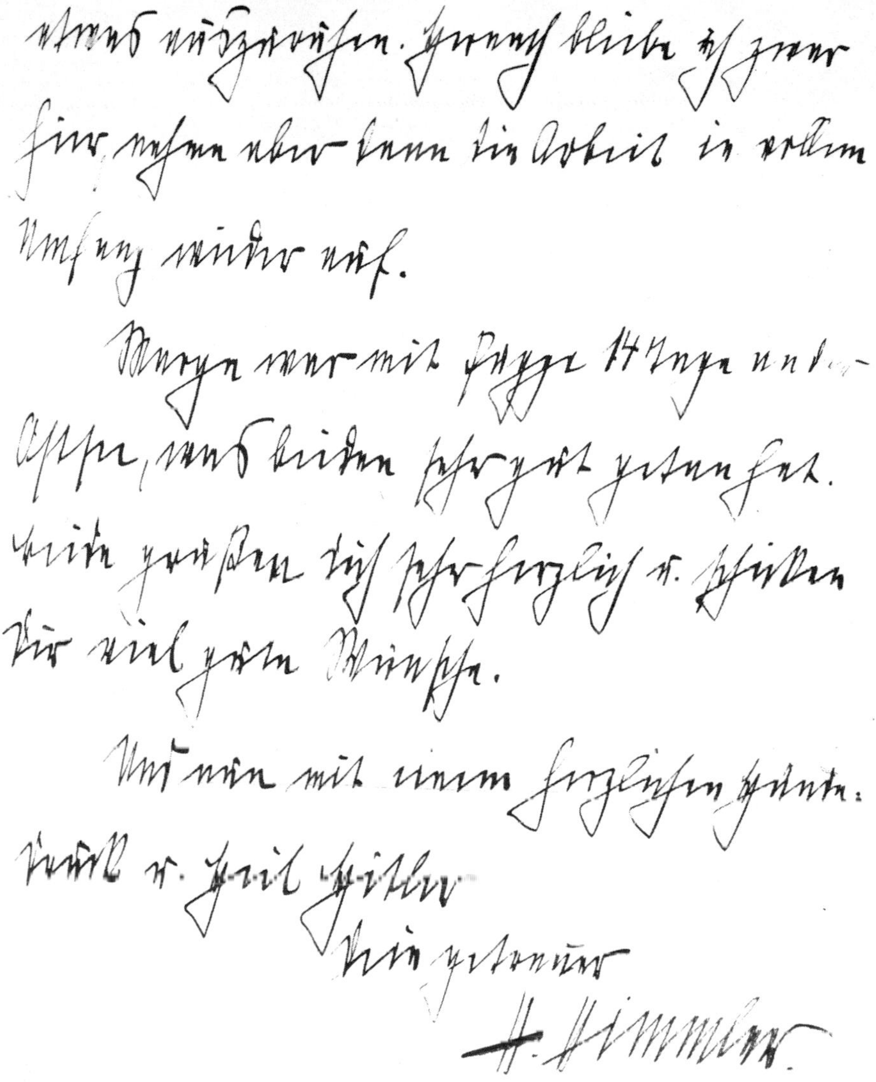

Last page of a handwritten letter signed by Heinrich Himmler. The fierce sharpness of Himmler's script has always fascinated me, and I asked the famous graphologist, Marie Bernard, to interpret it for me. She wrote:
"Himmler's cruel, razor-sharp script gives his writing the appearance of shark's teeth. The pointed triangular lower lengths belong to an inflexible and inhuman creature.
"The inner structure of Himmler's signature shows hysterical, compulsive and neurotic traits. All demons of the subconscious are let loose. The crossing of his narrow capital H is the sword of a murderer, a club-like weapon used in the naked, high prison walls of his regulated m formations.
"The capital H in Himmler has a bent, powerful upstroke shaped like a scourging whip. Himmler is a dangerous fanatic. There is not one curve in his whole script, only sharp angles."

Heinrich Himmler in death after biting on a cyanide capsule. His arrest report reveal that he was trying to escape from the Allies under the name Heinrich Hizinger.

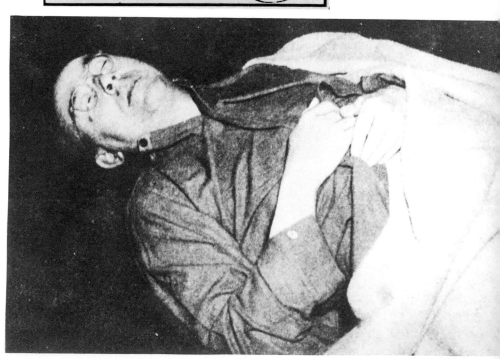

MARGARETE BODEN HIMMLER. Wife of Heinrich Himmler. The daughter of a German landowner from Concerzewo, West Prussia, Margarete, known as Marga, was seven or eight years older than Himmler. She worked as a nurse during World War I and after a brief first marriage moved to Berlin where she used her father's money to establish a clinic. She specialized in homeopathy and herbs and when Himmler met her in 1927 he was fascinated by her work and tumbled for her charms. Despite the fact that she was divorced and a Protestant, the two were married on July 3, 1928. Marga sold her clinic and she and Heinrich bought a chicken farm and populated it with 50 laying hens. At first they had a terrible struggle. On May 6, 1929, Marga wrote to Heinrich: "The hens are laying frightfully badly--two eggs a day. I worry so much about what we're going to live on..." Later Marga had a little girl, Gudrun, whom Himmler adored. Although Marga called Himmler her "naughty darling," the couple gradually drifted apart. Himmler was constantly away from home and did not like his wife to mingle with the social set in Munich and Berlin. Lina Heydrich, wife of Reinhard Heydrich, said of her: "Size 50 knickers..narrow-minded, humorless blonde female. She ruled her husband and could twist him round her little finger."

As Reichsfuehrer, Himmler acquired a mistress named Hedwig to whom he wrote scores of gossipy love letters signed with runic asterisks. Hedwig was Himmler's private secretary and by her he had two children, Helge, a son, and Nanette Dorothea, a daughter. Hedwig, born in 1912, was almost 20 years younger than Marga and after Himmler met her he rarely visited his wife. Marga dutifully remained on the chicken farm. She survived the war.

Frau Margarete ("Marga") Himmler

Identification book of Marga Himmler, with her photograph, description, and signature.

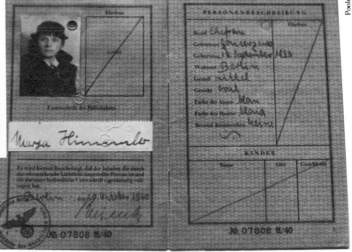

ALBERT SPEER (1905-1981), Nazi Minister of Armaments and War Production. One of the youngest of the inner circle, Speer was a brilliant architect who at 26 fell under the hypnotic spell of the Fuehrer, joined the Nazi party, and soon was put to the task of redesigning Berlin and Munich. The brick-and-marble ambitions of Hitler, a frustrated architect, were vested in Speer.

On February 9, 1942 Speer succeeded Fritz Todt as Reich Minister for Armaments and Munitions, and on September 2, 1943 was redesignated Reich Minister for Armaments and War Production. He performed miracles and largely by the use of impressed and slave labor kept the Nazi armies in the field. He was awarded the coveted Golden Party Badge and became Hitler's trusted friend.

Speer's eventual disillusionment led him to plot the Fuehrer's murder in 1945, a plan he was forced to abandon. In 1946 Speer was found guilty of war crimes at Nuremberg and sentenced to twenty years in prison. He was released from Spandau in 1966 and afterward wrote several unusual and illuminating books about Hitler and the Nazis. He died in London (during a visit) on September 1, 1981.

Albert Speer

Eva Braun, Hitler, his dog Blondi, "Sepp" Dietrich, and Albert Speer pause during their walk to the teahouse at Obersalzberg in 1944.

BERLIN-~~CHARLOTTENBURG 2~~ W 8, d.20.12.43
~~VERLÄNGERTE JEBENSSTRASSE~~ Pariser Platz 3
FERNSPRECHER: 11 00 52

DER REICHSMINISTER
FÜR
RÜSTUNG UND KRIEGSPRODUKTION

M 257/43

An den
Chef des Oberkommandos der Wehrmacht
Herrn Generalfeldmarschall K e i t e l

Führerhauptquartier

Lieber Generalfeldmarschall,

in dem in Abschrift beiliegenden Erlass des Führers über die Steigerung der Zulieferungs-Industrie vom 6.12.43 werden auch alle Dienststellen der Wehrmacht verpflichtet, der Zulieferungs-Industrie jede nur mögliche Hilfe zu geben. Ich bitte Sie um Bekanntgabe des Erlasses an die Wehrmachtdienststellen.

H e i l H i t l e r !

1 Anlage!

OKW/149

Letter signed by Albert Speer to Field Marshal Wilhelm Keitel, December 20, 1943, requesting assistance for all industries supplying the army. With a lengthy handwritten note signed "K" by Wilhelm Keitel in the upper right portion of the letter.

Signature of Albert Speer.

Architectural sketch by Speer, November 22, 1945. Inscribed: "First Hitler's architect, then Minister of War Production, and now - Cell 17 in the Nuremberg Prison."

Albert Speer (between Hess and Hitler) reviews architectural plans.

Photograph signed by Albert Speer, about 1975.

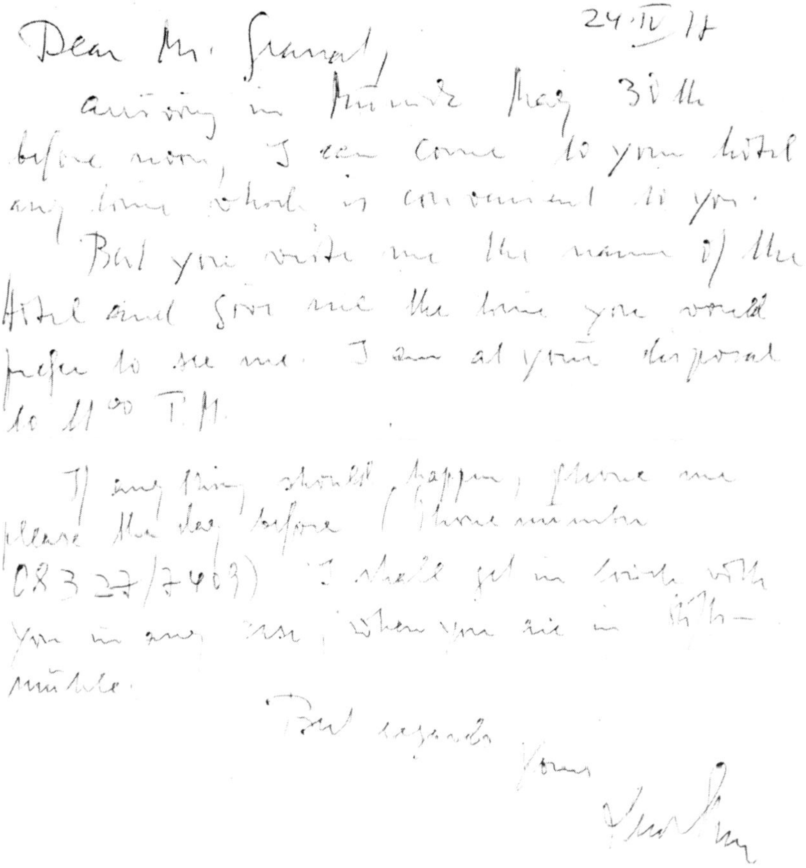

Dear Mr. *[illegible]*,   24.IV 78

Arriving in Munich May 31th
before noon, I can come to your hotel
any time which is convenient to you.

But you write me the name of the
hotel and give me the time you would
prefer to see me. I am at your disposal
to 11⁰⁰ T.M.

If anything should happen, phone me
please the day before (Phone number
0832 7/7463) I shall get in touch with
you in any case, when you are in Mü-
nich.

                    Best regards
                         yours
                              [signature]

Handwritten letter signed by Albert Speer in English, April 24, 1978.

Hitler with adjutants and staff in May 1940. (front row, L. to R.) Brueckner, Dietrich, Keitel, Hitler, Jodl, Bormann, v. Below, Hoffmann. (Middle row) Bodenschatz, Schmundt, Wolff, Dr. Morell, Hansgeorg Schulze. (Back row) Engel, Dr. Brandt, Puttkamer, Heinz Lorenz, Hewel, unidentified, Schaub, and Wuensche.

The Fuehrer's "Inner Circle"

Staff, Adjutants & Friends

ALWIN-BRODER ALBRECHT (1903-   ). Albrecht was Hitler's naval adjutant from June 1938 to June 1939, with the rank of Korvettenkapitan. Because Albrecht's wife did not match the high standards of the officer corps (labeled a woman with "a large-scaled zest for life"), he was forced to leave the navy by Admiral Raeder. Hitler was fond of him, however, and appointed him as a personal adjutant on July 7, 1939. He was given the rank of NSKK-Oberfuehrer and was flown out of Berlin on April 22, 1945.

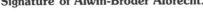

Signature of Alwin-Broder Albrecht.

Hitler, Wuensche, and Albrecht on April 20, 1939, the Fuehrer's 50th birthday.

HANS BAUR (1897-   ). Hitler's personal pilot. So skillful was this airman that Hitler rarely flew with any other pilot. Baur served as a Lufthansa pilot before he joined Hitler's personal entourage. He quickly became a favorite with the Fuehrer. Hitler often joked with him and greatly enjoyed his companionship. During the final days of the war, Baur was in the Berlin bunker with Hitler.

On the morning of April 30, 1945, as Hitler prepared to kill himself, he shook hands with Baur. The pilot said: "Let me fly you to Argentina or Japan.

We can still get out." Hitler replied: "One must have the courage to face the consequences. I am ending it all here. I know that by tomorrow millions of people will curse me." Hitler then offered Baur a treasured portrait of Frederick the Great in recognition of his long and faithful service. Then the Fuehrer proposed a sardonic epitaph for himself: "I want them to write on my tombstone 'He was the victim of his generals.'" Baur's escape attempt from besieged Berlin failed. He lost a leg in the attempt, and was not released from Russian captivity until 1955.

In 1956, Baur wrote a book about his experiences, published in English under the title, *Hitler's Pilot.*

Signed portrait of Hans Baur

Hans Baur signing autographs for youthful collectors on December 3, 1938, the Day of National Solidarity.

NICOLAUS VON BELOW (1908-   ). Colonel (Oberst) von Below served from 1937 to 1945 as Hitler's Luftwaffe Adjutant. He was with Hitler during his moments of greatest triumph and most awesome disaster. When Hitler signed the "peace pact" with Russia, his final bloodless coup, on August 24, 1939, von Below stood with him on the Berghof terrace watching an enormous red glow from the Northern Lights. Hitler said: "Looks like a great deal of blood. This time we won't bring it off without violence." The violence Hitler predicted was to end in the Berlin bunker nearly six years later. Below, now a colonel, was still with the Fuehrer. On April 29, the date before Hitler's suicide, he witnessed the Fuehrer's last will and testament. Then, as Below abhorred the idea of suicide, he asked Hitler's permission to leave the bunker. It was granted. Hitler gave him a bitter, recriminatory message to carry to Field Marshal Keitel.

Signature and titles of Nicolaus von Below: Major and Adjutant of the Wehrmacht (Luftwaffe) to the Fuehrer and Reich Chancellor. Fuehrer's Headquarters, 1942.

Von Below, Goering, and Bodenschatz look on as Hitler awards Hanna Reitsch her Iron Cross in February 1941.

ALBERT BORMANN. Adjutant to Hitler; high officer in the NSKK (paramilitary motor training unit). Born in September 1902 at Halberstadt, Albert was the younger brother of Martin Bormann. Albert studied banking and by age 23 was helping to support his widowed mother. In April 1931, at the depth of the depression, his brother Martin, even then a powerful Nazi leader, got Albert a job in Munich with the Relief Fund. Albert was very unlike his famous brother. Albert was tall, pleasant and handsome, cultured and unassuming. He soon made friends with Philipp Bouhler, general manager of the Nazi party. Within six months, much to the envy and chagrin of Martin, Albert was transferred to the Private Chancellery of Hitler.

Albert Bormann

Although Albert avoided the limelight and remained a shadowy figure, he became a trusted aide to Hitler. Those who knew him well found him dependable and honest, utterly without a lust for power. In 1938 the Fuehrer, who was very fond of Albert, assigned him to a small group of adjutants who were not subordinate to Martin Bormann. Albert became chief of Hitler's Private Chancellery and handled much of the Fuehrer's routine correspondence. He survived the war and in 1978 refused to dictate his memoirs.

ADOLF HITLER
KANZLEI

BERLIN W8
WILHELMSTRASSE 55 ¹¹
FERNSPR.: A.2.FLORA 7601

DEN   20. Febr. 34.

Herrn

TAGEBUCH-Nr. 6072/I. Kl.
BEI RÜCKFRAGEN UNBEDINGT ANZUGEBEN

Leland O. R h o d e s,

A d a m s   N.J. U.S.A.
----
23 Wachwell Str.

Sehr geehrter Herr Rhodes !

Jhr Schreiben an den Führer ging hier ein.

Die ausserordentlich starke Jnanspruchnahme des Führers und die grosse Zahl gleicher Bitten macht es jedoch leider unmöglich, Jhnen Jhre Bitte um persönliche Unterschrift zu erfüllen.

Jch bedaure Jhnen keinen günstigeren Bescheid geben zu können.

Mit deutschem Gruss!

Albert Bormann

Letter signed by Albert Bormann, Berlin, February 20, 1934. To an American, explaining why Hitler cannot send his autograph.

Albert Bormann, (second from right). After the bombing attempt on Hitler's life on July 20, 1944, Bormann stands next to the wounded Jodl. Hitler holds his injured right arm and Martin Bormann poses behind Hitler's right shoulder.

136

FROHE WEIHNACHTEN UND EIN
GLÜCKLICHES NEUES JAHR!

[signature]

LEITER DER PRIVATKANZLEI DES FÜHRERS

IM DEZEMBER 1937

Christmas and New Year's greetings from Albert Bormann.

DR. KARL BRANDT (1904-1948). One of Hitler's personal physicians. In 1933 Brandt, then only 29, was called to Upper Bavaria to treat Hitler's aide, Wilhelm Brueckner, who had been injured in an automobile accident. The impression he made upon this prominent patient led to his joining Hitler's personal circle. Brandt eventually became a Brigadefuehrer in the Waffen-SS and in 1942 Reich Commissioner for Sanitation and Health. He soon became one of Hitler's physicians. He and Theodor Morell, Hitler's favorite doctor, vied for the Fuehrer's favors. Morell injected Hitler with countless dangerous drugs, and Dr. Brandt, in turn, warned Hitler against the use of such drugs. The Fuehrer rebuffed all criticism of Morell, and in October 1944 Brandt was sacked, being replaced by Ludwig Stumpfegger.

Two weeks before his suicide, the Fuehrer learned that Dr. Brandt had placed his wife and child in a position where they could surrender to the advancing Americans rather than the Russians. Furious, he charged Brandt with treason. Brandt was tried by a summary court that included Dr. Goebbels. Found guilty, he was condemned to death, but Heinrich Himmler and Albert Speer managed to stall the execution by continuously calling for new witnesses.

At the Nuremberg trials, Dr. Brandt was accused of criminal experimentation on humans. His excuse, that "any personal code of ethics must give way to the total character of the war," did not convince the court and Brandt was sentenced to be hanged. He offered his body for experimental purposes such as the "freezing" to which he had subjected his own victims but the offer was declined. Denouncing his execution as "political revenge," Brandt's farewell speech on the scaffold was cut short when the black hood was pulled over his head. He was hanged on June 2, 1948.

A. Southard

Signature of Dr. Karl Brandt

BERLIN W 8, DEN
WILHELMSTR. 7?

FHO., den 7. Sept. 1942.

Herrn

Ministerialrat G o e r n e r t

B e r l i n W 8 /Leipziger Pl. 3

Büro Reichsmarschall Göring

Herr Feldmarschall K e i t e l sprach mich gestern auf die
Zusammensetzung des Präsidialrates des Reichsforschungsrates an.
Er hat Allerlei daran auszusetzen und hat wohl das Gleiche Ihnen
oder dem Herrn Reichsmarschall schon gegenüber geäussert. Ich
gebe nur ordnungshalber die Mitteilung an Sie weiter:

1.) war er der Auffassung, daß Herr Generaloberst F r o m m
    nicht Vertreter der Wehrmachtsführung sei und

2.) hielt er es für notwendig, daß Generaloberstabsarzt H a n d
    l o s e r ebenfalls als Gegengewicht zu Herrn Staatssekre-
    tär C o n t i dem Präsidialrat angehören müsse.

Ich habe Herrn Feldmarschall Keitel von mir aus gesagt, daß ich
der Meinung sei, Herr Staatssekretär Conti sei als einziger
Angehöriger des Reichsinnenministeriums im Präsidialrat , und
die Medizin bezw. Gesundheitsführung sei durch mich allein vertreten. Zu der Angelegenheit des Generaloberst Fromm habe ich
keine Stellung genommen, da ich das nicht beurteilen oder über-
sehen kann.

Ich glaube, daß der Feldmarschall Keitel die Angelegenheit als
erledigt betrachtet und es nicht notwendig ist, den Reichsmarschall nochmals darüber zu unterrichten.   3852

Mit freundlichem Gruß und

                              Heil Hitler

        Ihr   Karlbrandt.

**Letter signed by Dr. Karl Brandt to Wilhelm Keitel. Writing on his letterhead as
General Commissioner of the Fuehrer for Health and Sanitation, Dr. Brandt dis-
cusses with Keitel the assignments of General Fromm and Dr. Leonardo Conti.**

WILHELM BRUECKNER (1884-1954). SA lieutenant general (SA-Obergruppenfuehrer) and Hitler's chief personal adjutant. Brueckner was born on December 11, 1884, in Baden-Baden. After service in the First World War, he joined the Freikorps Epp and in 1922 the Nazi party. He commanded the SA Regiment "Muenchen" during the Beer-Hall Putsch and was one of Hitler's co-defendants after the failure of the uprising. Because of disagreements with Hitler, Brueckner left the NSDAP on May 1, 1925. He rejoined, however, on September 1, 1930 and became Hitler's adjutant. On February 20, 1934 he was appointed to the post of Chief Personal Adjutant to the Fuehrer.

In 1940, after a decade of service to Hitler, Brueckner was abruptly dismissed by his master. During a visit of the Italian Crown Prince at Obersalzburg, Hitler's butler, Arthur Kannenberg, complained that some of the young SS ordnance officers were not behaving correctly. Hitler agreed and ordered that Max Wuensche should be returned to the LAH immediately. Brueckner interceded on Wuensche's behalf, criticized Kannenberg, and was

Angolia

Signed photograph to Gretl Braun, Eva's sister.

immediately released by Hitler from his personal staff. He officially left on April 1, 1941. He then served in occupied France as an army captain and eventually as a colonel. After the war Brueckner ran a filling station in Bavaria. He died on August 20, 1954 in Herbsdorf.

GERDA "DARA" DARANOWSKY CHRISTIAN (1913-   ). Hitler's "best" secretary. A good-natured, pretty girl, Dara was born in Berlin on December 13, 1913. She left a job with Elizabeth Arden to join the Fuehrer's staff and was at Hitler's side during many of the great crises in his life. Dara was present with the Fuehrer when England declared war on Germany. Years later she recalled the pallor that spread over his face when he heard the terrible news that the British had called his bluff. Dara left Hitler's employ for a while after she married Eckard Christian, Jodl's chief staff officer, subsequently a general. Dara later rejoined Hitler and was one of two secretaries who volunteered to remain with him in the Berlin bunker in April 1945. She was a guest at Hitler's wedding to Eva Braun on April 29. After the ceremony Hitler invited her to join a little champagne party in his private suite.

Dara, who had been engaged to Erich Kempka, divorced Eckard Christian in 1946 because he did not remain with her in Berlin but escaped on April 22, 1945. She stated, "I am glad I survived the war just to be able to divorce that laut." After the war she retired to a quiet life in Duesseldorf.

Photograph signed by Gerda Christian (Dara). Dara stands between Julius Schaub (far left) and Adolf Hitler. At far right is Johanna Wolf.

Gerda Christian with Martin Bormann

FRITZ DARGES (1913-   ). Darges was Martin Bormann's SS adjutant from 1936 to 1939 and from October 1940 was an SS aide with periods of frontline duty until he was eventually wounded. From March 1, 1943 to July 18, 1944 he was a personal adjutant to the Fuehrer. During a conference Hitler became irritated when a fly kept returning to a point on a map he was concentrating on. As he angrily tried to shoo it away he looked up and saw Darges grinning. He immediately took him aside and had him transferred to the front. He won the Knight's Cross on April 5, 1945 as commander of the 5th SS Panzer Regiment, 5th SS Panzer Divison "Wiking."

Signed photograph of
Fritz Darges

GERHARD ENGEL (1906-1976). Hitler's army adjutant from 1938 to 1943. The first time Hitler met Engel he was immensely impressed by his intellect and efficiency. In 1937, during combat maneuvers, Captain Engel had filled in for the absent commander of his regiment. Hitler inspected Engel's battle positions, asked Engel several questions, then turned to General Hossbach and said: "Please take note of the name of this officer." A brilliant, energetic young artillery captain, Engel had served as General Fritsch's aide. Although Fritsch was accused of homosexuality and forced to resign in 1938, Hitler nevertheless chose Engel as his army adjutant. For months afterward, Engel risked the Fuehrer's disfavor by urging the reinstatement of Fritsch. Engel kept a diary that told of his prolonged and unremitting struggle to save his old commanding officer from disgrace. Despite Engel's persistence in a fruitless cause, he won the respect and affection of Hitler. The Fuehrer invariably used his youthful adjutants Colonel Rudolf Schmundt from the OKW, Captain Nicolaus von Below from the Luftwaffe, Captain von Puttkamer from the navy, and Captain Engel from the army to test the validity of his own ideas. He also leaned heavily upon them for suggestions and fresh interpretations.

Engel was subsequently promoted to colonel and eventually to major general. During the final year of the war he commanded a frontline unit, the 12th Peoples Grenadier Division. A man of great courage and integrity, Engel secretly arranged with the enemy for a cessation of hostilities to rescue the wounded. Hitler regarded such pauses in the conflict as a sign of weakness and was opposed to them. He died on December 9, 1976 at Duesseldorf.

Adjutants von Below and Engel.

Gerhardt Engel

Signature of Gerhardt Engel.

Colonel Heinrich Borgmann succeeded Gerhard Engel as Hitler's army adjutant in October 1943. On April 2, 1945 he was appointed commander of Infantry Division "Scharnhorst" and killed on April 6 when his staff car was attacked by an Allied fighter-bomber near Magdeburg.

HERMANN OTTO FEGELEIN (1906-1945). SS-Gruppenfuehrer in the Waffen-SS. Born in Ansbach on October 30, 1906, Fegelein received two years of advanced schooling and in 1923 enlisted in the 17th Cavalry Regiment. In 1933 he joined the SS. He was appointed leader of the first Reiter-SS unit. He commanded the SS-Kavallerie-Brigade in Russia until May 1942. During World War II Fegelein was wounded in action three times and received nine decorations for bravery. In 1944 he was chosen as Himmler's liaison officer with Hitler. He was wounded on July 20, 1944, during the bombing attempt on Hitler's life. His marriage on June 3, 1944, to Gretl Braun, sister of Hitler's mistress, Eva Braun, strengthened Fegelein's position in Nazi circles.

On April 27, 1945, three days before the Fuehrer's suicide, Fegelein vanished mysteriously from the Berlin Bunker. Hitler noticed his absence and ordered a search. Fegelein was arrested by the Gestapo at his home in Berlin. He was dressed in civilian clothes and had on him a large amount of jewelry and Swiss francs, an indication to Hitler that Fegelein intended to abandon the sinking ship and escape to Switzerland or some other neutral country. By this time Hitler had begun to suspect Himmler of treachery. He turned his wrath upon Fegelein who protested his innocence. Eva Braun pleaded for Fegelein's life, pointing out that Gretl was pregnant. The Fuehrer simmered down enough to spare Fegelein. He berated him for cowardice, however, and ripped off his Knight's Cross. A few hours later the BBC reported that Himmler had offered to surrender the German army unconditionally. Convinced now that Fegelein had planned to go to Switzerland to begin the peace talks for Himmler, Hitler immediately had Fegelein court martialed, found guilty, and condemned to death. Eva had, meanwhile, heard a rumor that some of the jewelry in Fegelein's suitcase was hers and that Fegelein intended to run off with a beautiful Hungarian woman, abandoning her pregnant sister. This time she made no attempt to save her brother in law. An SS squad took Fegelein into the Chancellery garden and shot him on April 28th.

Hermann Otto Fegelein

Fegelein and Gretl Braun on their wedding day, June 3, 1944. Himmler and Bormann were best men.

Signature of Hermann Fegelein.

**Signed portrait of
Hermann Fegelein.**

IM NAMEN
DES DEUTSCHEN VOLKES
VERLEIHE ICH
DEM ᛋᛋ-OBERFÜHRER
HERMANN FEGELEIN
DAS EICHENLAUB
ZUM RITTERKREUZ
DES EISERNEN KREUZES

FÜHRERHAUPTQUARTIER
DEN 22. DEZEMBER 1942

DER FÜHRER
UND OBERSTE BEFEHLSHABER
DER WEHRMACHT

**Fegelein's award document for the Knight's Cross with Oak Leaves, signed by
Hitler, December 22, 1942. One of 21 decorations received by General Fegelein.** 147

OTTO GUENSCHE (1917-   ). SS major (SS-Sturmbannfuehrer) and personal adjutant to Hitler. Guensche was present at the July 20, 1944 bombing attempt on the Fuehrer's life. The explosion burst his eardrums. His head was cut and his eyebrows scorched away. He helped Hitler, whose clothes were partially blown off, to limp from the burning building. Less than a year later Guensche was with Hitler in the Bunker. The Fuehrer said to him: "Eva and I are going to commit suicide. Be sure to burn our bodies. I don't want to be put on display in some Russian wax museum."

The Russians were closing in on Berlin and the city was under heavy bombardment. Guensche ordered Kempka to search for the gasoline necessary to immolate the corpses. He only found 160 liters in his Reich Chancellery garage and "borrowed" 20 liters from the Chancellery chief technician, Hentschel. After Hitler shot himself, Guensche was the first to see his body. The bodies were drenched with gasoline and Bormann ignited them. For three hours faithful servants of the dead Fuehrer continued to douse the flaming corpses with gasoline. Then they were wrapped in a tent shelter half and buried in a shell hole by three SD officers.

Guensche was arrested by the Russians and imprisoned for ten years in the Soviet Union and in East Berlin.

Photograph signed by Otto Guensche. Guensche is conferring with the Fuehrer.

Guensche joined the SS-Begleit-Kommando on May 1, 1936. He was an SS ordnance officer from 1940-41, followed by training and frontline duty. From January to August 1943 he was a personal adjutant (with Darges) with a period of combat duty again. In March 1944 he was once more appointed as a personal adjutant and remained in this position until the end of the war.

Photograph of Otto Guensche, inscribed and signed to Roger James Bender.   149

ERNST FRANZ SEDGWICK HANFSTAENGL (1887-1975). Hitler's representative with the foreign press, 1931-1937. Born in Munich of mixed German-American parentage, Hanfstaengl was descended from two American Civil War generals and was the son of an art dealer who owned a shop on Fifth Avenue. Ernst attended Harvard and was graduated in 1909. Unable to serve his fatherland during World War I, Hanfstaengl returned to Munich after the war and became close friends with Hitler. Hanfstaengl's ability to play the music of Wagner on the piano, his constant practical joking and his sense of humor appealed to Hitler. An enormous man, six feet four inches in height, Hanfstaengl won many friends among the leading Nazis. One man who was not his friend was Dr. Paul Joseph Goebbels. Hanfstaengl publicly called Goebbels "a swine." Eventually the Nazis who resented Hanfstaengl's frankness and conservative views plotted to murder him by pushing him out of an airplane. Hanfstaengl fled from Germany and despite assurances from Goering that the whole "plot" was just a joke, he remained in exile. He served as an expert on Nazi affairs in the White House during World War II. He died in Munich on November 6, 1975.

**Ernst Franz
Sedgwick Hanfstaengl
(nicknamed "Putzi")**

Signed photograph of Ernst Hanfstaengl (at right), Hitler's unofficial jester, about 1934. Notice the remarkable "swastika" signature.

ist paflos die Materialisation, der deutschen Jugend und des deutschen Idealismus —

So much for today —

Sincerely yours,

Ernst F. S. Hanfstaengl

Last page of a letter written and signed by Ernst Hanfstaengl. He mentions "German idealism" and displays his knowledge of English in the final two lines.

HEINRICH HOFFMANN (1885-1957). Official photographer of Hitler and the Nazi party. Born in Fürth on September 12, 1885, Hoffmann was the son of a successful photographer and learned the trade from his father. Almost from the beginning of Hitler's career, Hoffmann sensed that the wild-eyed politician would have a brilliant future. He became his constant companion. For many years he had an "exclusive" on photographing the Nazi leader and his magnificent portraits added to Hitler's political stature. Hoffmann introduced Hitler to Eva Braun, the Fuehrer's future wife, then working in Hoffmann's Munich studio.

Hoffmann produced many photographic books, all of which had large sales. Hitler had great confidence in Hoffmann's artistic acumen and permitted him to select the paintings to be shown in the annual German Art Show. When Hoffmann insisted that Hitler receive royalties from the use of his portrait on postage stamps, it added greatly to the personal fortune already built up for Hitler by Amann, publisher of *Mein Kampf*.

In 1938 Hitler conferred the title of professor on Hoffmann. Long before the outbreak of World War II the photographer had become a millionaire. In 1947 Hoffmann was tried for "profiteering" before a West German court. He was sentenced to ten years in prison and stripped of all his wealth except three thousand marks. The sentence was changed several times, ending up as five years. Hoffmann died in Munich on December 16, 1957.

PROFESSOR
HEINRICH HOFFMANN

MÜNCHEN
EBERSBERGERSTRASSE 5

Herrn

Gauleiter Paul Giesler

M ü n c h e n

Sehr verehrter Herr Gauleiter !
Lieber Parteigenosse Giesler !

Sie haben mir mit der Uebersendung Ihrer Geburts-
tagsgrüsse und mit dem damit verbundenen Geburts-
tagsgeschenk eine grosse Freude bereitet.
Ich danke Ihnen dafür auf das Herzlichste.

Mit freundschaftlichen Grüssen und

Heil Hitler !
Ihr ergebener

Letter signed by Heinrich Hoffmann. Thanks for birthday greetings.

Photograph of Heinrich Hoffmann (at right) with Lt. Colonel (formerly Major) R.H. Stevens. (See the biographical sketch of Walter Schellenberg for information on Stevens.)

Hoffmann and his favorite photographic subject, Hitler.

153

Hoffmann is shown taking photographs of Hitler and his entourage at a railway station in 1940.

GERTRUD "TRAUDL" JUNGE. One of Hitler's private secretaries. Born in Munich on March 16, 1920, Frau Junge, known as "Traudl" to her friends, was with Hitler in the bunker during his final days. She was married to Hitler's valet, SS-Obersturmfuehrer Hans Junge, who was killed in action in Normandy in 1944. Hitler often dined with the pretty, young widow and sometimes even flirted with her. Traudl was a guest at Hitler's wedding to Eva Braun on April 29, 1945. After the marriage ceremony and the brief celebration that followed, Traudl and Hitler left together around 2:00 in the morning and entered a small study in the lower bunker. Here Hitler dictated his will and his final political testament to Frau Junge. The following day Hitler committed suicide. Traudl was one of a half a dozen of the Fuehrer's inner circle in the bunker to escape capture by the Russians. Later, however, as Traudl and two other secretaries of Hitler were leaving Berlin, they were captured by a marauding group of Russian soldiers. The Russians raped them all. Traudl fought back and got badly beaten. She was rescued by a Russian doctor who took her to Berlin and enjoyed her exclusive ownership for a year before releasing her. Traudl now lives in Munich.

154

Gertrud "Traudl" Junge

Gertrud and Hans Hermann Junge. Junge was one of Hitler's personal valets, second to Heinz Linge. He requested a transfer to a combat unit and was killed in Normandy in August 1944.

Sehr beehrter Mr. Swearingen,

gerne mache ich von Ihrem Angebot Gebrauch, der Einfachheit halber in Deutsch zu antworten.

Ich sende Ihnen beiliegend die beiden Fotos der Schreibmappe zurück mit der Bestätigung, daß sie sicherlich aus Hitlers persönlichem Besitz stammt. Ich habe mich auch noch bei einer älteren Kollegin vergewissert, die sein Arbeitszimmer in München besser kennt als ich (da ich ja nur in den letzten Kriegsjahren und die meiste Zeit im Führerhauptquartier für Hitler arbeitete). Es ist anzunehmen, daß er die Mappe in seinem Schreibtisch aufbewahrte. Ich kenne die Briefbogen und kann bestätigen, daß sie für seine persönlichen Briefe benutzt wurden. Die Fotos habe ich wunschgemäß signiert und habe mich gefreut, sie gesehen zu haben.

Mit freundlichen Grüßen

Traudl Junge

Letter signed by Traudl Junge, Hitler's secretary in the bunker, written from Munich to the noted collector, Ben Swearingen. Frau Junge authenticates a relic of the Fuehrer: ". . .I worked for Hitler only in the last years of the war and mostly in the Fuehrerhauptquartier. . .I recognize the [correspondence] folder and can state that he used it for his personal letters. . . ."

ERICH KEMPKA (1910-1975). Hitler's chauffeur and SS-Obersturmbannfuehrer (lieutenant colonel). Born on September 16, 1910, Kempka joined the Nazi party and the SS, serving in Hitler's bodyguard formation. He was Josef Terboven's chauffeur before joining Hitler's staff on March 1, 1932. He succeeded Julius Schreck as Hitler's chauffeur in 1936.

Kempka personally knew most of the important people in Hitler's circle. He once described Eva Braun, the Fuehrer's mistress, as "the unhappiest woman in Germany." After Eva's joint suicide with Hitler in the Bunker (April 30, 1945), Kempka carried her body halfway up the staircase where he was relieved by Guensche. Her corpse was placed next to Hitler's and, in accordance with the Fuehrer's last instructions, were sprinkled with gasoline and ignited in a Viking-like funeral pyre.

In 1952 Kempka set down his recollections of Hitler in a volume dramatically entitled, against his wishes, *I Burned Hitler*. He died on January 24, 1975.

Erich Kempka

Erich Kempka (at wheel) with Hitler.

Erich Kempka (signature)

Signature of Erich Kempka

KARL WILHELM KRAUSE. Hitler's personal orderly and bodyguard, 1934-1939. Born on March 5, 1911 in Michelau, West Prussia, near Danzig, Krause studied cabinet making and architecture. In 1931 he joined the navy. Three years later Hitler chose Krause, from a line-up of other naval prospects, to be his personal orderly. Although Krause was not a Nazi, he impressed the Fuehrer with his tall, erect, "Nordic" appearance.

Krause's most important job was to protect the Fuehrer from assault or assassination by following directly behind him at public appearances and on tours. Hitler often jokingly called him *Schatten* (Shadow) since, at times, he appeared to blend with the shadow of the Fuehrer. Between 1934 and the attack on Poland in 1939, Krause was constantly with Hitler. Once Krause helped the Fuehrer to wrap Christmas presents. The Fuehrer laughed when Krause accidentally tied Hitler's thumb to a package. On Christmas Eve, in 1937, Krause crept out with Hitler on an incognito jaunt by night through Berlin. The pair managed to elude the SS guards and took a taxi into the city where they had an exciting midnight stroll. Hitler was not recognized. The next day Krause was reprimanded by Himmler for allowing his master to expose himself to nocturnal dangers.

As an intimate of Hitler during his early years as Fuehrer, Krause later recorded many intimate details of the dictator's life. Hitler slept in a nightgown, read telegrams and newspapers on awakening, and bathed and shaved himself. He used a fresh razor blade for each cheek. For breakfast he often had a glass of milk and apple and cheese with a cup of peppermint tea.

Krause intimated that Hitler was secretly enamoured with Rudolf Hess, known to fellow homosexuals as "Fräulein Anna," but he never made a direct accusation of this. He recalled that Greta Garbo was Hitler's favorite actress. The Fuehrer also enjoyed watching the courage displayed by a handful of British soldiers in *Lives of a Bengal Lancer* and viewed the film three times.

In September 1939, after a petty squabble over some "spring" water that Krause had represented to Hitler as "bottled mineral water" (Hitler's favorite beverage), the Fuehrer sacked Krause. During the war years Krause served briefly in the navy, then as an ordnance aide in the Reich Chancellery, and finally as a captain in an SS Panzer flak unit. Credited with shooting down 45 Allied aircraft, Krause was personally awarded the German Cross in Gold by Hitler.

At the end of the war Krause escaped from the Soviets and surrendered to the Americans. Ultimately, after various interrogations, he was fined seven marks and released. He found a job as assistant waiter and interior decorator. Except for an occasional interview, he leads a quiet life in retirement.

Schwab

Signed photograph of Karl Wilhelm Kraus.

The ever-present Krause is seated behind Hitler during one of his public appearances.

HEINZ LINGE (1913-1981). Hitler's valet and major in the SS (SS-Sturmbannfuehrer). Born on March 22, 1913, Linge was originally a bricklayer. In 1933 he joined the SS and was soon attached to the SS-Begleitkommando, the SS detachment entrusted with the Fuehrer's personal safety. In July 1935 he became Hitler's ordnance officer, and in 1939, after the departure of Karl Krause, he was appointed as Hitler's head valet.

As head valet he was in daily contact with Hitler, who was quite fond of him. After Hitler's suicide on April 30, 1945, Linge helped to wrap the body in a

Linge holds Hitler's gloves and cap as the Fuehrer prepares to take off his greatcoat.

159

brown blanket and carry it into the garden of the besieged chancellery. Following Hitler's orders to burn his body, Linge aided in dousing the Fuehrer's corpse, together with Eva Braun's, with gasoline until they were swept with flames. He then helped bury the charred remains in a shell-hole. Linge attempted to break out of Berlin, but was captured, and spent ten years in Soviet captivity. He became a prosperous businessman in Hamburg after his return. He composed a volume of memoirs entitled *Bis zum Untergang* and died on March 9, 1981 in Hamburg.

Signed photograph of Heinz Linge

EMIL MAURICE (1897-1972). Hitler's personal bodyguard and chauffeur. Maurice was born on January 19, 1897, in Westermoor, and was one of the very few individuals to be mentioned by name in *Mein Kampf*. He held SS Number 2, and Nazi party Number 39.

Maurice, a watchmaker by trade, joined the German Workers Party, the forerunner of the NSDAP, in 1919, and was sent to Landsberg Prison for his part in the 1923 Beer-Hall Putsch. In prison he became an intimate of Hitler, and following his release, remained in Hitler's inner circle. He acted as a bodyguard and, subsequently, as Hitler's chauffeur. Tensions broke out between Hitler and Maurice in 1927, however, and he was ultimately ousted from the inner circle because of an unwanted liaison (from Hitler's point of view!) with Geli Raubal, Hitler's niece.

By 1935 the tensions between the Fuehrer and Maurice had begun to subside, when Maurice applied for permission to marry. At this time he was an SS colonel (SS-Standartenfuehrer) and a Ratsherr (city councillor) of the city of Munich. Maurice and his bride had to submit proof of Aryan origin before they could wed, when it was discovered, in the words of Heinrich Himmler, that "Without question, SS-Standartenfuehrer Emil Maurice is, according to his ancestral table, not of Aryan descent." Hitler refused, however, to purge Maurice from the SS or the party. Himmler was outraged over this, but the debacle did not hurt Maurice's career significantly: by 1939 he had been promoted to SS brigadier general and remained a Ratsherr of Munich. From 1940 to 1942 he served as a Luftwaffe officer, and in 1948 was sentenced by a denazification court to four years in a labor camp. Emil Maurice, the partly Jewish holder of SS Number 2, died in Munich on February 6, 1972.

Hitler in Landsberg prison with (L. to R.) Emil Maurice, Hermann Kriebel (military leader of the Putsch), Hess and Dr. Friedrich Weber.

Signature of Emil Maurice

E. Voelker

THEODOR MORELL (1886-1948). Hitler's personal physician. After graduation from medical school, Morell took a post as ship's doctor, then began a practice as specialist in skin and venereal diseases in Berlin. His office was soon crowded with actors and film stars. In 1936 Heinrich Hoffmann, Hitler's court photographer, developed a dangerous infection and Dr. Morell cured it with a new wonder drug, sulfanilamide, that he had imported from Hungary. Hoffmann told Hitler about Morell's skills and Morell soon had the privilege of injecting "vitamins" into the Fuehrer. After an initial rash, Hitler improved greatly and said: "What luck I had to meet Morell. He has saved my life."

Over a period of nine years Morell continued to shoot serums made from bull's testicles and cow's intestines into Hitler. Over twenty-eight drugs, including some untested amphetamines, were injected into the Fuehrer. Hitler's skin took on a strange color and his hands shook. Morell acquired a fortune, not just from his patients, but from the "Morell Russian Lice Powder" that was compulsory for the Nazi armed forces.

Some of the Nazi leaders were too smart to fall for this maestro of the needle. Goering called Morell "Herr Reich Injection Master." Eva Braun said he had the manners of a pig. Dr. Karl Brandt insisted that Morell was poisoning Hitler. The Fuehrer, however, kept Morell on until almost the very end, dismissing him on April 21, 1945.

Dr. Morell died at Tegernsee on May 26, 1948.

Hoover Institution

Dr. Theodor Morell on February 26, 1944.

Prof. Dr. Theo Morell.   **Entwurf**

F.H.Qu.   2.3.1944
über Reichskanzlei, Bln-W8

E i n s c h r e i b e n

An das
Finanzamt für Körperschaften in Hamburg
H a m b u r g 1
Steinstra. 1o/III

Betr.: Steuernummer Kö 1o8/72o
        Ihr. Schr. vom 14.1. und 1.2. d.Js. an die
        Hamma- G.m.b.H. Olmütz- Radisch 16 wegen Belassung eines
        Teils der Gewinnabführung 1942 und örtl. Zuständigkeit.

Infolge dienstlicher Abwesenheit und einiger inzwischen noch
erforderlich gewordener Rückfragen beim Herrn Finanzminister
kann ich zu den Fragen der oben angeführten Schreiben erst heute
abschliessend Stellung nehmen:

1.) Die Leitung der Hamma- G.m.b.H. Hamburg 39, deren alleiniger
    Geschäftsführer ich bin, ist nur vorübergehend nach
    Olmütz- Radisch 16 verlegt.

2.) Es besteht die Absicht, die Leitung der Hamma in abseh-
    barer Zeit wieder nach Hamburg zurückzuverlegen.

3.) Ich bitte, die Hamma weiter beim dortigen Finanzamte zu
    führen. Die Genehmigung zur zeitweiligen Verlagerung des
    Betriebes von Hamburg nach Olmütz nach den Bombenangriffen
    auf Hamburg wurde von der Gauwirtschaftskammer Hamburg nur
    unter der Bedingung erteilt, dass Hamburg der Sitz des
    Unternehmens bleibt. Eine dahingehende bindende Erklärung
    wurde abgegeben.

Wegen der Belassung eines Teiles des Gewinnabführungsbetrages
1942 für wissenschaftliche Forschungen ergeht noch ein
besonderer Bescheid des Finanzministers, dem ein entsprechen-
der Antrag vorliegt.

                            Heil Hitler!

                    H a m m a - G.m.b.H. Hamburg

Letter signed by Dr. Theodor Morell about his taxes, March 2, 1944.

163

HANS PFEIFFER (-1944). Captain (SS-Hauptsturmfuehrer) Pfeiffer was Ludwig Bahls' successor as Hitler's second SS ordnance officer from October 23, 1939 to July 31, 1942, and was later killed in action in Normandy (June 1944).

Signature of Hans Pfeiffer

Hans
Pfeiffer

...eritz, Engel, Brueckner, Meissner, Schmundt, and Ludwig Bahls. Bahls was
...itler's SS ordnance officer from 1938 to September 1939 when he died from an
...pendicitis attack.

165

KARL-JESKO VON PUTTKAMER (1900-1981). Admiral Puttkamer served as Hitler's naval adjutant from March 1935 to June 1938, and from September 1939 to May 1945. As the Fuehrer's adjutant, Puttkamer was often at Hitler's side during times of crisis or emergency. After the victory over the British at Dunkirk, Hitler planned "Sealion," code name for the invasion of England. He planned to send troops in barges. Puttkamer eventually persuaded the Fuehrer to abandon the dangerous project.

Puttkamer was with Hitler at the headquarters in Rastenburg on July 20, 1944, when von Stauffenberg triggered the bomb that almost killed Hitler. Puttkamer was dazed by the shattering explosion. The next day Hitler told his slightly injured naval adjutant that the unsuccessful plot had "only confirmed the conviction that Almighty God has called me to lead the German people-- not to final defeat but to victory."

Puttkamer survived the war to record in 1970 and 1971 seven lengthy tapes of his recollections. He died on March 4, 1981, at the age of 81.

Sims

Admiral Karl-Jesko von Puttkamer

[handwritten letter conclusion]

Conclusion of a handwritten letter signed by Karl-Jesko von Puttkamer.

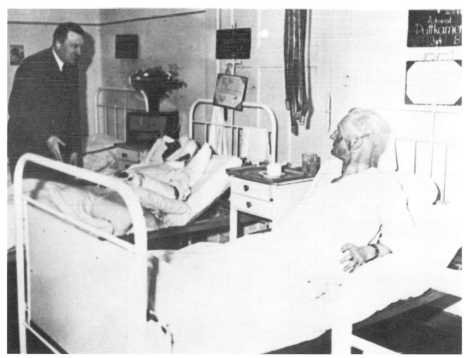

Hitler visits the wounded from the July 20 bomb blast. Admiral Puttkamer is in the foreground.

JULIUS SCHAUB (1898-1967). Schaub, born in Munich on August 20, 1898, was a constant companion of Adolf Hitler for twenty years. An early member of the NSDAP (Number 81), he was also a member of the Stosstrupp Hitler, the forerunner of the SS. He was imprisoned with Hitler after the Beer-Hall Putsch, and soon became a member of the Fuehrer's immediate entourage, ultimately becoming Hitler's No. 2 adjutant. When Wilhelm Brueckner was dismissed, he became the Fuehrer's chief personal adjutant.

Hitler became increasingly isolated during the war years, and men like Schaub gained great influence as they controlled access to the dictator. It was to Schaub that Hitler confided his secret dislike of Himmler. "I need such policemen," he told Schaub, "but I don't like them." When Hitler met with his Gauleiters for the last time in February 1945, his left leg was partially paralyzed and his left hand shook badly. It was Schaub who supported him as he walked. Shortly before Hitler's suicide, Schaub was sent from Berlin to destroy the Fuehrer's personal papers in Munich and Berchtesgaden. He fell into American captivity in Bavaria. Schaub, who had also held SS Number 7, became an apothecary after the war and died on December 27, 1967 in Munich.

Signed photograph of Julius Schaub, inscribed to Ben Swearingen.

Dr. Seyss-Inquart, Schaub, von Below, Bormann, Hitler, Himmler, Engel, and Wolff in Austria, October 6, 1938.

RUDOLF SCHMUNDT (1896-1944). Chief adjutant of the armed forces to Hitler; general of infantry. Born at Metz on August 13, 1896, Schmundt was a career officer who rose steadily through the ranks until he became Hitler's adjutant, a post he took over when only a major and held until his death. Schmundt attended all military conferences with the Fuehrer and took voluminous notes, some of which were confiscated by the Allies after the war. Schmundt was intimately associated with Hitler and frequently dined with him. When news of England's declaration of war against Germany arrived, Schmundt was standing with a group of top Nazi leaders. Goering was stricken with horror. He turned to Schmundt and said: "If we lose the war, then Heaven have mercy on us!" Jodl said: "It's like a blow from a club." Goebbels was pale and speechless.

Hitler and Schmundt converse during a walk on a country road.

Note:
Schmundt succeeded Friedrich Hossbach as army adjutant on January 28, 1938, became chief adjutant of the Wehrmacht on March 10, 1938, and was made chief of the army personnel office, succeeding Bodewin Keitel, on October 2, 1942. He was posthumously promoted to general of infantry on October 7, 1944 and awarded the German Order.

Belgium Army Museum

Garibaldi, Halder, Schmundt (in background), Keitel, and Hitler at the Fuehrer's headquarters on May 14, 1942.

General Schmundt was present at the Rastenburg conference on July 20, 1944 when the bomb planted by Colonel Claus von Stauffenberg nearly killed Hitler. Schmundt was fatally injured by the blast and died on October 1, 1944. When news of his adjutant's death reached Hitler, the Fuehrer broke down and cried. "Don't expect me to console you," he told Frau Schmundt. "You must console me for my great loss."

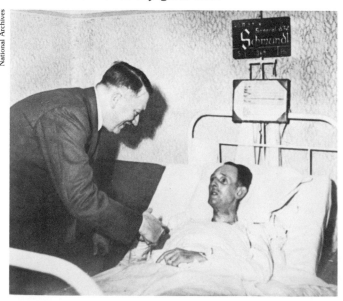

National Archives

Hitler consoles Schmundt in the hospital following the July 20 bombing.

Generalfeldmarschall von M a n s t e i n , Oberbefehlshaber
der Heeresgruppe Süd, Rangdienstalter: 1.7.42, Friedensdienststelle: Kommandeur 18.Div.;

Generalfeldmarschall von K l e i s t , Oberbefehlshaber der
Heeresgruppe A, Rangdienstalter: 1.2.43(1), ~~Friedensdienst-~~
~~stelle: Oberbefehlshaber einer Heeresgruppe~~

in die Führer-Reserve des Heeres zu meiner Verfügung.

Mit Wirkung vom gleichen Tage werden beauftragt:

Generaloberst M o d e l , mit der Führung der Heeresgruppe
Nord beauftragt, mit der Führung der Heeresgruppe Süd unter
gleichzeitiger Beförderung zum Generalfeldmarschall.
Rangdienstalter als Generaloberst: 1.2.42 (2), Friedensdienststelle: Chef des Generalstabes IV.A.K.;

Generaloberst L i n d e m a n n , Oberbefehlshaber der
18.Armee, mit der stellv. Führung der Heeresgruppe Nord.
Rangdienstalter: 3.7.42, Friedensdienststelle: Kommandeur
36.Div.;

General der Gebirgstruppe S c h ö r n e r , Chef des NS-Füh-
rungsstabes des Heeres, mit der Führung der Heeresgruppe A
unter gleichzeitiger Beförderung zum Generaloberst und unter
Festsetzung eines RDA dieses Dienstgrades mit dem 1.8.43.
Rangdienstalter als Gen.d.Geb.Tr.: 1.6.42(10),
Friedensdienststelle: Kommandeur Geb.Jäg.Rgt.98;

General der Artillerie L o c h , Kommandierender General des
XXVIII.Armeekorps, mit der stellv. Führung der 18.Armee.
Rangdienstalter: 1.10.41(1e), Friedensdienststelle: Kommandeur
17.Div.;

Generalleutnant M a t z k y , Kommandeur 21.Jnfanterie-
Division, mit der stellv. Führung des XXVIII.A.K.
Rangdienstalter: 1.4.43(2c), Friedensdienststelle: Ober-
quartiermeister im Generalstab des Heeres.

Führerhauptquartier,den 30. März 1944

Der Führer

Der Chef
des Heeres-Personalamts

Generalleutnant

Second page of a document signed by Hitler and Rudolf Schmundt (as major general) about three months before Schmundt was fatally wounded in the bombing attempt on Hitler's life. A re-assignment of officers, including four who were or would become field marshals: Manstein, Kleist, Model, and Schoerner.

JULIUS SCHRECK (1898-1936). Hitler's chauffeur. Schreck was born in Munich on July 13, 1898, and was an important figure in the development of both the SA and the SS. In addition, he was a prominent member of Hitler's personal entourage until his death in 1936. Schreck was an early member of the party (No. 53), one of the first members of the SA, and a co-founder of the Stosstrupp Hitler. Like many others of this group, he was sent to Landsberg Prison for his part in the Beer-Hall Putsch. In 1925 he founded the "Schutzkommando," a group responsible for the Fuehrer's safety and a direct forerunner of the SS. He held SS No. 5.

Julius Schreck (second from left) poses in a signed photograph with Julius Schaub (far left), Adolf Hitler, Hansjoerg Maurer and Edmund Schneider. Schreck, Schaub, Maurer, and Schneider were all members of the 1925/26 "Schutzkommando." Note that Emil Maurice (between Schreck and Hitler) was removed from all copies of this photo.

Schreck is remembered with fondness by the surviving members of Hitler's inner circle. A well-liked man, he was apparently on very good terms with Hitler, who was distraught when he died. From 1925 to 1936 he was never far from Hitler's side. His last position, succeeding Emil Maurice, was that of Hitler's personal chauffeur. Hitler once said of him: "Schreck is the best driver you can imagine and our supercharger is good for over a hundred. We always drive very fast. But in recent years, I've told Schreck not to go over fifty. How terrible if something had happened to me." He died of cerebrospinal meningitis on May 16, 1936 and was given a state funeral.

Julius Schreck

CHRISTA SCHROEDER (1908-   ). Hitler's personal secretary. A friend and confidant as well as a secretary. Fräulein Schroeder often was the recipient of Hitler's most intimate thoughts. She was with Hitler during the Blood Purge, or Night of the Long Knives, when many of the leading SA officers were murdered at Hitler's orders. Once the Fuehrer confided to her: "Eva (Braun) is very nice but, in my life, only Geli (Raubal) could have inspired me with genuine passion. I can never think of marrying Eva." During the war, Fräulein Schroeder recorded, at Hitler's dictation, the orders of the day. She was with Hitler when the news of the French request for an armistice reached him. "He was literally shaken by a frantic exuberance," she later recalled.

When events began to conspire against Hitler and his troops failed to take Moscow, Fräulein Schroeder noticed the change in his table talk. He repeated himself like a gramophone record. "It was always the same: his early days in Vienna. . .the history of man, the microcosm and the macrocosm. On every subject we knew in advance what he would say. . .These monologues bored us. But world affairs and events at the front were never mentioned. Everything to do with the war was taboo."

Christa Schroeder (right) chats with Gerda Daranowsky while waiting for a train.

Signature of Christa Schroeder

On the evening before the bombing attempt on Hitler's life (July 20, 1944) Fräulein Schroeder noticed that Hitler was nervous and preoccupied. "I hope nothing is going to happen to me," he explained. "I cannot allow myself to fall ill, since there is no one who can replace me in the difficult situation Germany finds herself in." The following evening, the injured Fuehrer showed up in the dining room, his face youthful and calm. He told his secretary: "I had incredible luck." Then he explained how the heavy legs of the conference table had protected him from the full force of the bomb. Fräulein Schroeder accompanied Hitler into the Berlin bunker but on his last birthday (April 20, 1945), after dining with her and Johanna Wolf, his two older secretaries, Hitler announced that he was sending them out by the last plane to leave Berlin. He telephoned Fräulein Schroeder later to say that Berlin was surrounded. Then his voiced trailed away and she could not understand his last words.

In 1949 Christa Schroeder dictated the story of her twelve years as Hitler's confidential secretary; they appeared under the title, *Hitler Privat.*

HANSGEORG SCHULZE (-1941). An SS ordnance officer to Hitler from October 1939 to August 1941 (and brother of Richard Schulze), Hansgeorg Schulze was killed in action in late 1941, while serving with the LAH (Leibstandarte Adolf Hitler) in Russia. (He was nicknamed "Frettchen.")

Signature of Hansgeorg Schulze.

Schulze-Kossens

Hansgeorg Schulze

175

RICHARD SCHULZE (1914-   ) SS lieutenant colonel (SS-Obersturmbannfuehrer). Schulze began his career as the youthful adjutant of von Ribbentrop. His younger brother was then Hitler's SS ordnance officer. Later, Schulze was himself promoted to the post of adjutant to the Fuehrer. Hitler was genuinely fond of him and bestowed upon him an almost avuncular attention. In 1942 the Fuehrer made Schulze responsible for all men serving in the SS-Begleitkommando, the SS men entrusted with Hitler's personal safety. Schulze finished up the war as the last commander of the SS training school at Bad Toelz.

Schulze as von Ribbentrop's adjutant.

Note:
Richard Schulze was Ribbentrop's adjutant from April 1939 to January 1941, from October 3, 1941 an SS ordnance officer (with short intervals of combat duty), and from October 27, 1942 to mid-December 1944 (again with intervals of combat duty and at Bad Toelz), a personal adjutant to Hitler.

Richard Schulze's signature

Schaub, Mussolini, Schulze, and Hitler at the Berghof in 1942.

National Archives

Schulze (far left) hands a "July 20, 1944 Wound Badge" to Lieutenant Colonel von Amsberg, who had been Keitel's aide, during award ceremonies. From July 20 to late October 1944, von Amsberg served as one of Hitler's adjutants in the absence of Schmundt, Borgmann, and von Below.

CHRISTIAN WEBER (1883-1945). Weber was born in Polsingen on August 25, 1883. He was an early member of the party and belonged to the Stosstrupp Hitler as well. As a prominent member of Hitler's entourage during the early period of the struggle for power, Weber faded from view during the Third Reich. Hitler did, however, entrust this "Old Fighter" with the responsibility for his personal safety during the annual gathering of the Old Guard in Munich, on November 8. This had serious repercussions when on November 8, 1939, a bomb explosion nearly killed the Fuehrer. Had the SS or police been responsible for security on these occasions, it is likely that the bomb would have been detected before it went off.

Weber, a lifelong horse fancier, held many equestrian posts during the Nazi era, including that of Inspector of the SS Riding Schools. He was also a city councillor (Ratsherr) of Munich. He was killed during the abortive Bavarian uprising in late April 1945.

Signed photograph of Christian Weber

FRITZ WIEDEMANN (1891-1970). One of Hitler's personal adjutants. Born in Augsburg on August 16, 1891, Wiedemann was a career army officer. He was promoted to lieutenant in 1912 and at the outbreak of World War I was made a captain and battalion adjutant of the 16th Bavarian Infantry Regiment. His dispatch bearer, with whom he became friendly, was Lance Corporal Adolf Hitler. After the war Wiedemann turned to farming. In 1934 he joined the Nazi party and was appointed Hitler's personal adjutant. During the World's Fair in 1939 Wiedemann was dispatched to San Francisco as the German Consul General. He returned to Germany in 1941. He then became General Consul in Tientsin, China, where he was captured by the Americans. In 1964 he wrote an amusing and informative volume of recollections about the Fuehrer. He spent his last years as a farmer in southern Germany.

BERLIN W 8. DEN 1.4.37
REICHSKANZLEI

DER FÜHRER UND KANZLER DES DEUTSCHEN REICHES
ADJUTANTUR

Hauptmann a.D. Wiedemann

W/Mi

Streng persönlich und vertraulich !
Ungeöffnet zu übergaben !

Hochverehrter Herr Minister !

In der Anlage übersende ich Ihnen in Beant-
wortung Ihres Schreibens vom 26.3.37 das mir zur
Verfügung gestellte Material.

Für gelegentliche Rückgabe wäre ich dankbar.

Mit deutschem Gruss!

Adjutant des Führers

Herrn

Reichsminister D a r r é

B e r l i n

Letter signed by Captain Fritz Wiedemann, Berlin, April 1, 1937. To Richard-Walther Darre, about some requested material. With Darre's initials at upper right under the typewritten date.

NOTE:
Wiedemann was a personal adjutant to the Fuehrer from February 1, 1934 to February 1939.

Captain Fritz Wiedemann (second from right, next to Hitler), examining a photograph album with the Fuehrer.

ADOLF HITLER
ADJUTANTUR

1. 4. 35

Hptm.a.D.Wiedemann
    W/Mü.

An den

Adjutanten der Wehrmacht
beim Führer und Reichskanzler
Herrn Major H o s s b a c h

    i/H a u s e

v. 27.3.35

persönlichen Referenten d.Reichsministers, Pg. Hanke,Bln.-W.8,

Wilhelmstr.(betr.:einen Bericht über die Heldengedenkfeier im
    Potsdamer Lustgarten). u. 3 Photos.

    xxxxxxxx

Adjutant des Führers.

Note signed by Captain Fritz Wiedemann as Hitler's adjutant, April 1, 1935, written to Major (later General) Friedrich Hossbach, also then an adjutant of Hitler's.

JOHANNA WOLF (1900-   ). Hitler's chief private secretary. It was the fate of this middle-aged spinster to be with Hitler before and during some of the fateful events of World War II. When Czechoslovakia surrendered to Hitler without a battle in March 1939, the Fuehrer told Johanna: "I shall go down in history as the greatest German." And he called Johanna and his other secretary, Christa Schroeder, to him and exclaimed: "Children, quickly, give me a kiss!" Fräulein Wolf stayed with Hitler all through his career and left him only at the very end. In ordering her to leave the Berlin bunker, Hitler said: "I will join you as soon as possible." But, as she got ready to board the last plane out of Berlin, he whispered: "It is all over."

Johanna Wolf and Hitler.

Note:
Wolf was Hitler's secretary from January 1930 to April 1945.

Members of the Fuehrer's Inner Circle. At top, left to right: Christa Schroeder (Hitler's secretary), Otto Guensche (Hitler's SS adjutant), and Gerda ("Dara") Christian (Hitler's secretary). Bottom row, left to right: Hans Baur (Hitler's pilot), Johanna Wolf (Hitler's chief secretary), and Frau Gertrud Junge (Hitler's fourth secretary to whom he dictated his personal and political wills on April 29, 1945). This photograph was taken on Johanna Wolf's 80th birthday, June 1, 1980.

Handwritten letter signed by Johanna Wolf with her nickname, "Wolfsel." A gossipy letter to Hitler's pilot, Hans Baur.

MAX WUENSCHE (1914-   ). Lieutenant colonel in the SS (SS-Obersturmbannfuehrer). Wuensche served as Hitler's ordnance officer from March 1938 to October 1940. (For reasons of dismissal, see Brueckner section.) He then transferred to an active combat unit and served in frontline positions throughout the war. He was awarded the Knight's Cross on February 28, 1943, the Oak Leaves on August 11, 1944, and was captured in France on August 24, 1944.

On May 27, 1941, when the Greek army surrendered to Sepp Dietrich, Wuensche was present. After the victory at Kharkov, he was personally congratulated by Goebbels in Berlin. Wuensche survived the war and in 1971 taped his recollections of Hitler.

SS adjutant Wuensche escorts a guest from the Berghof after a meeting with Hitler in 1940.

Signed photograph of Max Wuensche.

Photograph of Hitler with some of his intimates taken on March 28, 1924, only four days before Hitler was sentenced to five years' imprisonment (of which he served only nine months) for his part in the Beer-Hall Putsch. The women are Irene Kriebel, wife of Colonel Hermann Kriebel, Frau Weber, wife of Dr. Friedrich Weber, Margarethe Poehner, wife of Ernst Poehner, and Helene Bechstein, wife of piano manufacturer Carl Bechstein and early sponsor and mentor of Hitler. The man behind the women is unidentified but is probably Carl Bechstein. The men standing on the right are Hitler's adjutant, Lieutenant Wilhelm Brueckner, Hitler, Colonel Hermann Kriebel, Ernst Roehm, Dr. Friedrich Weber, and Ernst Poehner.

Dr. Weber, Dr. Frick, and Hermann Kriebel on February 24, 1924.

The women who signed the photograph are listed under the caption to the photograph. Wilhelm Brueckner's signature appears at the top right, directly under Hitler's. The two signers at the bottom are:

LIEUTENANT COLONEL HERMANN KRIEBEL. Commander of the Working Union of Patriotic Combat Leagues, a nationalist group that supported Hitler in 1923. Kriebel was the military leader of the Beer-Hall Putsch and marched by the side of Hitler. He was sentenced with Hitler to five years in Landsberg prison on April 1, 1924. He was placed in Cell 8, next to Hitler in Cell 7, and was released with Hitler. In 1929 Kriebel was sent to China as military adviser to Chiang Kai-shek. He died on February 16, 1941.

DR. FRIEDRICH WEBER. A veterinarian by profession and a tough brawler by avocation, Weber organized the *Oberland Bund,* a quasi-military group. He marched beside Hitler in the Beer-Hall Putsch (1923) and was tried with Hitler. On April 1, 1924 he was sentenced to serve five years in Landsberg prison. He died in 1954.

ERNST POEHNER, who did not sign the photograph, was the ex-police president of Munich. He also took part in the Beer-Hall Putsch and was sentenced to five years' imprisonment. He was killed in an automobile accident on April 11, 1925.

Hitler and Eva Braun leaving the Berghof.

The Women
in Hitler's Life

EVA BRAUN (1912-1945). Hitler's mistress and wife. An unassuming woman, Eva worked in Munich for Heinrich Hoffmann, Hitler's photographer who, early in the 1930s, not long after the suicide of Geli Raubal, introduced her to the Fuehrer. Her dark blond hair and quiet manner appealed to Hitler, and before long she became his mistresss, the sole woman in his life until he died.

Eva was not a glamorous or romantic woman, but to Hitler she represented a complete escape from the pressures of political and military problems. Only seldom did he see her and few Germans even knew she existed. In time Eva accepted the role of companion to Hitler in the brief moments he could spare. The Fuehrer's chauffeur, Erich Kempka, said: "She was the unhappiest woman in Germany. She spent most of her life waiting for Hitler."

On April 15, 1945, Eva Braun arrived in Berlin for her moment of supreme grief and glory. In the deep-delved bunker where Hitler was directing the death agonies of the Third Reich, she joined her lover. A few days later, the Fuehrer urged her to leave on the last airplane out of Berlin, protesting that he would soon join her, but she elected to stay and die with him.

Just before dawn on April 29, 1945, Hitler and Eva were married and there were a few champagne toasts before Hitler slipped away to write his will, in which he stated: "My wife and I choose to die in order to escape the shame of overthrow or capitulation. It is our wish that our bodies be burned immediately..."

At 3:30 on the afternoon of April 30, Hitler and his bride retired to their room, armed with two revolvers. Only a single shot rang out, but when Goebbels and Bormann entered the room, they found the Fuehrer sprawled on the sofa in a pool of blood. He had shot himself in the mouth. Eva had preferred a quieter, less dramatic death. She had swallowed poison.

Then, in the manner of the ancient Vikings, their bodies were burned.

Full signature of Eva Braun

Eva Braun

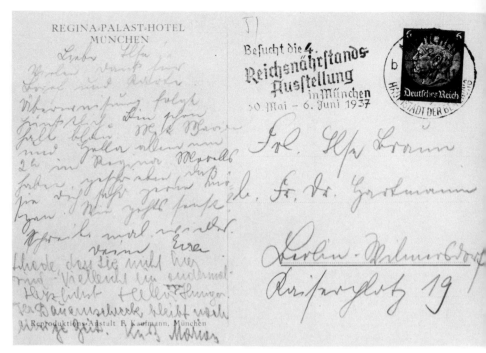

Handwritten note signed "Eva" to Frau Ilse Braun, sending greetings. This note of Hitler's future wife is in German [Sütterlin] script, rarely used by Eva Braun.

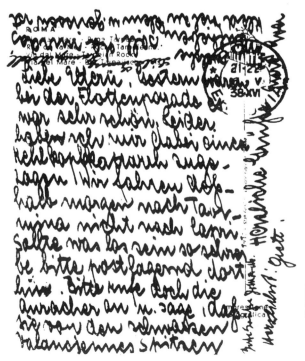

Eva Bra
at the o

Handwritten letter from Eva Braun to her parents. She describes a naval "parade."

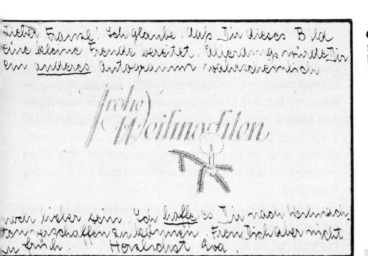

Christmas greetings from Eva to her brother-in-law, Franz.

Handwritten note from Eva Braun to her mother, praising a hotel. There is a note by Eva's sister under Eva's message.

Eva Braun

191

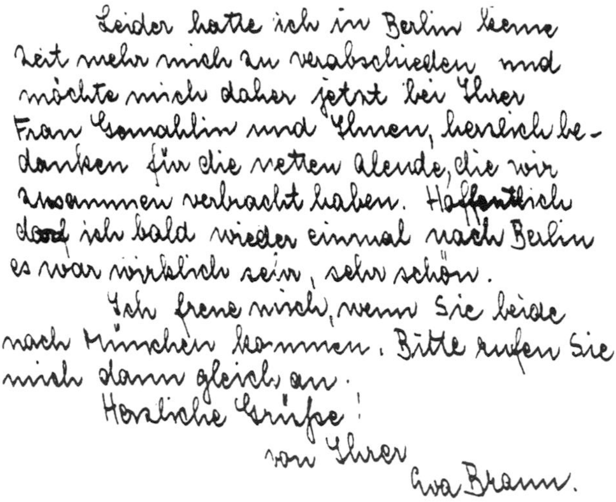

[Handwritten letter in German cursive:]

Leider hatte ich in Berlin keine
Zeit mehr mich zu verabschieden und
möchte mich daher jetzt bei Ihrer
Frau Gemahlin und Ihnen, herzlich be-
danken für die netten Abende, die wir
zusammen verbracht haben. Hoffentlich
darf ich bald wieder einmal nach Berlin
es war wirklich sein, sehr schön.
    Ich freue mich, wenn Sie beide
nach München kommen. Bitte rufen Sie
mich dann gleich an.
    Herzliche Grüße!
        von Ihrer
            Eva Braun.

Handwritten letter of Eva Braun to Dr. Theodor Morell [Hitler's personal physician].

UNITY VALKRYIE MITFORD (1914-1948).   English friend of Adolf Hitler. One of six daughters of Lord Redesdale, Unity was an enthusiastic, unpredictable, golden blond. While studying art in Munich in 1933 she met Adolf Hitler. From the moment he bowed and kissed her hand, she was wildly in love with him. The Fuehrer, in turn, adored her classic Nordic beauty and delighted in her whimsical wit. When Unity's disapproving parents cut off her allowance, she managed to survive on a few marks a month just to be near Hitler.

Hitler at an outdoor café with Unity Mitford and Sir Oswald Mosley, British Fascist leader.

oth Dec.
1935

Dee droudled Boudededdle,
Jung va ja leddra. I'm
had you missed me at Christmas. I
hope you will be missing me for the
next 50 Christmasses at ledot, because
I mean to always spend the Festtage
here in future.
I had a long letter
from Dolly, which I consider is a
triumph considering she is said never
to write to anyone. She described you
as "sitting like a round-eyed kitten
by the hearth," which I call rather
nice for you, dont you. Her letter
was 7 pages long, terrible handwriting.
I am looking forward to seeing her.
Did Tom really like her. I think she is
heaven. I loved the bit about "Bobo
wouldnt have hesitated". Nor I would
have. I now see, on re-reading her
letter, that it runs "sweet Decca sitting
like a . . . "etc etc.
I had a new perm
to-day, & have had my hair done in a
completely new way, with a sort of
crown of curls, I certainly like it much

First page of a handwritten letter from Unity Mitford to her sister Jessica. Unity, signing with her nicknames "Bond" and "Decca," salutes her sister with the nickname "Boudededdle." Of Hitler, Unity writes: "I love him more & more each time though it doesn't seem possible to love him any more than I always did. . . ." 193

better. It looks much nicer.

You've no idea how sweet th Führer was yesterday, I love him more & m each time though it doesn't seem possible love him any more than I always did.

I hope you will have a love time in Paris, are you excited to go back. Gi Dolly my best love when you see her.

Poor sweet Erich had to return to Konstanz this morning, how he h it there, & I was unkind to him here so c together its dreadful. Max talks of you a lot sends you lots of greetings. I must scram away now. Goodbye & Heil Hitler!

Je Boud

DECCA

DECCA

Second page of a handwritten letter from Unity Mitford to her sister, Munich, December 30, 1935.

Unity was a patriotic Englishwoman, but she also loved Germany. Frequently she tried to discuss the future of England and Germany with Hitler, but he adamantly spurned all talk of politics during their social meetings. No doubt Unity hoped to become his wife and thus strengthen the bond between the two nations she loved. She told her sister, "If England and Germany go to war, I shall kill myself."

On September 3, 1939, the day England and France declared war on Germany, Unity shot herself in the head with a small-caliber pistol. The wound was serious but not immediately fatal. The Munich surgeons provided by Hitler were hesitant to remove the embedded bullet from her temple. Finally the Fuehrer sent her home in a special railway car via Switzerland, his last gesture of kindness toward the woman he may have loved.

Unity lived on for almost nine years until the bullet finally worked its way into her brain and killed her. On her gravestone in Swinbrook is inscribed the famous line by the British poet, Walter Savage Landor, "Say not the struggle nought availeth."

RENATE MUELLER. German movie star; intimate of Hitler and Goebbels. Renate was introduced to Hitler by Goebbels' wife, Magda, who suggested to Renate that she have an affair with the Fuehrer. Evidently Hitler was beguiled by Renate's beauty, for he presented her with a horse. After an argument with the SS who were maltreating one of her lovers, a young Jewish millionaire named Karl Simon, Renate hurled herself under the wheels of Hitler's limousine. Both her legs were broken. The Fuehrer sent her a bouquet of flowers and visited her in the hospital. Renate appeared on the way to recovery when she had a sudden relapse and died of an internal hemorrhage. She was born on April 26, 1906 and died on October 7, 1937 in Berlin.

Aufnahme Walther Jaeger, Berlin

Renate Müller

„Ross" Verlag

Signed photograph of Renate Mueller

ANGELA (GELI) RAUBAL (June 4, 1908-September 18, 1931). Hitler's niece and sweetheart; daughter of his half-sister, Angela Raubal. In the summer of 1925, Hitler rented, for $25 a month, a small villa near Berchtesgaden to which his widowed half-sister Angela came as housekeeper. With her was Geli, her seventeen-year-old daughter, a beautiful girl with long blonde hair and a joyous disposition. Hitler, who was always partial to attractive women, at once fell deeply in love with Geli. He took her with him everywhere, not only to cafés and festivals, but even to political meetings and conferences. In 1929 he rented a luxurious apartment in Munich and installed his niece in it, with her own room. There was vicious gossip in Munich that Hitler should stop cavorting with Geli or marry her.

It is likely that Hitler's relationship with Geli was platonic for he adored her and, according to many of his intimates, intended to marry her. Hitler's photographer, Heinrich Hoffmann, expressed a different view: "Geli was deeply revered, indeed worshipped, by her uncle, and any idea of an affair between them certainly never entered his head. To him she was. . .beautiful, fresh and unspoiled, gay, and intelligent." Hoffman comments that Hitler told him: "I love Geli and I could marry her. But you know my views. I am determined to remain a bachelor."

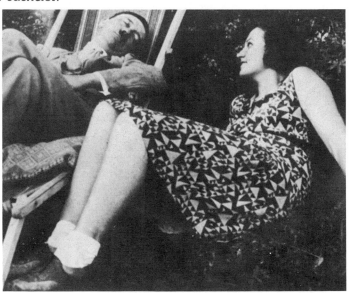

Hitler relaxing with Geli Raubal

Geli was flattered by Hitler's attentions and no doubt was very fond of him, but her beauty attracted other suitors, and Hitler became increasingly possessive and jealous. So zealously did he guard Geli that in the end she was little more than·a slave to his whims.

In the summer of 1931 Geli announced to her uncle that she planned to continue her voice studies in Vienna. Hitler objected violently. The storm between the two intensified, and on September 17, 1931, as Hitler entered his

Geli Raubal

car to drive to Hamburg, Geli called out from the window: "Then you won't let me go to Vienna," and Hitler hurled back a sharp "No."

The next morning Geli was found dead in her room, a bullet in her heart. She had shot herself with Hitler's pistol. Her suicide was so great a tragedy to Hitler that for two days and nights his friend, Gregor Strasser, had to stay with him to prevent him from taking his own life. For years Hitler could rarely speak of Geli without tears coming into his eyes.

Geli's room was preserved as a shrine. Frau Anny Brunner-Winter, Hitler's confidant and housekeeper, sealed off the room at Hitler's orders and opened it only on the anniversary of Geli's birth and death to brighten it with flowers. Stephen Bumball, a Special Agent with the United States Army Counter-Intelligence Corps, recalls a visit to Hitler's apartment on the Prinz Regentenstrasse in Munich where Geli killed herself: "There was an eeriness in the room. The shade on the only window was drawn. All of Geli's clothes and cosmetics were just as she left them. Frau Brunner-Winter said, 'After Geli shot herself, Hitler never once entered this room.'"

Handwritten postcard signed "Geli" to Adolf Hitler. "On a stroll to Berchtesgaden we came across this picture postcard of our house. Wolf [Hitler's dog] feels very well here. We don't have him on a leash; he always runs about free. Only his qualities as a watchdog are very poor. He has forgotten how to bark. . .Greetings from your little niece. Geli."

HANNA REITSCH (1912-1979). Nazi test pilot and friend of Hitler. Born in 1912 in Silesia, Hanna became Germany's outstanding woman stunt flier and was picked by Ernst Udet in 1937 to be a test pilot in the new Luftwaffe. During World War II she was one of the only women to be awarded the Iron Cross, First and Second Classes.

A small, intense person, hysterically devoted to Hitler, Hanna flew with General Robert Ritter von Greim to visit the Fuehrer in Berlin on April 25, 1945, five days before he died. With von Greim at the controls, the two flew roof-high through a blistering barrage of flak. When von Greim was wounded in the foot, Hanna successfully landed the aircraft.

Both Hanna and von Greim wished to stay and die with Hitler, who told her: "If I die, it is for the honor of our country...but, my dear Hanna, I still have hope." The Fuehrer then gave both Hanna and von Greim (now appointed to Field Marshal as successor to Goering) a vial of poison to use in case of necessity and ordered them out of the bunker to join the defense of Germany. Miraculously they flew back as they had come, through skies black with flak and red with fire.

Von Greim committed suicide less than a month later. Hanna Reitsch was arrested by the Americans, held in an interrogation center for 15 months, then released in 1946. After the war Fraulein Reitsch won many gliding championships. In 1959 she visited India and became friendly with Indira Gandhi and Prime Minister Nehru. She took Nehru for a glider flight over New Delhi. In 1962 she set up the National School for Gliding in Ghana. Near the end of

Signed photograph of Hanna Reitsch.

7ᵗ of March 79

Dear David Carlson

Thank you very much for sending me this Magazine. I am sorry to be so busy, that I can thank you only with a hurried line.

Best wishes — sincerely

Hanna Reitsch

Handwritten letter signed in English by Hanna Reitsch, March 7, 1979.   199

her life she admitted that the political events in Nazi Germany had left her
shaken and disgusted. Hanna Reitsch died at Frankfurt am Main on August
24, 1979.

Hanna Reitsch's signature

LENI RIEFENSTAHL (1902-   ). Actress and film director. Greatly admired by Hitler for her artistic movies, Leni became the unofficial documentary
camerawoman of the Third Reich. When Hitler first approached her on the
possibility of making a feature-length film of the Nazi's 1934 Party Day, she
protested, "I'm not a member of the party and I don't even know the difference between SA and SS."

Signed photograph
of Leni Riefenstahl

1902-2003

LENI RIEFENSTAHL

BERLIN-WILMERSDORF
HINDENBURGSTRASSE 97
TELEFON: H2 UHLAND 1456

Dienstag Abend
nach der Vorführung

Mein Führer —

ich bin glücklich, daß Ihnen der Film gefallen hat — während der Arbeit war ich immer nur von dem einen Wunsch beseelt — etwas Schönes für Sie zu schaffen. Heute weiß ich es nun — daß ich durch meine Arbeit Ihnen Freude bereiten konnte —

Ihre glückliche Leni Riefenstahl

Handwritten letter from Leni Riefenstahl to Adolf Hitler, commenting on her famous movie, "Triumph of the Will." Leni is happy that Hitler liked it and is grateful that she has given him pleasure.

"That's why I want you to do it," replied the Fuehrer. "This will give it a fresh approach."

Riefenstahl's films were enormously successful. But when Hitler asked to have a few changes made, Leni adamantly refused, stamping her foot and shouting, "I won't do it." After his usual theatrical threats, the Fuehrer gave in meekly and allowed Leni to finish the documentary as she wished. Later she filmed a spectacular two-part documentary on the Olympic games, held in Berlin in the summer of 1936.

Historians still debate about whether Hitler and Leni Riefenstahl were lovers, but it appears likely that the Fuehrer admired only her artistic genius.

GERTRUD SCHOLTZ-KLINK. Head of the NS-Frauenschaft, the Nazi women's organization. Born in Adelsheim on February 9, 1902, Frau Scholtz-Klink worked first for the German Red Cross in Berlin. Later she became the Reichsfrauenfuehrerin. An able worker and mother of four children, she adroitly avoided controversial issues and proved that women could work effectively in the party. Frau Scholtz-Klink tactfully stated that the goal of a woman in the Third Reich was "to minister in the home and in her profession to the needs of life from the first to the last moment of man's existence. Her mission in marriage is comrade, helper, and womanly complement of man--this is the right of woman in the new Germany."

Frau Scholtz-Klink was the prototype of the militant Nazi woman. She was forceful and tough and spoke with a rasping, masculine voice. After the war she hid for almost three years under a false name. She was finally discovered and arrested by the French. A French military court sentenced her to 18 months' imprisonment on November 18, 1948. In 1949 a de-Nazification court at Tuebingen included her in its list of "Major Offenders" as a diehard Nazi, but she was acquitted of any war crimes.

Gertrud Scholtz-Klink

Gertrud Scholtz-Klink's signature.

SISTER PIA (1886-1981). Nazi nurse. A warm admirer of Adolf Hitler, Sister Pia (whose real name was Elenore Baur) supported the Nazi cause with zeal. She marched in the ranks during the ill-fated Beer-Hall Putsch of 1923 and tended the wounded. She organized the first Nazi mobile hospital and became the first SA (Brown Shirts) sister. During World War II Sister Pia served again as a nurse. After several years in an Allied internment camp she retired to a small village near Munich, always hoping that the days of Nazi glory would return to Germany. She died on May 18, 1981, at the age of 95.

Signed photograph of Sister Pia (Elenore Baur).

Handwritten letter signed by Sister Pia to Ben Swearingen, Oberhaching (near Munich), April 7, 1975. "Can you understand my attitude as a German? I love my Fatherland, for which I have fought and suffered my entire life. For Germany I was imprisoned five years and struck by an American. . . . Don't think badly of the German people. It was not so. . . .
" 'If Germany perishes, then shall the earth tremble.' "

PROFESSOR GERDY TROOST. Architect and wife of architect Paul Ludwig Troost. Frau Troost's husband, a creative architect much admired by Hitler, built the famous Nazi headquarters, the *Braun Haus*. Hitler approved of Troost's spartan style and classical approach and commissioned him to design the *Haus der Deutschen Kunst* (House of German Art) in Munich. When Troost died on March 21, 1934, his attractive young wife Gerdy took his place and soon became an intimate of the Fuehrer.

Gerdy Troost was interviewed by author John Toland in 1971 and described her constant aesthetic disputes with Hitler. The Fuehrer found her ideas provocative but Frau Professor Troost resigned in a huff from the art committee of the House of German Art when Hitler criticized her taste. Frau Troost was present, however, at the grand opening of her husband's architectural masterpiece on July 18, 1934. That Hitler was genuinely fond of Gerdy is clear. When she asked that a Jewish composer, Arthur Piechler, be reinstated in the school of music, Hitler, after an anti-Semitic tirade and a few weeks of thought, ordered that Piechler be reinstated in his former post.

Frau Professor Gerdy Troost (center), with Hitler and Professor Wacherie

Signature of Gerdy Troost, May 3, 1938

WINIFRED WAGNER (1897-1980). Born in England in 1897 as Winifred Williams, she married Siegfried Wagner, son of Richard Wagner, and 25 years her senior. In 1923 she met Adolf Hitler, a fervent admirer of Wagner's music, who soon became a close friend. After 1930, when Siegfried died, their friendship deepened and it was rumored that Hitler intended to marry Winifred. He even looked upon her children as his own. The intimacy between Hitler and Winifred excited the jealousy of Geli Raubal, the Fuehrer's beloved niece, and resulted in a violent argument between Geli and Adolf during which Hitler fumed and cursed. Eventually Hitler decided not to marry Winifred, but

Geli, weary of the violent disputes with her uncle and grieving over the death of a pet canary, shot and killed herself with Hitler's revolver on September 17, 1931. To the end of her life Winifred Wagner remained an impassioned admirer of Hitler. "To have met him," she said in 1973, "is an experience I would not have missed."

Winifred Wagner (in white) greets Frau Goebbels and Joseph Goebbels at Bayreuth.

Handwritten note signed in German by Winifred Wagner.

BAYREUTH
SIRGFRIED WAGNER-HAUS
Eingang Wahnfriedstraße
Telefon 5900

4th June 1975

Dear Sir.

As far as I can remember the happenings of I923 Göring
was seriously wounded in front of the Feldherrnhalle in November
I923 and managed to escape to Austria - I <u>believe</u> he went to
Klagenfurt - but can't swear that it was in Klagenfurt that my
husband Siegfried Wagner, who was on an Austrian concert-tour
(conducting) shortly after the Putsch of November I923 in
Munich visited Göring there or in another Austrian town. - I
did not accompany my husband but <u>suppose</u> that they talked about
Walters hotel in Venice - as Siegfried was a friend of the
<u>conductor Carlo</u> Walter- I believe his Christian name was Carlo -
and that Rudolfo Walter washis father, who owned the Hotel Venezia
in Venise ! Both my husband and I were guests of this Hotel in
the twenties - but Göring wwa not staying there at the same time a
we did. -
For further imformation perhaps Görings Daughter EDDA Göring -
8 Munich - Bürkleinstr. I6 could give you the addresses of one
or the other person still alive, who might be able to give you more
information than I can.
I think Carlo Walter was calles Carletto - If the Hotel id still
property of the family Walter you might get information from there
too. I think Carlo had a married sister - who might have inherited
the hotel - it is all so long ago 52 years !
Hoping to have given you a tiny bit of useful information I am.
dear Mr. Swearingen

sincerely Yours

Winifred Wgnr

Letter signed by Winifred Wagner, June 4, 1975.

**Winifred Wagner greeted
by Adolf Hitler**

ANNY BRUNNER-WINTER. Hitler's housekeeper and friend. According to Frau Winter, Hitler was not in love with Geli, but looked upon her with the eyes of a father.

Anny Brunner-Winter

Signature of Anny (Brunner-) Winter, 1956.

BESCHEINIGUNG

Ich Anny Brunner - Winter war 16. Jahre beim deutschen Fuehrer
u. Reichskanzler Adolf Hitler in seiner Wohnung in Muenchen,
Prinzregentpl. 16, als Hausdame taetig. Ich bestaetige Herrn
Stephen W. Bumball dass, das Buch "Mein Kampf" aus der Muenchner
Wohnung stammt und Eigentum von Adolf Hitler war. Das Bucheig-
nerzeichen wurde von einen Mitglied der Partei entworfen und
Adolf Hitler zugedacht. Es duerfte von den Dichter Dietrich
Eckart gezeichnet sein. Ich bestaetige hiermit, dass ich dieses
Buch als Freundschaftsgeschenk Herrn Bumball im Mai 1945 ueber-
reichte.

                              Anny Brunner - Winter

Signed statement of Anny Brunner-Winter, Hitler's housekeeper, about Hitler's special bookplate. Anny writes that the bookplate may have been designed by the author, Dietrich Eckart, and presented to Hitler. It appears, however, that Hitler seldom, if ever, used it.

PAULA HITLER WOLF (1896-1960). Hitler's sister. Although Paula helped her brother Adolf during his struggling years as an artist, she later drifted away from him, only visiting his home on rare occasions. Hitler remembered her in his will, leaving "my relatives (Paula Wolf and Eva Braun's mother) everything that is of value as a personal memento."

Frau Wolf lived modestly in a ramshackle house in Berchtesgaden not far from her brother's famed retreat, "The Eagle's Nest." Few knew of her existence, and she died of stomach cancer on June 1, 1960.

Paula Hitler Wolf

)he Weihnacht und ein frohes Neues Jahr !
Ihre

Hitler and his sister, Paula, relaxing at Berchtesgaden.

"MARIA" -- the Mystery Woman in Hitler's Life

Two recently discovered letters of "Maria," both penned in affectionate terms, suggest a secret intimacy with the Fuehrer. Maria addresses Hitler as "Dear Adolf" and writes in the intimate second-person singular, used in German only with relatives, servants, close friends, or lovers.

The two letters were written and posted during the "Götterdammerung," those anguished final weeks in the bunker when no mail from civilians reached the reclusive dictator.

They are the sort of letters a lover reads and then burns, but Hitler never received them. They appear to be a part of a much larger correspondence with the Fuehrer. No doubt they survived only because they never came into his hands. They were discovered at the end of the war, sealed and undelivered, by an American soldier.

Who was this strange woman who wrote in such endearing terms to one of the most unapproachable men of modern times? Possibly, just possibly, the writer was fantasizing about having an affair with Hitler. It seems much more likely, however, that Maria knew Adolf and knew him intimately. We may never discover a picture of Maria, but doubtless she was the Fuehrer's "type"--a little plump, blonde, phlegmatic, and frowsy.

In the earliest letter, dated from Prien on April 8, 1945 and postmarked from Prien on April 9, 1945, Maria refers to her "Sunday letter" to the Fuehrer and sends "fond kisses until we can meet again." The fact that her letter carried no postage but was dispatched by *Feldpost* (military courier) indicates that either Maria had a special dispensation to send her letters to Hitler without postage or was an auxilliary member of the armed forces, possibly a nurse or secretary. Here is the full text of the first letter:

> Prien, 8.4.1945
> Dear Adolf:
>
> I am sorry I cannot write a longer Sunday letter to you today.
>
> I am in a good mood and my confidence in you and my belief in Germany's victory is undaunted.
>
> I am sending you the heartiest greetings and remain with fond kisses until we can meet again
>
> Your unwavering always true
> Maria

My. M. Tomzih Prien a Giensee (13b) Hinterwanger in Obal

Maria's full name and return address on verso of the envelope addressed to Hitler.

Trier d. 8. 7. 1945

Lieber Adolf!

Leider kann ich dir heute keinen
langen Sonntagsbrief schreiben.

Die guten Wünsche und mein
Herz eilen zu dir und mein
Gebet an dem Tag Deutschlands sind
unerschüttert.

Sende dir die herzlichsten Grüße
und verbleibe mit innigen Küssen
bis zum erhofften Wiedersehen
Deine innerzarte
innertreue

Maria

<u>Feldpost</u>

Adolf Hitler

<u>Führerhauptquartier</u>

The second letter, penned the day before Hitler's last birthday and eleven days before his suicide, reads:

Prien, 19.4.1945
Dear Adolf:

It is a special pleasure for me today to congratulate you on your birthday.

Most of all I wish with all my heart that all your wishes may come true and that you won't have to be alone for long.

May our Lord keep you a very very long time in good health and grant you and your courageous troops a speedy victorious peace.

On your birthday I greet and kiss you especially fondly in love and loyalty.

Your Maria

Envelope addressed by Maria to Adolf Hitler at the Fuehrer's headquarters, postmarked from Prien, April 19, 1945.

The "mystery woman" who wrote these passionate letters to Hitler is quite possibly Maria Reiter, a Nordic blonde who became Hitler's mistress in 1926 when she was sixteen and he was thirty-seven. They met while walking their German shepherds in a Berchtesgaden park and almost at once fell in love. He called her his child "Mimilein" and she called him by his favorite nickname, "Wolf." When rumors about their relationship, fostered by their constant appearance together in his Mercedes, jeopardized his political reputation, Hitler gradually put an end to their intimacy. In 1928 Maria attempted to hang herself. Had she succeeded, she would have joined the three other beautiful women whose love for Hitler brought them death--Geli Raubal, Unity Mitford, and Eva Braun.

Maria wished to marry Hitler, but he explained (as always) that his political destiny and his "desire to save Germany" took precedence over his personal wishes. Apparently Maria continued to see Hitler from time to time. In 1936 she married an SS officer named Kubisch who was killed in France in 1940. Hitler sent her one hundred roses. A number of Hitler's letters to Maria survive, although it is believed she did not see him after a farewell meeting in Munich in 1938. The blonde, buxom Maria survived the war and lived quietly in a Munich suburb. In 1959 she received wide publicity after an interview on British television.

These two letters, perhaps the only letters of Maria that survive from a lengthy, torrid correspondence, are now in the personal collection of Stephen W. Bumball.

The commemorative march of the "Old Fighters" in Munich on November 9, 1936.

Builders of the New Reich

RICHARD-WALTHER DARRÉ (1895-1953). Reich Farmer's Leader and Minister of Food. Born in Buenos Aires, Argentina, on July 14, 1895, Darré was educated in Heidelberg and at Wimbledon near London. After World War I, during which he served as an artillery officer, Darré turned to agriculture, organizing farmers for the German labor party. In 1929 he wrote a book entitled *The Peasantry as a Life Source of the Nordic Race,* the title of which attracted the attention of Rudolf Hess, who brought him to Hitler. At the Fuehrer's request, Darré prepared a farm program for the Nazi party which favored Aryan farmers and established the hereditary system of medieval days by which no farm land could ever be sold or mortgaged. Only a German who could establish the purity of his blood could own such a farm and bear the honored title of *Bauer,* or peasant.

Darré was an SS-Obergruppenfuehrer (lieutenant general) and from January 1932 to February 1938 was head of the Central Office of Race and Resettlement. He was dismissed from this office in May 1942, because of incompetence and the failure of his policies. He died in Munich from a liver disorder on September 5, 1953.

Richard-Walther Darré as prisoner of war.

Richard-Walther Darré

Signature of Richard-Walther Darré

The entrance to Darré's headquarters bears a tapestry with the ironic inscription: "No people lives longer than the documents of its culture."

OTTO DIETRICH (1897-1952). Reichsleiter and Reich Press Chief. Born in Essen on August 31, 1897, Dietrich served in World War I and was awarded the Iron Cross (First Class). In 1931 he was appointed press chief of the Nazi party, in which post he showed extraordinary skill at fabrication and dissimulation. Almost every publicized atrocity of Hitler and his cohorts was effectively camouflaged by Dietrich in his press releases. After Hitler murdered many SA leaders in the brutal Blood Purge of 1934 Dietrich described the Fuehrer's "shock" at the "moral degeneracy" of the old comrades he had butchered. When Hess flew to England, Dietrich reported his death in an accident over enemy territory. Even as the Russians were winning on the eastern front Dietrich continued to assert that "the Soviet Union is finished."

Dietrich, who was also a State Secretary in the Propaganda Ministry and President of the Reich Press Chamber, was dismissed by the Fuehrer in March 1945. In 1949 he was tried by a military tribunal at Nuremberg and sentenced to seven years' imprisonment. He was released the following year and died on November 22, 1952 in Duesseldorf.

Heil Hitler!

Ihr

Dietrich

Signature of Otto Dietrich

Signed photograph of Otto Dietrich

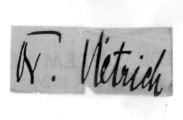

Dr. Otto Dietrich

Handwritten note signed by Otto Dietrich, sending thanks.

Dr. Otto Dietrich

ANTON DREXLER (1884-1942). Intellectual founder of the Nazi party. Born in Munich on June 13, 1884, Drexler was a harmless looking, bespectacled man. He sought his fortune in Berlin, ultimately becoming a railway locksmith. During and after World War I he worked with the Fatherland Party, an organization devoted to getting a fair peace for Germany. In January 1919, Drexler fused two tiny groups of malcontents into the German Workers' Party, an organization with no assets except a cigar box in which to put contributions. Hitler joined the party in 1919 and was impressed with Drexler's ideas. Drexler was bitterly opposed to the "capitalist Jews" and the "Marxist conspiracy." From these wild theories, already germinating in Hitler's mind, sprang the very quintessence of Nazism.

Drexler wrote to a friend about Hitler: "An absurd little man has become steering committee member No.7 of our party." No doubt Drexler was already envious of the sudden impact of Hitler's personality and the fire and zeal of his oratory. It soon became obvious that Hitler would replace Drexler as the party leader. Six years later Hitler wrote of Drexler in *Mein Kampf:* "His whole being was weak and uncertain...nor did he have the ability to use brutal means to overcome the opposition to a new idea inside the party. What was needed was one fleet as a greyhound, smooth as leather, and hard as steel."

Within a year the "absurd little man" was the dominant force in the party. Soon afterward, when Hitler merged the German Workers' Party with the Nationalist Socialist German Workers' Party, Drexler faded into the background. Although he participated in the Munich Beer-Hall Putsch and served a brief prison term, Drexler never again took an active part in the movement he had done so much to create. He died in Munich on February 25, 1942.

Anton Drexler

Hitler's membership card in the D.A.P. (German Workers' Party) signed with a facsimile signature of Anton Drexler. Hitler was steering committee member number 7 when he joined in 1919. In 1920 the membership was numbered from 500 upwards (to make it appear larger) and Hitler, whose name was spelled incorrectly by the party clerk, was accorded membership number 555.

FRANZ RITTER VON EPP (1868-1947). Franz Epp was born in Munich on October 16, 1868. After completing his education he became a professional soldier. His pre-World War I service record included tours in China and in German Southwest Africa. During the First World War he was personally ennobled for bravery by the king of Bavaria and received the Pour le Mérite. After Germany's defeat he organized a Freikorps to "liberate" Munich from its Communist government (this was accomplished with much bloodshed). He joined the Nazi party on April 1, 1928.

Like Hermann Goering, Epp, who joined the NSDAP early, was used as "window dressing" by the party. In return for his services, he became one of the first Nazi Reichstag deputies, and soon after the Nazis came to power was made Reichsstatthalter (governor) of Bavaria. He held this post until the fall of Nazi Germany. He was also a Reichsleiter and leader of the Colonial Political Office of the NSDAP from May 5, 1934 to the time of its closing on February 17, 1943.

More of a figurehead in his role as governor of Bavaria, Epp fell into American hands at the end of the war. Aged and in ill health, he died in an internment camp on December 31, 1946.

General von Epp as prisoner of war.

General Franz Ritter von Epp

Signature of Franz Ritter von Epp

WILHELM FRICK (1877-1946). Nazi Minister of the Interior from 1933-1943. As a police officer at Munich headquarters, Frick joined the Nazi party and worked as a spy for Hitler, reporting all anti-Nazi police activities. A colorless, self-effacing man, blindly loyal to the Fuehrer and eager to handle the most thankless tasks, Frick became the leader of the Nazi delegation in the Reichstag and subsequently Minister of the Interior (1933-1943). In 1934 Frick tried to limit the number of concentration camp victims but was dissuaded by Himmler and quietly joined in the madness. Also a Reichsleiter, Frick was made "Reichsprotektor" of Bohemia and Moravia in 1943. Frick was tried at Nuremberg, found guilty of war crimes, and hanged on October 16, 1946.

Wilhelm Frick

Signature of Wilhelm Frick.

MY ADDRESS IS: Dr. Wilhelm Frick

MEINE ADRESSE IST WIE FOLGT: Internal Security Detachment

IL MIO INDIRIZZO È: Nürnberg, Justizpalast

W. D., P. M. G. Form No. 4
June 11, 1943

16—33458-2   U. S. GOVERNMENT PRINTING OFFICE: 1943

Handwritten letter from Wilhelm Frick, Nuremberg, March 24, 1946, to his wife, "Oh, in these beautiful days of spring, the longing for you, dear Grete, and the children, is twice as great. How wonderful it would be to walk with you. . .and listen to awakening nature."

WALTHER FUNK (1890-1960). Minister of Economics; President of the Reichsbank. Funk, editor of a leading financial newspaper, became convinced that Hitler's star was rising and quit his job as editor in 1931 to join the Nazi party. He became contact man between Hitler and the leading industrialists of Germany. A squat, furtive little man, Funk wormed his way into Hitler's favor and was appointed Minister of Economics in 1938. He served as President of the Reichsbank from 1939 to 1945.

Funk's ministry received gold, jewels and other valuables confiscated from Jews in the concentration camps, as per a secret agreement with Heinrich Himmler. He was sentenced to life imprisonment as a war criminal in 1946. Released from Spandau Prison because of illness in 1957, he died at Dusseldorf on May 31, 1960.

Funk at Nuremberg, sketc by fellow prisoner, Alfrec Rosenberg.

Walther Funk's signature.

A. Southard

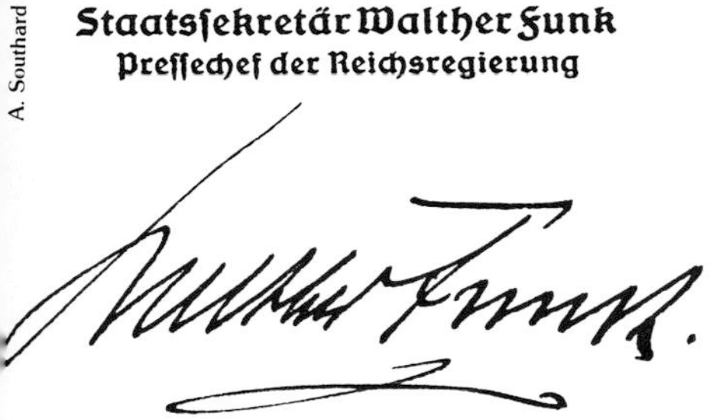
Staatssekretär Walther Funk
Pressechef der Reichsregierung

Walther Funk

Walther Funk's signature, January 4, 1937

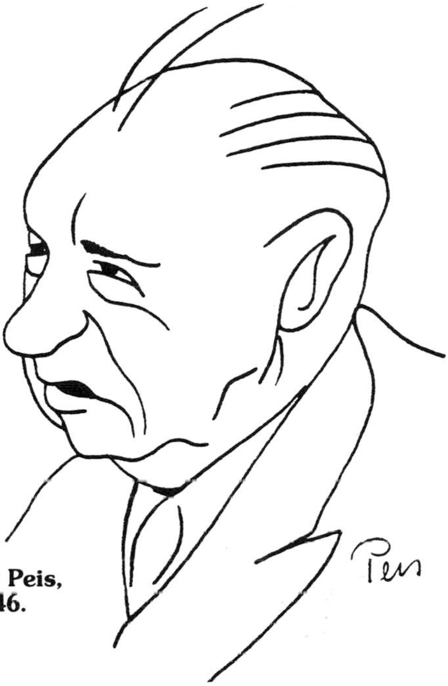

Caricature of Funk by Peis, Nuremberg, about 1946.

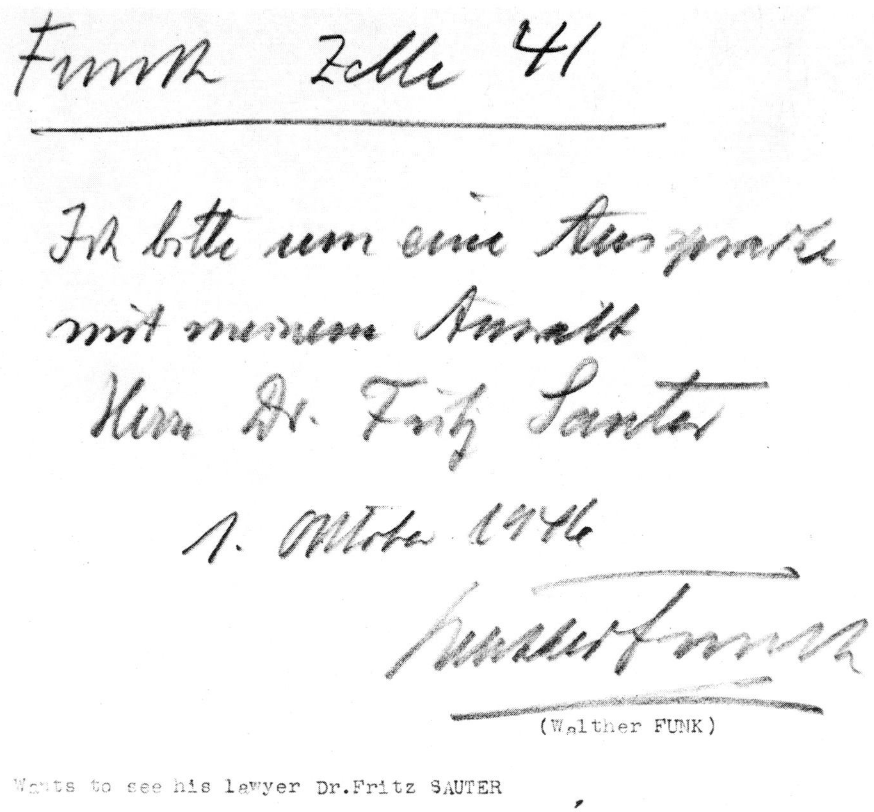
Funk Zelle 41

Ich bitte um eine Aussprache mit meinem Anwalt Herrn Dr. Fritz Sauter

1. Oktober 1946

Walther Funk

(Walther FUNK)

Wants to see his lawyer Dr.Fritz SAUTER

Handwritten note signed by Funk asking to consult with his lawyer.

Dr. FRANZ GUERTNER (1881-1941). Reich Minister of Justice. Born in Regensburg on August 26, 1881, Guertner studied law at the University of Munich. He served in World War I as a captain and was awarded the Iron Cross (First and Second Classes). After the war Guertner resumed his legal career. He was Minister of Justice in Bavaria at the time of the Beer-Hall Putsch in 1923 and helped to get a light sentence for Hitler. Subsequently, Guertner got Hitler out of prison. He discretely helped to re-establish the NSDAP in 1925.

Guertner was Minister of Justice from June 2, 1932 in von Papen's and Schleicher's cabinets, and Hitler retained him in his new cabinet of 1933. It appears that he was appalled by the atrocities committed by the regime, but like Frick, was powerless to stop them.

Guertner held his post as Minister of Justice until his death in Berlin on January 29, 1941.

Franz Guertner stands with Hitler's cabinet almost directly in front of the portrait at left. Guertner, the tall man, is between Franz Seldte and Goebbels. At Hitler's left are Goering, Blomberg, Frick, von Neurath, Schacht, and Schwerin von Krosigk.

Dr. Franz Guertner

Die besten Wünsche zum
Weihnachtsfest und *Neuen Jahre*

Dr. frang Gürtner

New Year's message signed by Dr. Franz Guertner, about 1936.

KONSTANTIN HIERL (1875-1955). Reichsleiter; head of the German Labor Service (RAD). Born on February 24, 1875, Hierl was a professional soldier, serving from 1893 to 1924 at various posts within the army. He joined the NSDAP in 1929 and became leader of Organization Department II in 1929. In 1933 he was made State Secretary in the Reich Labor Ministry, and in 1935 was appointed Reich Labor Leader. He was promoted to Reichsleiter in 1936 and became a Reichsminister in 1943. He also helped to organize the Women's Labor Service Corps at Hitler's urging for more female labor. This body was originally a volunteer group but later became compulsory for all girls between the ages of 17 and 26 who were not engaged in industrial, agricultural, or household work. After the war Hierl was tried and convicted as a "major offender." He was sentenced to five years in a labor camp. He was soon released, however. Following his release he lived in Heidelberg until his death on September 23, 1955.

Signature of Konstantin Hierl

Signed photograph of Konstantin Hierl.

Der Reichsarbeitsführer   Berlin-Grunewald, den 15. Juni 1943

    Lieber Parteigenosse Bormann !

        Zu Ihrem Geburtstage spreche ich Ihnen
meine herzlichsten Glückwünsche aus.
        In nationalsozialistischer Verbunden-
heit

                Heil Hitler !
                Ihr

Letter from Konstantin Hierl to Martin Bormann, Berlin, June 15, 1943.
Birthday greetings.

HANNS KERRL (1887-1941). Reich Minister for Ecclesiastical Affairs from 1935-1941. Born in Fallersleben on December 11, 1887, Kerrl was a son of a Lutheran schoolmaster. He served as a lieutenant in World War I and was awarded the Iron Cross (First and Second Classes). An enthusiastic Nazi, Kerrl was, in 1933, appointed as Reich Commissar in the Prussian Ministry of Justice. He became Reich Minister without portfolio in 1934 and Minister of Ecclesiastical Affairs in 1935, a position in which he had some success in bringing the church in line with Nazi ideology. He was a staunch defender of the Nazi doctrine of Race, Blood, and Soil. In 1937 Kerrl said: "Positive Christianity is National Socialism. . .National Socialism is the doing of God's will. . .God's will reveals itself in German blood. . .True Christianity is represented by the party. . .The Fuehrer is the herald of a new revelation." Kerrl, who also served in the Reichstag, died in Berlin on December 15, 1941.

Reichsminiſter Kerrl

Berlin W 8, den   5.Dezember 1941
Preußenhaus
Fernruf: 11 66 51

Lieber Parteigenosse Brückner !

    Für Deine mir mit Deiner Feldpostkarte

vom 28.November d.J. übermittelten Glückwünsche

zu meinem Geburtstage danke ich Dir bestens, Dein

Gedenken hat mich sehr erfreut.

    Auch ich möchte Dir zu Deinem Geburtstage

herzlich gratulieren.

    Mit den besten Grüßen und Wünschen für

Dich, verbleibe ich

                mit Heil Hitler !

           Dein

Letter signed by Hanns Kerrl, 1941.

Hanns Kerrl

DR. ROBERT LEY (1890-1945). Head of the German Labor Front. A chemist by profession, Dr. Ley was an aviator in World War I and spent nearly three years as a French prisoner. In 1925 he joined the Nazi party. That year he became Gauleiter for Gau Rheinland-South until 1931, when he was made Reich Inspector of the NSDAP. One year later he was appointed Reich Organization Leader of the party.

In 1933 Dr. Ley founded the German Labor Front. He effectively destroyed the free trade unions, forcing them into the Labor Front (DAF). He was also head of the "Kraft durch Freude" organization (the Strength through Joy movement sponsored cheaply priced tours, sports activities, etc., for laborers).

In 1938 Dr. Ley said: "I believe on this earth in Adolf Hitler alone. I believe in one Lord God who made me and guides me, and I believe that this Lord God has sent Adolf Hitler to us." During the war years (1939-1945), Dr. Ley confiscated the old-age pensions of workers, looted the treasuries of the unions, lowered wages and lengthened hours, and, perhaps the ultimate indignity, forced exhausted workers to attend his drunken meanderings at mass meetings. (He was facetiously called the "Reich Drunk Master".)

Slated for prosecution at Nuremberg, the imprisoned Dr. Ley rigged a noose from towel rags, hitched it to a toilet pipe, and hanged himself on October 25, 1945.

Handwritten letter signed by Dr. Ley, Weisdorf, October 24, 1927, protesting against a tax fine.

Heil Hitler!

Complimentary close of a letter
signed by Dr. Robert Ley.

Dr. Robert
Ley

30. Sept. 1945. Lieber Hugo! Lebst du noch? Wenn ja, so bitte ich dich, hilf meinen Kindern. Nimm dich Rottland an, damit es den Kindern erhalten bleibe. Ich gebe dir hiermit alle Vollmacht in meinem Namen zu handeln. Die Kinder sind in Imst (Tirol) oder in Wiesbaden. Suche sie u. führe sie heim. Dein Dr. Robert Ley. Internal. Security Detachment. O.U.S.C.C. P.A.C. A.P.O. 403. U.S. Army.

Handwritten letter signed by Dr. Ley, September 30, 1945, less than three weeks
before his suicide in his prison cell. Dr. Ley asks "Dear Hugo" to take care of his
children. "You are to act for me...Look for them and take them home...."

232

JOACHIM VON RIBBENTROP (1893-1946). Foreign Minister, 1938-1945. The son of an army officer, Ribbentrop studied in France as a youth, then served in the German army in World War I. He was awarded the Iron Cross for bravery in action and was transferred into the intelligence department, where he was trained by von Papen.

A handsome and arrogant man, Ribbentrop became a vintner and married the daughter of a rich grower of champagne grapes. His new wealth inspired him to enter society, add a *von* to his name, and even hobnob with the Rothschilds, the richest Jews in Germany.

Most of those who knew von Ribbentrop considered him rather incompetent and lazy and short-changed on brains, but Hitler was impressed by his connections and solicited his help in organizing his cabinet in 1933. As ambassador to Great Britain in 1936, he saluted King George V with "Heil Hitler," possibly exhibiting the worst taste of any ambassador in history. In 1938 he was

Joachim von Ribbentrop

![Signature of Joachim von Ribbentrop]

Signature of Joachim von Ribbentrop.

appointed Foreign Minister by Hitler and in August 1939 negotiated the agreement between Russia and Germany by which these two nations agreed to attack and divide Poland.

The outbreak of World War II in 1939 effectively ended von Ribbentrop's career as a diplomat. To curry favor with Hitler, he encouraged Germany's allies to join in the plan to exterminate the Jews. At the Nuremberg trials he was found guilty of war crimes and crimes against mankind and was the first of the condemned Nazis to mount the scaffold at exactly eleven minutes after one a.m. on October 16, 1946.

Handwritten note signed by Joachim von Ribbentrop on his visiting card (1935), sending thanks and greetings.

Joachim von Ribbentrop in his cell during the Nuremberg trials.

ALFRED ROSENBERG (1893-1946). Reichsleiter, editor of the *Voelkischer Beobachter* and Minister for the Occupied Eastern Territories. The son of an Estonian cobbler, Rosenberg studied in Russia and received a diploma in architecture from the University of Moscow. Having fled to Germany after the Russian revolution, Rosenberg settled in Munich and joined the Thule Society, whose members specialized in anti-Bolshevik and anti-Semitic myths. In 1920 he joined the Nazi party and his muddled theories about Judaism won him Hitler's approval.

In 1920 Rosenberg wrote the first of many books attacking the Jews, setting down in exalted and confusing terms his philosophical concepts of racism. His *Myth of the Twentieth Century* (1930), an overblown and pretentious discourse on Nordic superiority, was regarded as a major text of Nazism, but even Hitler found it unreadable.

Although accepted as the mentor of Nazi ideology, Rosenberg was looked upon by the more intelligent Nazis as shallow and intellectually limited. "On each telegraph pole from Munich to Berlin," he once wrote, "we must display the head of a prominent Jew."

From 1933 to 1945 Rosenberg headed the party's Foreign Affairs Office. In 1934 Hitler made him "Deputy to the Fuehrer of the National Socialist Party for the Entire Spiritual and Ideological Training of the Party." From 1941 to

Heil Hitler !

Rosenberg's signature from a typed letter.

Caricature of Rosenberg at Nuremberg by Peis, about 1946.

A. ROSENBERG
REICHSLEITER DER N.S.D.A.P.

Signed photograph of Rosenberg, about 1943.

DER REICHSMINISTER
FÜR DIE
BESETZTEN OSTGEBIETE

BERLIN W 8, den 20. Juli 1943
UNTER DEN LINDEN 63

Nr. 945/43 g – R/H. –

Geheim !

An den

Chef des SS-Hauptamtes
SS-Obergruppenführer und General
der Waffen-SS B e r g e r

Berlin-Wilmersdorf 1
Hohenzollerndamm 31

Sehr geehrter Parteigenosse Berger!

  Ich bitte Sie, beiliegenden Brief an den Reichsführer
SS und Chef der Deutschen Polizei H i m m l e r weiter-
zuleiten.

Heil Hitler!

Rosenberg

Anlage

Typewritten letters from Rosenberg to General Gottlob Berger, July 20, 1943, requesting that a certain letter be given to Himmler. Beneath Rosenberg's signature
appears a handwritten note from Berger to Himmler.

NOTE:
From March 1925 to 1938 Rosenberg
was also editor-in-chief of the
Voelkischer Beobachter.

1945 he was Minister for the Occupied Eastern Territories. His personality was far too weak, however, to seriously impede men like Himmler, Bormann and Goering — all of whom had different plans for the occupied territories. Rosenberg had so little influence in his post as Reichsminister for the Eastern Occupied Territories that he resigned in a fit of pique. His most important work for the Nazis was in supervising the looting of art treasures from France.

At the Nuremberg trials, Rosenberg was accused of complicity in the plan to exterminate the Jews, found guilty, and hanged on October 16, 1946.

DIENSTAUSWEIS

Nr. 14

für

Reichsleiter

ALFRED ROSENBERG

geboren 12. Januar 1893

in Reval (Estland)

Parteimitglieds-Nr. 18

Ausgestellt:

München, den 1. Januar 1943

Eigenhändige Unterschrift

Der Leiter der Partei-Kanzlei

Rosenberg's party membership book, signed by him and countersigned by Martin Bormann.

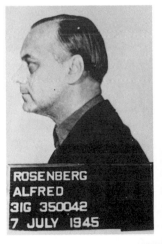

ROSENBERG
ALFRED
3IG 350042
7 JULY 1945

(Left) Rosenberg after being taken prisoner and (below) after being hanged.

Handwritten note signed by Alfred Rosenberg, Nuremberg, October 14, 1946, two days before he was hanged. Rosenberg asks that some letters from his family be turned over to his lawyer.

JULIUS STREICHER (1885-1946). Gauleiter of Nuremberg-Fuerth from 1925 until 1929, and of Franconia from 1929 until 1940. Born on February 12, 1885, Streicher was by profession an elementary school teacher. He served in World War I, rising from enlisted man to lieutenant. After the war he founded the anti-Semitic "Deutsch-Sozial Partei," and in 1922 joined the Nazi party, bringing all of his followers with him. Hitler never forgot this and remained loyal to Streicher. Streicher participated in the Beer-Hall Putsch and served a month in prison. In 1925 he was appointed Gauleiter of Nuremberg-Fuerth, in 1929 enlarged and redesignated Franconia. Streicher was Gauleiter until 1940.

A lifelong enemy of the Jews, he founded the infamous newspaper *Der Stuermer* in 1923, and remained its chief editor until 1945. *Der Stuermer* featured crude political cartoons, repulsive photos of Jews and other enemies of National Socialism, and periodic semi-pornographic outbursts. Although this "journal" was widely ignored, it had one very loyal reader - the Fuehrer.

Corrupt, brutal, sadistic, and bullying, Streicher quickly amassed a number of enemies in the party and government. Evidence was gathered about Streicher's many abuses of power and he was tried by a party court in 1940. (The hearing appears to have been triggered by remarks made by Streicher that Goering was impotent and had fathered a daughter by resorting to artificial insemination.) The Gauleiters unanimously voted for Streicher's dismissal. Hitler reluctantly agreed to this, but he never formally took away Streicher's title of Gauleiter or expelled him from the party.Streicher was banned from Nuremberg and did not enter the city again until shortly before its fall. He spent the war years editing *Der Stuermer*. Streicher was infamous even among the Nazis as a seducer of women. He carried, and often used, a whip, and was so personally revolting that most of the Nazis, including Hitler, despised him.

A prison guard at Nuremberg, where Streicher was confined after the war, told me: "The other Nazi prisoners refused to speak to him. Whenever women entered the prison, Streicher called out vulgar remarks."

A bald and broken "dirty old man," Streicher insisted that his judges at Nuremberg were all Jews and was not astonished when he was found guilty of war crimes and he was hanged on October 16, 1946.

Autograph greeting signed by Streicher to Walther Darré. "To an old comrade. . ." Christmas, 1939.

Signed photograph of Julius Streicher

Julius Streicher

Letter from Streicher to Reinhard Heydrich about an army officer, Nuremberg, November 3, 1937.

Julius Streicher

Nürnberg-O
Hitler-Haus

Aufg. 2

3. 11. 1937.

An den

SS-Gruppenführer
Reinhard H e y d r i c h ,

B e r l i n   SW 11.
===================
Prinz Albrechtstr.8.

Lieber Parteigenosse Heydrich!

Ich bitte Sie von der Abschrift eines Schreibens des Oberstleutnant F l e i s c h h a u e r Kenntnis zu nehmen. Ich glaube er hat recht. Wenn Sie derselben Überzeugung sind, halte ich es für notwendig, dass man das in Frage kommende Buch beschlagnahmt.

H e r z l i c h e   G r ü s s e !

Streicher's full signature in German (Sütterlin) script.

Streicher's full signature in Roman script.

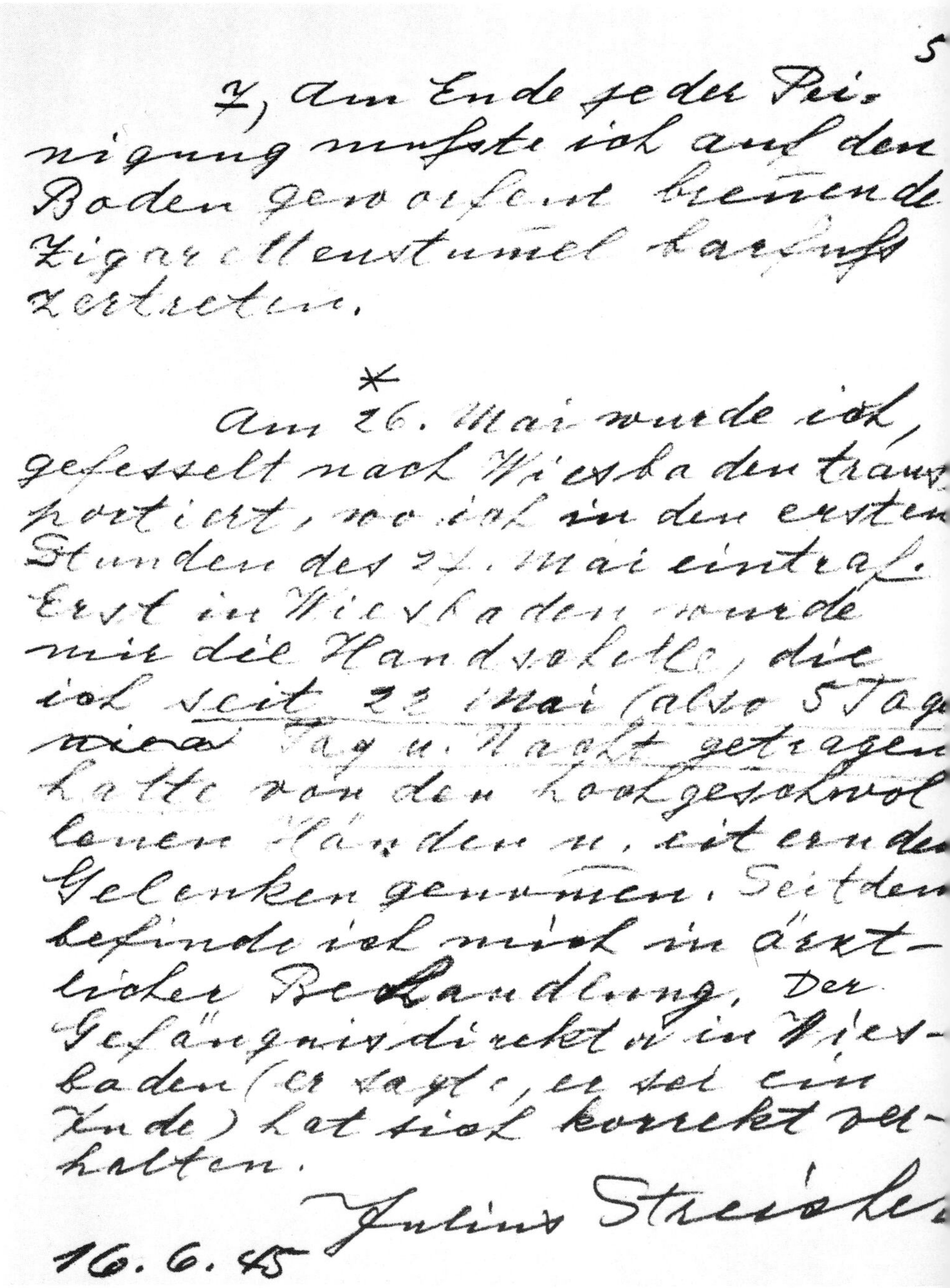

7, Am Ende jeder Reinigung mußte ich auf dem Boden gewesene brennende Zigarettenstummel barfuß zertreten.

*

Am 26. Mai wurde ich, gefesselt nach Wiesbaden transportiert, wo ich in den ersten Stunden des 27. Mai eintraf. Erst in Wiesbaden wurde mir die Handschellen, die ich seit 22 Mai (also 5 Tage vier Tag u. Nacht getragen hatte von den hochgeschwollenen Händen u. eiternden Gelenken genommen. Seitdem befinde ich mich in ärztlicher Behandlung. Der Gefängnisdirektor in Wiesbaden (er sagte, er sei ein Ende) hat sich korrekt verhalten.

Julius Streicher

16. 6. 45

Last page of a handwritten letter to the prison officials at Nuremberg, bitterly complaining about his treatment by American guards. "I was forced to kiss the feet of the Negroes. At the end of each torture I had to put out with my bare feet burning cigarette butts thrown on the ground..."

242

Caricature of Streicher by Peis, Nuremberg, about 1946.

Peis

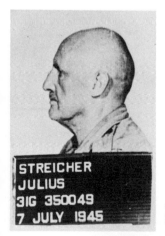

STREICHER
JULIUS
3IG 350049
7 JULY 1945

Julius Streicher as prisoner of war.

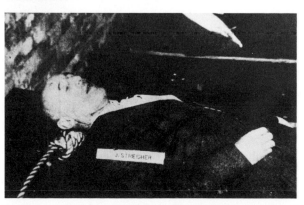

J. STREICHER

Julius Streicher after his execution, Nuremberg, October 16, 1946.

Hitler and other high party officials at the opening of the 1935 Reich Party Rally of the NSDAP in Nuremberg. Hess (left of Hitler) holds a presentation sword given to the Fuehrer by the city of Nuremberg.

Personalities
of the Third Reich

MAX AMANN (1891-1957). Reichsleiter in charge of the Nazi Press. Born in Munich on November 24, 1891, Amann served in a Bavarian infantry regiment during World War I and was Hitler's company sergeant. Amann was awarded the Iron Cross (Second Class) and joined the Nazi party when it was first organized. In 1921 he became the party's first business manager. A rough, uncouth man, Amann nevertheless was shrewd and sharp. When Hitler wrote a book called *Four and a Half Years of Struggle Against Lies, Stupidity and Cowardice*, Amann changed the title to *Mein Kampf.* As director of *Eher Verlag,* the official Nazi publishing house, Amann supervised the dozens of editions which were published during Hitler's career. Partly because of his financial and publishing adroitness, *Mein Kampf* ultimately outsold every book in Germany except the Bible. Brought before de-Nazification courts after the war, Amann had his property confiscated and died in poverty on March 31, 1957 in Munich.

NOTE:
He lost his left arm in 1931 in a firearms accident, while on a hunting trip with Ritter von Epp.

Signed photograph
of Max Amann.

München, 19.Nov.1937.
Thierschstraße 11

Herrn

    Adjutant Wilhelm B r ü c k n e r,

        M ü n c h e n.

        ———————————

Lieber Pg. Brückner,

      zur Geburt Ihres Stammhalters sende ich Ihnen
und Ihrer verehrten Frau Gemahlin auch im Namen meiner Frau
die aufrichtigsten und herzlichsten Glückwünsche.

                  Heil Hitler!

                Ihr

Letter signed by Max Amann congratulating Hitler's adjutant Wilhelm Brueckner on the birth of a child.

ARTUR AXMANN (1913-   ). Reich Youth Leader. Born on February 18, 1913 in Hagen, Axmann studied law and in 1928 founded the first Hitler Youth group in Westphalia. In 1933 he was appointed Chief of the Social Office of the Reich Youth Leadership. At the outbreak of war he entered the army and was in combat until May 1940 on the western front. In August of the same year he succeeded Baldur von Schirach as Reich Youth Leader. In 1941, while on active service on the Russian front, Axmann was badly wounded, losing an arm. Faithful to Hitler until the end, he led a battalion of boys in the Berlin street fighting and arrived in the Bunker in time to view Hitler's body in death and to witness the funeral pyre of the Fuehrer and Eva Braun.

Axmann claimed that two days later, on May 2, 1945, he saw the body of Martin Bormann in the moonlight under a bridge. There were no visible wounds on the corpse and Axmann assumed that Bormann had swallowed a capsule of poison. Axmann was arrested in December 1945 and tried for war crimes at Nuremberg. He was sentenced to three years and three months as a "Major Offender" in 1949. In 1958 a West Berlin de-Nazification court fined Axmann 35,000 marks for "indoctrinating" German youth, but found him not guilty of war crimes. He left Germany and became a businessman in the Canary Islands.

Artur Axmann and Baldur von Schirach, September 1942.

C. Hannahs

DER JUGENDFÜHRER DES DEUTSCHEN REICHS

REICHSJUGENDFÜHRER

Signature of Artur Axmann on a Hitler Youth certificate

HERBERT BACKE (1896-1947). Reich Food Minister. Backe was born in Batum in the Caucasus on May 1, 1896. After attending the Russian Tifliser Gymnasium from 1905 to 1914 he studied at the University of Goettingen. He spent most of the years 1914 to 1918 as a Russian war prisoner. From 1933 to 1942 he was a state secretary in the Ministry of Food. He assumed the position of Food Minister in 1942 and held this post until the end of the war. He hanged himself at Nuremberg Prison on April 6, 1947.

Obergruppenführer!

      Zu Ihrem Geburtstage gratuliere ich Ihnen herzlich und wünsche Ihnen für Ihre Arbeit und auch für Ihr persönliches Wohlergehen für die Zukunft von Herzen alles Gute.

        H e i l   H i t l e r !

Ihr sehr ergebener

Herbert Backe.

Brigadeführer.

Letter signed by Herbert Backe to Hitler's adjutant Wilhelm Brueckner.   Birthday greetings.

Herbert Backe

GOTTLOB BERGER (1896-1975). SS-Obergruppenfuehrer (lieutenant general). Born on July 16, 1896, the son of a sawmill owner, Berger volunteered for service in World War I. He was severely wounded in action while commanding a battle group. After the war Berger became an athletic instructor and studied military tactics in his spare time. With a skill that would have awed Machiavelli, Berger insinuated himself into Himmler's confidence and became his chief adviser, as well as an adviser to Alfred Rosenberg. An early member of the SA, Berger changed his loyalty to the SS after the murder of SA chief Ernst Roehm. With Himmler's approval, Berger helped to organize the Waffen-SS. By this time a general, Berger was looked upon by many Waffen-SS officers as a leper. General Bittrich dubbed him "a mountebank, a swindler."

Berger was also in charge of the SS Main Office; was Himmler's liaison representative to Rosenberg's ministry; and from 1944 was in charge of all P.O.W. affairs.

In August 1944 Berger was put in charge of military operations in Slovakia where he "imposed the peace of the graveyard" after an uprising. He was tried at Nuremberg for the wartime murder of Jews and in April 1949 was sentenced to 25 years' imprisonment. He was released in 1951 and died on January 5, 1975.

Gottlob Berger

Handwritten note signed by Gottleb Berger, written to the *Reichsfuehrer* (Heinrich Himmler), enclosing a letter addressed to Alfred Rosenberg, July 23, 1943.

PHILIPP BOUHLER (1899-1945). Reichsleiter. Born in Munich on September 2, 1899, Philipp Bouhler was severely wounded in World War I. After the war he became involved with the publishing world, and in 1921 joined the NSDAP. From 1925 to 1934 he was the business manager of the Nazi party and in 1933 was promoted to Reichsleiter. Bouhler served briefly as Police President of Munich in 1934 and later that year was named head of Hitler's Private Chancellery (in effect, Hitler's secretariat). He simultaneously held a number of posts associated with the German publishing industries, and was a member of the Reichskultursenat.

In 1939 Bouhler was entrusted with the sinister task of supervising the "mercy killings" of the hopelessly ill and insane. Some lethal medical "experiments" were also carried out under his auspices.

Public protests about the euthanasia program forced Hitler to cancel it in 1941, and Bouhler returned to his literary and party tasks. Gradually the Private Chancellery was absorbed by the Party Chancellery, under Martin Bormann, and in 1944 it was totally merged with the Parteikanzlei. Bouhler retained his rank, but had little to do

When the Americans tried to arrest him at the end of the war, he (and his wife) committed suicide on May 10, 1945.

**Signed photograph
of Philipp Bouhler**

Presentation inscription signed by Philipp Bouhler to Hitler's adjutant Wilhelm Brueckner.

WERNHER FREIHERR VON BRAUN (1912-1977). German rocket expert. Born at Wirsitz, Prussia (now part of Poland), von Braun dreamed even as a boy of propelling a rocket into outer space. My friend, Dr. Constantin Morales, an expert on space medicine, was an intimate friend of von Braun. "I met von Braun when we were both students at Zurich in 1930," Dr. Morales told me. "The first day we met we formed an instant attachment and talked nearly all afternoon. I asked him: 'What is your ambition?' and he said: 'I have only one ambition and that is, to put a man on the moon.'" Von Braun took his engineering degree in 1932 at Berlin and in the same year became head of a rocket-research station established by the German army. In 1936 Hitler constructed a rocket facility at Peenemuende where von Braun and his associates worked on V-1 and V-2 rockets. Our B-26 medium bomber air force, of which I was a member, was aware of the V-1 launching ramps along the French coast, all aimed at London. Long before the first buzz bomb was launched we were urged by the French underground to destroy the ramps, known to us by the code name of "No-Ball targets." For months the No-Balls served as secondary targets when our bombers could not attack the primary targets (bridges, factories, railroad yards) because of cloud cover. We knocked out scores of the ramps.

I vividly recollect the starless night of June 12, 1944 when the Nazis first peppered us with von Braun's secret weapon. All night long the air-raid sirens alternately sounded alerts and then all-clears as dozens of these low-flying, fire-tailed projectiles flew over us. Some cut out near us and glided in lethal silence to the earth where they exploded with thunderous impact. It was a week before we learned what these projectiles really were. At first we had thought they were enemy aircraft, shot down, and descending to the earth in flames. Von Braun and his associates followed the buzz bombs with the V-2, a projectile fired straight up in the air that would descend on its target with no previous warning.

National Archives

Von Braun, on May 3, 1945, with a group of German scientists following their surrender to the 44th Division, 7th U.S. Army.

After the war, in 1945, von Braun was imported to the United States where his great technical knowledge of rockets ultimately enabled him and other experts to build the Saturn V and put an American team on the moon. Von Braun was recently described as a "twentieth century Columbus who pushed back the new frontiers of outer space." He died of cancer in Alexandria, Virginia, on June 16, 1977.

Signed photograph of Wernher von Braun

WALTER BUCH (1883-1949). Reichsleiter; Chief judge of the Nazi party court and father-in-law of Martin Bormann. Born in Bruchsal, Baden on October 24, 1883, the son of a prominent judge, Buch served as a major in World War I and thereafter used the title of major. As president of the Nazi Supreme Court, Major Buch judged all crimes according to Hitler's views. After an explosion of anti-Semitic riots in Germany on November 9, 1938, Major Buch ruled that the Nazis who had raped Jewish women during the outbreak were to be expelled from the party and turned over to the civil courts, but wanton murderers were dismissed or given minor punishments since "party members who kill Jews are merely carrying out orders." Buch was not only a virulent anti-Semite but a sadist. In 1934 during the notorious Blood Purge in which Ernst Roehm and other SA leaders were murdered, Major Buch played a prominent role. Eye-witnesses described his enjoyment as he watched his victims die, some of them old comrades whom he butchered with his own hands.

Major Buch became the supreme executioner of the Nazi party, a vengeful man from whom nobody was safe. In an article in *German Justice* on October 21, 1938, Buch wrote: "The Jew is not a human being. He is an appearance of putrescence. Just as the fission-fungus cannot permeate wood until it is rotting, so the Jew was able to creep into the German people, to bring on disaster only after the German nation...had begun to rot from within." Buch's power was short-lived, however. Hated and ignored by his son-in-law, and with most of his functions taken over by the SD (Security Service), he gradually slipped into obscurity. Arrested and tried at the war's end, Major Buch was sentenced to five years' hard labor. He committed suicide on September 15, 1949 by slashing his wrists and drowning himself in Ammer Lake in Bavaria.

Signed photograph of Major Walter Buch.

JOSEF BUERCKEL (1895-1944). Born on March 30, 1895 in Lingenfeld in the Palatinate, Buerckel served four years in the army during World War I. After a stint at teaching, he became Gauleiter in the Rheinpfalz. In 1935 he was appointed Reich Commissioner for the Saar. After the *Anschluss* of Austria, Buerckel was named Reich Commissar of Austria on April 23, 1938. He was given a year to incorporate Austria, culturally and economically, into the Reich. Buerckel was appalled by the anti-Semitic outbreaks in Austria and took measures to stop indiscriminate looting and violence. He started criminal proceedings against Nazis who had stolen Jewish property. He was obliged to cooperate, however, in the deportation of Jews into unoccupied France in the fall of 1940. Buerckel was Gauleiter of Gau Saarpfalz (renamed Gau Westmark) from 1935 to 1944, and also Gauleiter of Vienna from 1939 to 1940. On September 28, 1944 Buerckel committed suicide, fearing the consequences of a premature flight from the city of Metz.

A. Southard

**Josef
Buerckel**

In Verehrung und Hochschätzung

Ihr Ihnen sehr ergebener

**Last lines of a letter signed
by Josef Buerckel**

DR. LEONARDO CONTI (1900-1945). Chief physician of the Third Reich. Conti was born in Lugano, Switzerland on August 24, 1900. He moved to Berlin after taking his medical degree, joined the old guard of the Nazi party and in 1923 became the first SA physician in Berlin. In 1939 he was appointed by Hitler to be Reich Health Leader and State Secretary for Health. In these posts he instituted a program for destroying Germans of unsound mind to purify the Nordic race. He killed huge numbers of his countrymen. On April 20, 1944 he was promoted to SS-Obergruppenfuehrer.

> "Liebe Ingard, Viele herzliche Grüsse sende ich Dir. Sei lieb und brav. Sei auch tapfer wo Du nun jetzt deine Eltern nicht hast. Frau Kelly und Frau Silhiller werden sehr lieb zu Dir sein. Denke immer lieb an deinen Vati.
> 19. 8. 45. LEONARDO CONTI.

Handwritten letter signed by Dr. Leonardo Conti, August 19, 1945, written from prison shortly before his suicide (October 6, 1945). Dr. Conti tells his daughter to behave, now that she is without her parents.

While awaiting trial in Nuremberg Prison in 1945, Conti committed suicide and four years later his estate was fined 3,000 marks by the Berlin de-Nazification tribunal.

B. Tomberlin

Signature of Dr. Leonardo Conti.

(above and at right) Dr. Leonardo Conti

HANS HEINRICH DIECKHOFF (1884-1952). German ambassador to the United States from 1937 to 1938. A wary and perceptive envoy, Dieckhoff sensed the impending conflict between Germany and the United States. He cautioned Hitler that if Germany resorted to force against England, "the whole weight of the United States would be thrown into the scale on the side of Britain. I consider it my duty to emphasize this very strongly." Dieckhoff feared that Hitler might, as did the Kaiser in 1917, underestimate the power and determination of the United States. As American animosity towards the Nazis increased after *Kristallnacht* (the Night of Broken Glass) on November 9, 1938 in which the Nazi demonstrators murdered 36 Jews and arrested 20,-000, President Roosevelt recalled the American ambassador to Germany and Hitler retaliated by recalling Dieckhoff on November 18, 1938. Later, at the Fuehrer's request, Dieckhoff drew up a lengthy list of President Roosevelt's anti-German activities for use in Nazi propaganda. From 1943 to 1944 he was German ambassador to Spain. Dieckhoff died on March 21, 1952 in Lenzkirch, Germany.

AUSWÄRTIGES AMT   Berlin, den 21. November 1932

Lieber Herr Viereck!

              Sie haben mir mit der Übersendung
Ihres Buches "The strangest friendship in history"
eine große Freude gemacht und ich habe das spannend
geschriebene Werk mit großem Interesse gelesen. Es
bringt, wie mir scheint, wichtige neue Tatsachen ans
Licht, deren Kenntnis von erheblicher Bedeutung für
die Beurteilung der historischen Zusammenhänge in
den letzten Jahren des Krieges ist. Ich würde es
sehr begrüßen, wenn Ihr Buch, das sicher in der eng-
lisch sprechenden Welt schon viele Leser gefunden hat,
auch in Deutschland Verbreitung fände.

       Mit aufrichtigen Grüßen bin ich

              Ihr sehr ergebener

rrn

George Sylvester V i e r e c k

     Hôtel Kaiserhof

Hans Heinrich Dieckhoff

Letter signed by Hans Heinrich Dieckhoff to George Sylvester Viereck, Berlin, November 21, 1932, sending thanks for Viereck's new book.

RUDOLF DIELS (1900-1957). The first head of the Gestapo. Diels was born in Berghaus, in the Taunus, on December 16, 1900. He joined the Prussian Ministry of the Interior in 1930, and soon became a high-level police official. By 1932 he had joined the Nazis. In 1933 he persuaded his friend, Hermann Goering, that a secret police force was necessary to keep an eye on the Communists. Goering appointed Diels to head a new department (Gestapo) in the Prussian State Police affiliated with the Ministry of the Interior. Gradually Diels became aware that the Nazi party was engaged in widespread illegal activities. He clashed with Himmler, then rising to power and eager to take over the Gestapo. On the night the Reichstag burned down (February 27, 1933) Diels told Hitler it was the work of a single, demented pyromaniac, already in custody, but Hitler blamed the Communists and burst out in fury: "This is a cunning plot! Every Communist official must be shot...All Communist deputies must be hanged this very night."

Diels, who was married to Goering's cousin, was forced out of the Gestapo and Himmler took over. Later Diels was reconciled with Himmler and allowed to wear an honorary colonel's uniform. Through Goering's aid, Diels held a number of government posts, such as assistant police commissioner of Berlin and administrative president of Cologne. He refused, however, to participate in the anti-Jewish measures of the 1940s.

After the July bomb plot to kill Hitler (1944), Diels was seized by the Gestapo and thrown into prison. Miraculously he survived. After the war he worked as a provincial official in Lower Saxony. Diels accidentally shot and killed himself on November 18, 1957 while on a hunting expedition.

Rudolf Diels (right) chats with Himmler.

Rudolf Diels

 **Signature of Rudolf Diels**

JULIUS DORPMUELLER (1869-1945). Reich Transport Minister. Born at Elberfeld on July 24, 1869, Dorpmueller attended high school in Aachen and studied engineering at the Aachen Technical College. After nine years with the Prussian Railway System, he embarked on a career in China with the Imperial Railway, making a spectacular escape in 1914 through Siberia and Russia. He was appointed Reich Minister of Transport in 1937 and remained in that post until 1945. He died on June 5, 1945.

**Julius
Dorpmueller**

Julius Dorpmueller (second from right, standing between a smiling Goebbels and the president of the Reichbank, Dr. Hjalmar Schacht. Also in the photo, taken in 1935, are left to right, General von Blomberg, Hitler, and Dr. Fritz Todt.

Der führer

Bottom portion of a document signed by Julius Dorpmueller, with a printed signature of Hitler, appointing a railroad director, August 14, 1944.

DR. HUGO ECKENER (1868-1954). German aeronaut. A brilliant engineer and a skilled promoter, Eckener got his first important job in 1908 when he joined Count Zeppelin in building dirigibles. Although he made many passenger flights, Eckener always looked upon the Zeppelin as a military weapon. Eventually he persuaded the German government to use Zeppelins in attacking England during World War I. Eckener was president of the pioneer German Aerial Navigation Company, established in 1911. He formed and became head of the Zeppelin Company in 1924. Eckener's activities were followed with great interest by Hitler. Goebbels realized their publicity value. Eckener built the celebrated *Graf Zeppelin* in which he circled the globe in 1929. A series of rigid airship accidents, however, eventually convinced the Fuehrer and other Nazi leaders that the dirigible was not practical as a bombing weapon. He died on August 14, 1954 in Friedrichshafen.

Signed photograph of Dr. Hugo Eckener.

CARL EDUARD, DUKE OF COBURG. Born on July 19, 1884 in Esher, the Duke of Coburg was a lieutenant general in the NSKK (Motor Corps). He was President of the German Red Cross from 1934 to 1945 and died on March 6, 1954 in Coburg.

**Carl Eduard,
Duke of Coburg**

Heil Hitler

Ihr

Carl Eduard

Complimentary close of letter and signature of Carl Eduard, Duke of Coburg.

THEODOR EICKE (1892-1943). Chief inspector of concentration camps. Born in Huedingen, Alsace-Lorraine in 1892, Eicke resigned his career as an army paymaster to join the police forces in Thuringia. He lost several posts because of his erratic conduct and his outspoken hostility towards the Weimar Republic. In 1928, after losing his final job with the police, Eicke joined the Nazi party. Transferred to the SS (Elite Guard), Eicke was promoted to colonel in 1931. He was sentenced to two years in prison in March 1932 for preparing political bomb attacks. Eicke escaped to Italy and the following year, upon

Div.St.Qu.,den 22.Oktober 1940

Anlagen: - 1 -

An den

R e i c h s f ü h r e r - SS
und Chef der Deutschen Polizei,
Heinrich H i m m l e r ,

B e r l i n SW 11.

Prinz-Albrecht-Str. 8

R e i c h s f ü h r e r !

Als Anlage überreiche ich wunschgemäß das Handschreiben des
Oberbefehlshaber der 7.Armee, Herrn Generaloberst D o l l -
m a n n , welches dieser anläßlich des Jahrestages der Auf-
stellung der SS-Totenkopf-Division an mich übersandt hat.

H e i l H i t l e r !
Ihr gehorsamer

SS-Gruppenführer.

**Letter signed by Theodor Eicke to Heinrich Himmler, October 22, 1940. With one
word and initials penned at upper right (circled) by Himmler.**

Hitler's ascension to power, returned to Germany. In July 1934 Himmler appointed him to command Dachau, the nucleus of a concentration camp
system about twelve miles northwest of Munich. His first important act as com-
mandant of Dachau was to issue a firm code of regulations that included:
     "Article 11. The following offenders, considered as agitators, will be hanged:
Anyone who. . .politicizes, holds inciting speeches and meetings, forms cliques,

Hitler and Theodor Eicke

loiters around with others; who, for the purpose of supplying the propaganda of the opposition with atrocity stories, collects true or false information about the concentration camp, receives such information, buries it, talks about it to others, smuggles it out of the camp into the hands of foreign visitors, etc.

"Article 12. The following offenders, considered as mutineers, will be shot on the spot or later hanged. . .Anyone. . .refusing to obey or to work while on detail. . .or bawling, shouting, inciting or holding speeches while marching or at work."

Eicke was, like Himmler, a rigid disciplinarian who never deviated from the regulations. He issued precise instructions for solitary confinement, corporal punishment, beatings, and reprimands. Eicke detested all forms of military weakness and instructed his men to banish all pity from their hearts. Any SS man with a soft heart, said Eicke, would do well "to retire at once to a monastery." He declared that he wanted only men who were ruthless and would obey without question every order. At the start of World War II he addressed his concentration camp commandants: "It is the duty of every SS man to identify himself body and soul with the cause. Every order must be sacred to him. . . ."

In 1940 Eicke was replaced as concentration camp inspector. Early in 1943 he was promoted to the rank of Waffen-SS lieutenant general. He was killed on February 16, 1943 during an air reconnaissance on the Russian front.

PAUL FREIHERR VON ELTZ-RUEBENACH (1875-1943). Reich Minister of Post and Communications in Hitler's first cabinet. Born in Wahn, Muelheim am Rhein on February 9, 1875, von Eltz attended *Gymnasium* (high school) before beginning a career in railroad work. He served in World War I as an expert on railroads and won the Iron Cross (First and Second Classes). After the war he was employed in the German railway system. He became its president in 1921. He became Minister of Transport in 1932, and he remained in that position after the Nazis came into power. An opponent of

Signature of Paul Freiherr von Eltz-Ruebenach.

In this photo of Hitler's first cabinet, von Eltz-Ruebenach is third from right.

Nazi ideology, von Eltz was forced to retire in 1937. He died on August 25, 1943 in Linz am Rhein.

KARL ERNST (1904-1934). Storm Trooper leader. Born in Wilmersdorf, Berlin, Ernst started his career as a bouncer and bellhop in a fancy restaurant frequented by intellectuals. He joined the Nazi party in 1923. Ernst was extremely handsome and Captain Ernst Roehm of the Storm Troopers quickly added the nineteen-year-old youth to his entourage of homosexual lovers. Ernst rose rapidly in the ranks and was elected a delegate to the Reichstag in 1932. By 1934 he was an SA-Gruppenfuehrer (major general), in charge of SA-Obergruppe 3. He was a victim of the 1934 Blood Purge. Ernst was heading for a Madeira honeymoon with his bride when members of the SS opened fire on his car. His bride was wounded and Ernst was knocked unconscious. He was flown back to Berlin and executed in the LAH barracks in Berlin-Lichterfelde.

264

Abteilung:

m :

efr :

nordnung des Gruppenführers:

Karl Ernst

üdlauf an mich!

wischenbescheid abgeben!

ericht und Vorlage an mich!

Gruppenführer.

Note signed by Karl Ernst, November 20, 1933. Ernst asks for the date of the next troop meeting.

HERMANN ESSER (1900-1981). Nazi political leader. Born on July 29, 1900, Esser was a founding member of the Nazi party and an intimate friend of Hitler. Esser was constantly involved in scandals and arrests. Hitler disliked and distrusted him, but said: "I must use him as long as he is of any use. I must keep him near me so that I can watch him." He was party member No. 20.

Esser turned out a series of anti-Semitic posters and wrote a book attacking the Jews. Only after he quarreled with Streicher and assaulted a young girl did Hitler finally decide to ease him into the background.

Esser edited the *Illustrierter Beobachter* from 1926 to 1932. During the 1930s he held a number of posts. At war's end he was Vice President of the Reichstag and State Secretary for Tourism in the Propaganda Ministry. Although arrested by the Americans after the war, he was considered an insignificant official and was released in 1947. Esser then went into hiding until he was arrested on September 9, 1949, this time by the German police. A Munich de-Nazification court reclassified him as a "Major Offender" for being the earliest propagator of Nazi ideas and for his anti-Semitic activities. He was given a sentence of five years at hard labor but in view of his previous detention he was released in 1952. He died at eighty on February 7, 1981.

Speer, Hitler, Esser, and Funk examine architectural plans on October 24, 1936.

19. OKTOBER 1945

ICH BESTÄTIGE, DASS DIES MEINE EIGENHÄNDIGE
UNTERSCHRIFT IST.

UNTERSCHRIFT: *[signature]*

HERMANN ESSER 13786

TITEL: STAATSMINISTER A.D.

LETZTE OFFIZIELLE: STAATSEKRETÄR FÜR FREMDENVERKEHR
FUNKTION

Hand-printed document, October 19, 1945, signed by Hermann Esser, certifying to the authenticity of his signature.

Hermann Esser

Signed photograph of Hermann Esser, about 1933.

267

MICHAEL VON FAULHABER (1869-1952). Cardinal of the Roman Catholic Church; tacit supporter of Hitler. Cardinal von Faulhaber was born in Lower Franconia on March 5, 1869. In 1892 he was ordained a priest. He was an expert on Old Testament theology. During World War I, as Bishop of Speyer, he defended the German cause as "a just war." With the advent of Hitler, von Faulhaber tried to steer a middle course but was soon compelled to protest the Nazi relapse into paganism. However, he was pacified by reassurances from Hitler and in 1936 gave the order: "Catholic men, we will now pray together a *Paternoster* for the life of the Fuehrer." In a three-hour conference later with Hitler, von Faulhaber was told: "If National Socialism does not succeed in defeating Bolshevism, then both Church and Christianity are finished in Europe."

During the anti-Semitic riots on the Night of the Broken Glass (November 9, 1938), von Faulhaber provided a truck for the Chief Rabbi of Munich to rescue religious objects from his synagogue before it was demolished. Despite continuous incidents that revealed the Nazi antipathy towards Catholicism, the cardinal refused to join the July 1944 conspirators in their attempt to murder Hitler. After the failure of the plot, von Faulhaber was grilled by the Gestapo but he denounced the assassination attempt and pledged his personal loyalty to Hitler. He died in Munich on June 12, 1952.

Michael Cardinal Faulhaber
Erzbischof

Promenade - Strasse 7   München

Signed visiting card of Cardinal Faulhaber.

GOTTFRIED FEDER (1883-1941). An early member of the German Worker's Party, out of which grew the Nazi party, Feder was an eloquent orator and during one of his tirades converted a spell-bound Adolf Hitler. Soon the two men became fast friends, but as Hitler's ideas developed, he came to look upon Feder as old-fashioned. Despite Feder's great contributions to the Nazi cause, he was dismissed by Hitler in 1934 from his post as State Secretary in the Ministry of Economic Affairs. Feder lived in retirement until his death on September 24, 1941 as a professor in the Charlottenburg Technical School.

Gottfried Feder

Heil H i t l e r !

   Ihr sehr ergebemer

Signature of Gottfried Feder.

269

KARL FIEHLER (1895-1969). Reichsleiter and SS-Obergruppenfuehrer (SS lieutenant general). An early supporter of Hitler, Fiehler was born on August 31, 1895 in Brunswick. He served in the Germany army in World War I and was severely wounded. After a minor political career in Munich, Fiehler joined the Nazi party (membership number 37) and in 1923 marched by the side of Hitler during the Beer-Hall Putsch. He served in prison with Hitler. By 1933 Fiehler was the head of the Nazi Office for Municipal Policy. From March 1933 until the fall of the Third Reich, he was mayor (Oberbuergermeister) of Munich. He died on December 8, 1969 in Diessen am Ammersee.

Munich, capitale du Mouvement, théâtre de centaines d'années d'histoire et de glorieuse tradition, lieu des premières victimes héroïques d'une forte Allemagne. Munich, ville de l'Art allemand, source des joies de l'existence et de la bonhomie cordiale.

Ces feuilles illustrées de nombreuses gravures dépei= gnent Munich dans sa diversité et sont dédiées aux amis de notre ville et à ceux qui le deviendront.

Fiehler

Signed, printed statement by General Karl Fiehler (as mayor), praising Munich as a cultural center.

Official portrait of Karl Fiehler, one of the more obscure Reichsleiters.

▲ Hitler is saluted by the heirarchy of the Nazi party. Reichsleiter Fiehler is in the
▼ center of the photo.

ALBERT FORSTER (1902-1954). Gauleiter of Danzig. Born on July 26, 1902 in Fuerth, Forster became a local Nazi and SA leader in his twenties. While working as a bank employee, Forster was appointed Gauleiter of Danzig in October 1930. In the same year he was elected to the Reichstag from Franconia. Forster directed the secret preparations for the Nazi seizure of Danzig and was subsequently appointed German regent there just before the outbreak of World War II. As Gauleiter of Danzig, Forster committed numerous atrocities against the Poles. In August 1946 he was extradited to Poland by the British. On April 29, 1948 he was sentenced to death by a Danzig court. The following accounts of his death have been reported: (a) the German Red Cross states he was executed just before Christmas 1955, (b) Polish authorities informed his wife that he had died in 1952, and (c) one source claims he was executed on March 31, 1954.

Der Gauleiter und Reichsstatthalter
in
Danzig-Westpreußen

**Albert
Forster**

Herrn
Major Wilhelm B r ü c k n e r
Fp.Nr. 18 566

Mein lieber Parteigenosse Brückner!

Es hat mich sehr gefreut, nach so langer Zeit wieder mal etwas von Ihnen zu hören.

Gern will ich Ihrem Wunsche nachkommen und habe veranlaßt, daß Ihnen 2 Flaschen Machandel und 200 Zigaretten zugehen. Leider sind auch wir hier durch die neuen Verfügungen und Erlasse mit diesen wohlbekömmlichen Sachen sehr beschränkt,sodaß es jetzt nur möglich ist,die obenangegebene Menge zu senden.

Ich darf hoffen, daß es Ihnen bei Ihrer Truppe nach wie vor gut geht und Sie alles gut überstehen, trotzdem die Kämpfe, wie aus allem zu ersehen,schwer und hartnäckig sind.

Indem ich Ihnen weiterhin alles Gute wünsche, bin ich mit den besten Grüßen und Wünschen für ein recht gesundes Weihnachtsfest für Sie und Ihre Einheit mit

Heil Hitler!

A. Forster

Letter signed by Albert Forster to Wilhelm Brueckner, Danzig, 1941.

ROLAND FREISLER (1893-1945). President of the People's Court. Known as "the hanging judge," Freisler was born in Celle on October 30, 1893. He served in the First World War and was captured in 1915 by the Russians. After five years as a prisoner in Siberia, he mastered the Russian language and became an ardent communist. When Hitler discovered this he found it difficult to accept. Freisler was, therefore, overlooked when Guertner's job became available in 1941. He managed to return to Germany in 1920. He studied law at Jena and was graduated with honors. In 1925 he joined the Nazi party. After serving in a number of minor posts, he was appointed a State Secretary in the Ministry of Justice in 1934.

From 1942 to 1945 Judge Freisler headed "the People's Court," a dreaded tribunal where most trials resulted in the death sentence. Freisler was brutal and without mercy. He heaped abuse on prisoners before he sent them to the gallows. He was especially vindictive towards the members of the July 20 plot to kill Hitler. Few people connected with the conspiracy were spared his wrath. Freisler escaped a dose of his own justice--for he surely would have been sentenced to hang at Nuremberg--when he was killed by an American bomb on February 3, 1945 in Berlin while presiding over a treason trial.

Dr. jur. Roland Freisler
Staatsfekretär

Berlin W 8, den
Wilhelmstraße 65

Heil Hitler!

Ihr sehr ergebener

Printed letterhead of Judge Roland Freisler, Berlin, with complimentary close and signature from a letter.

Roland Freisler

ULRICH GRAF (1878-1950). City Councillor of Munich. Graf was born in Bachhagel on July 6, 1878. A roughneck and an amateur wrestler, he left his job as a butcher to become the personal bodyguard of Hitler from 1920 to 1923. Graf was seriously wounded in the 1923 Beer-Hall Putsch in Munich. Had he not thrown himself in front of the Fuehrer, Hitler might well have been killed in the Putsch. In 1936 he was elected to the Reichstag. In 1943 he was promoted to SS-Brigadefuehrer (brigadier general). He died in March 1950.

Ulrich Graf

Ratsherr
der Hauptstadt der Bewegung
Ulrioh Graf

A n

Herrn Hans S c h m i d t

D e s s a u
Schloßstraße 19.

Sehr geehrter Herr Schmidt!

Anbei erhalten Sie das an mich gesandte Bild mit meiner eigenhändigen

Unterschrift zurück. Es freut mich, daß Sie in so netter Weise meiner

gedenken und bin mit deutschem Gruß

Heil Hitler!

Ihr Pg.

Ulrich Graf

des Führers alter Begleiter.

Letter signed by Ulrich Graf, sending a signed photograph to Hans Schmidt.

Graf with Hitler and Goering, on August 30, 1932.

ARTHUR GREISER (1897-1946). Gauleiter of the Wartheland. Born in Schroda, Posen (now Poznań) province, on January 22, 1897, Greiser was an aviator in World War I and co-founder of the Steel Helmet (*Stahlhelm*) veterans' organization in Danzig. He joined the Nazi party in 1929. After service in the Danzig senate, he was made Gauleiter of the Gau Wartheland in 1939 and remained in this position until the end of the war. He was extradited to Poland by the Americans where he was tried, found guilty of war crimes and hanged at Poznań on July 21, 1946.

Der Gauleiter und Reichsstatthalter
im Reichsgau Wartheland

Heil Hitler!

Ihr Ihnen stets ergebener

ℋ–Gruppenführer.

Printed letterhead of Arthur Greiser, with complimentary close and signature from a letter.

JAKOB GRIMMINGER (1892-1969). Bearer of the Blood Banner. Born on April 25, 1892, Grimminger served with distinction in World War I. An early member of the Nazi party and the SS, Grimminger took part in the famous Beer-Hall Putsch in Munich. He was later accorded the honor of being appointed the official bearer of the Blood Banner of November 9, 1923, a special flag carried during the unsuccessful Putsch. The flag was drenched with the blood of those killed on November 9, 1923, and was used in special rituals during the Nazi regime. Grimminger was an SS colonel (SS-Standartenfuehrer) and a City Councillor of Munich. He died in Munich in obscurity and poverty on January 28, 1969.

Jakob Grimminger holds the Blood Banner. Hitler grips the flag.

**Jakob
Grimminger**

Jakob Grimminger [signature]

Signature of Jakob Grimminger.

KARL HAUSHOFER (1869-1946). Army officer and geo-politician. Born in Munich on August 27, 1869, Haushofer served as a brigadier general during World War I. In 1921 he took a post as professor of geography at the University of Munich, where he founded the Institute for Geopolitics. Rudolf Hess was one of his students. Later Hess passed on to Hitler the ideas of his teacher.

Haushofer held the belief that the British Empire was in decline and a continental power (Germany, of course) would take over the leadership of Europe. Hitler was enthusiastic about Haushofer's ideas and one of his favorite expressions was cribbed from the Munich professor: "space as a factor of power." Haushofer, much to his embarrassment, became known as "the man

277

behind Hitler." Haushofer's son was involved in the anti-Hitler plot of July 20, 1944, and was shot by the Gestapo. Grieving for his son, and utterly disillusioned by the Nazis, Haushofer committed suicide on March 13, 1946.

**Karl
Haushofer**

Signature of Karl Haushofer

ERNST HEINKEL (1888-1958). German aircraft inventor and manufacturer. Born in January 1888 in Grunbach, South Germany, Heinkel was the son of a plumber. While a mechanical engineering student, he witnessed the burning of a Zeppelin that had been struck by lightning, and decided that the future of aviation lay in airplanes. In the summer of 1911, Heinkel built his first aircraft, a machine driven by a powerful 50-horsepower engine. Heinkel made ten successful flights in it before he crashed. By 1913 Heinkel was designing planes that flew faster, climbed higher, and operated without the impedimenta of wires and struts that characterized other aircraft of the period.

Heinkel built a number of successful seaplanes for the Hansa-Brandenburg aircraft company. After the war Heinkel continued to design powerful aircraft. Obsessed with speed, he began constructing aerodynamic planes that were not only aesthetically beautiful but broke records. He developed the famous Heinkel-111 twin-engined bomber which was used first in Spain. Goering valued it highly and made it the backbone of his bombing force. In 1934 Heinkel met the youthful Wernher von Braun, now remembered for his postwar work in astronautics in the United States, and together the two men designed the Heinkel-176, a tiny aircraft driven by rockets. At the same time Heinkel was at work developing a plane that would use gas-turbine power. The jet age began in August 1939 with Heinkel's 178 monoplane, the first aircraft ever propelled by a turbojet engine.

After the war Heinkel lived for a while in relative obscurity but in 1955 he re-established his aircraft company. He died on January 30, 1958.

Signed photograph of Professor Doctor Ernst Heinkel

A. Southard

August Heissmeyer

AUGUST HEISSMEYER (1897-   ). Lieutenant general (Obergruppenfuehrer) in the SS. In 1934 Heissmeyer was put in charge of SS-District Rhein, and from 1935 to 1940 was head of the SS Main Office (SS-Hauptamt). In 1943 he became the controlling authority for all political education institutions. He opposed the linking of the police and the SS but was overruled by his chief, Heinrich Himmler, He was married to Gertrud Scholtz-Klink, the Nazi women's leader.

Pooler

Signature of SS Lieutenant General August Heissmeyer

KONRAD HENLEIN (1898-1945). Sudeten German leader. Born in Bohemia on May 6, 1898, Henlein began his career as a bank clerk. On October 1, 1933, shortly after Hitler's ascension to power, Henlein founded a political party in support of the Nazis, a group subsequently known as the Sudeten Deutsche Partei. The new party was supported partially by financial

Konrad Henlein

Herrn
Professor Dr. med. Theo M o r e l l

Führerhauptquartier

Lieber Parteigenosse M o r e l l !

    Für Ihre lieben Zeilen danke ich Ihnen herzlichst.
Nach Rücksprache mit meinem Gauamtsleiter für Volksge-
sundheit kann ich Ihnen mitteilen, daß ich Gelegenheit
hätte, mir jeden zweiten Tag eine intramuskuläre Injektion
geben zu lassen. Ich wäre Ihnen daher sehr verbunden, wenn
Sie mir die versprochenen Ampullen Vitamultin-Calcium,
Vitamultin-forte, Leber-Hamma-Ampullen und auch das Tono-
phosphan-fortius zusenden würden.
    Für Ihre Liebenswürdigkeit im vorhinein bestens dankend,
bin ich mit besten Grüßen

                            Heil Hitler!

Letter signed by Konrad Henlein to Dr. Morell, November 1943, requesting drugs.

gifts from the Nazis. Henlein led his followers in a movement for independence from Czechoslovakia for the Sudeten Germans. He was enthusiastically
supported by Hitler, who told him: "I will stand by you...you will be my
viceroy." In October 1938 Henlein became Gauleiter (District Leader) of
Czechoslovakia. On June 21, 1943 he was promoted to SS-
Obergruppenfuehrer. In early May 1945 he was captured by the United States
Seventh Army. On May 10 he committed suicide in an Allied internment camp
at Pilsen by slashing his wrists with a razor blade he had concealed in a
cigarette case.

Signature of Konrad Henlein

OTTO HERZOG (1900-1945). A lieutenant general in the SA. Herzog was born on October 30, 1900. He was the leader of SA Group Schlesien from 1934 to 1936. From 1936 to 1939 he served in the SA High Command and in 1939 took over the leadership of SA Group Schlesien once more. He was killed in May 1945, while attempting to break out of besieged Breslau. Herzog was one of the few SA men to be awarded the Knight's Cross of the Iron Cross (on April 15, 1945).

Otto Herzog
SA-Obergruppenführer
Stabsführer der Obersten SA-Führung

München, den
Barer Straße 11

lo. Dez. 1936.

An   SA-Obergruppenführer B r ü c k n e r ,
      1. Adjutant des Führers

      B e r l i n,
      Reichskanzlei

      Anlässlich Ihres Geburtstages übermittele ich
Ihnen namens der Obersten SA-Führung wie auch persönlich, kameradschaftliche Gratulation, verbunden
mit den besten Wünschen für Ihre weitere verant-
wortungsvolle Arbeit zum Wohle der Bewegung.

      Heil Hitler!

Otto
Herzog

A. Southard

PRINCE PHILIPP VON HESSEN. (1896-   ). President of the
province of Hessen-Nassau, SA major general. In March 1938 the Prince was

Oberpräsident
der
Provinz Heſſen-Naſſau

Kaſſel, den 10. August 35.

8 AM. 12,8,—

Sehr geehrter Herr Wiedemann!

Den Empfang der Einladung zum Reichs-
parteitag 1935 bestätige ich und darf darum
bitten, dem Führer meinen gehorsamsten
Dank übermitteln zu wollen.

Mit deutschem Gruß und

Heil Hitler!

Philipp Prinz von Hessen.

SA-Gruppenführer.

Letter signed by Philipp, Prince of Hessen, written to Hitler's adjutant, Captain Fritz Wiedemann, Kassel, 1935.

Birthday greetings from Otto Herzog to Wilhelm Brueckner, Hitler's SA adjutant.

Hitler's envoy to Mussolini during the Austrian *Anschluss*, when the Fuehrer feared that Mussolini might object to Germany's territorial expansion. He later fell from grace with the Nazis and was arrested with his wife. His wife died on August 27, 1944 during an Allied air attack on Buchenwald concentration camp, but as of 1978 he was still reported as living.

Prince Philipp von Hessen

ERICH HILGENFELDT (1897-1945). Chief of the Office of Peoples Welfare. Hilgenfeldt was born on July 2, 1897 in Heinitz. He served in World War I and after the war became an economic statistician. He joined the Nazi party in 1929 and subsequently headed the annual winter relief program run by the party. Hilgenfeldt was also an SS major general and a member of the Reichstag.

Erich Hilgenfeldt

Ihr Glückwünsche zum Jahreswechsel haben mich besonders erfreut. Ich spreche Ihnen dafür meinen besten Dank aus und erwidere sie auf das herzlichste.

Heil Hitler!

Hilgenfeldt
Reichsbeauftragter für das W·H·W·

New Year's greetings signed by Hilgenfeldt

FIELD MARSHAL PAUL VON HINDENBURG (1847-1934). Never a Nazi, von Hindenburg led the German forces in a successful campaign against Russia during World War I and, with Ludendorff, directed all German strategy from 1916 to the war's end in 1918. From 1925 until his death, von Hindenburg was President of Germany and although he looked upon Hitler as an upstart Austrian corporal, he was compelled to appoint him chancellor in 1933. When Hindenburg died at 87 on August 2, 1934 at Neudeck, Hitler merged the offices of president and chancellor and declared himself Fuehrer.

Paul Hindenburg

Signature of Paul von Hindenburg

KARL HOLZ (1895-1945). Acting Gauleiter of Franconia. Born in Nuremberg on December 27, 1895, Holz joined the Nazi party in 1922 (membership number 77) and became friendly with Julius Streicher who appointed him editor of the anti-Semitic newspaper *Der Stuermer*. In 1934 Holz was made Deputy Gauleiter of Franconia. Like Streicher, his life was beset with scandals. In 1939 he was forced to resign his party posts. After a successful army career, serving in Rommel's 7th Panzer Division during the western campaign of 1940, Holz returned to Franconia as acting Gauleiter. He ran Streicher's Gau until the end of the war. Holz was killed in the battle for Nuremberg on April 20, 1945, while entrenched in the police headquarters building. He was awarded the German Order, the party's highest decoration.

**Karl
Holz**

Signature of Karl Holz

ADOLF HUEHNLEIN. (1881-1942). NSKK leader (Korpsfuehrer). Huehnlein served as a major in World War I. After the war he joined the SA (Brown Shirts). Huehnlein took part in the Beer-Hall Putsch in 1923. He rose

**Signature of
Adolf Huehnlein**

gradually in Nazi ranks, becoming, in 1934, chief of the NSKK (National Socialist Transportation Corps), an organization devoted to para-military transportation that developed many soldiers who subsequently served in Panzer divisions. Huehnlein died on June 18, 1942.

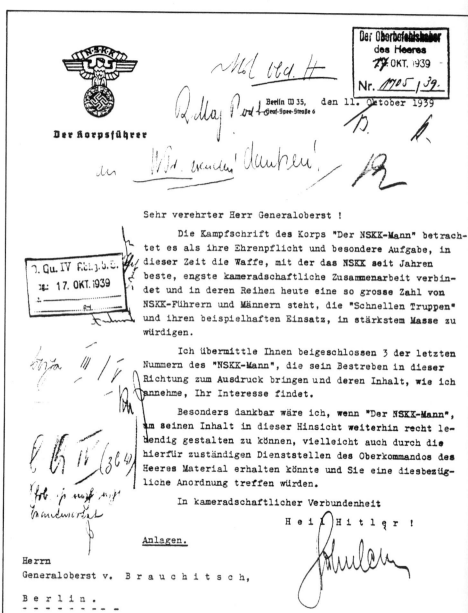

Der Korpsführer

Berlin W 35, den 11. Oktober 1939
Graf-Spee-Straße 6

Sehr verehrter Herr Generaloberst !

Die Kampfschrift des Korps "Der NSKK-Mann" betrachtet es als ihre Ehrenpflicht und besondere Aufgabe, in dieser Zeit die Waffe, mit der das NSKK seit Jahren beste, engste kameradschaftliche Zusammenarbeit verbindet und in deren Reihen heute eine so grosse Zahl von NSKK-Führern und Männern steht, die "Schnellen Truppen" und ihren beispielhaften Einsatz, in stärkstem Masse zu würdigen.

Ich übermittle Ihnen beigeschlossen 3 der letzten Nummern des "NSKK-Mann", die sein Bestreben in dieser Richtung zum Ausdruck bringen und deren Inhalt, wie ich annehme, Ihr Interesse findet.

Besonders dankbar wäre ich, wenn "Der NSKK-Mann", um seinen Inhalt in dieser Hinsicht weiterhin recht lebendig gestalten zu können, vielleicht auch durch die hierfür zuständigen Dienststellen des Oberkommandos des Heeres Material erhalten könnte und Sie eine diesbezügliche Anordnung treffen würden.

In kameradschaftlicher Verbundenheit

H e i l H i t l e r !

Anlagen.

Herrn
Generaloberst v. B r a u c h i t s c h ,
B e r l i n .
- - - - - - - - - -

Letter signed by Adolf Huehnlein on his letterhead as chief of the NSKK (National Socialist Motor Corps), Berlin, October 11, 1939. Huehnlein calls von Brauchitsch's attention to certain NSKK periodicals.

Adolf
Huehnlein

DIETRICH VON JAGOW (1892-1945). Lieutenant general in the SA (SA-Obergruppenfuehrer); German ambassador to Hungary 1941-1945. Born on February 29, 1892 in Frankfurt (Oder), von Jagow was appointed leader of SA Group Berlin-Brandenburg in 1934. He held the post until 1941, serving also as an officer at the front from September 1939 until May 1941. He was a holder of the Golden Party Badge and was a survivor of the Blood Purge of 1934 when Roehm, leader of the SA, was murdered. Von Jagow seized every effort to thwart Himmler and his recruiting officer, Gottlob Berger, in their recruiting efforts for the Waffen-SS in the Balkans. He died on April 26, 1945 in Merano, Italy.

Der Führer
der SA Gruppe Berlin=Brandenburg

Jhr

...ature of Dietrich von Jagow with his letterhead
...roup Leader of the SA for Berlin-Brandenburg.

289

FRIEDRICH JECKELN (1895-1946). Lieutenant general (Obergruppenfuehrer) in the SS. A leader of an *Einsatzgruppe,* or task force designed to exterminate Jews in Kiev, Jeckeln performed his liquidation task in 1941 with great skill and zeal. In the month of August 1941 alone, he reported 44,125 executions, mainly of Jews. As Higher SS and Police Leader for northern Russia, Jeckeln initiated a program called "Action Marsh Fever" in February and March of 1942. By the time the program was completed, Jeckeln reported 389 partisans killed, 1,274 persons shot on suspicion, and 8,-350 Jews liquidated. In 1944 Jeckeln was awarded the Knight's Cross of the Iron Cross. After the war he was tried by the Russians as a war criminal and executed on February 3, 1946 in Riga.

Pooler

The birthday gift above was presented with the facsimile signature of Friedrich Jeckeln.

Friedrich Jeckeln

HUGO JUNKERS (1859-1935). German aircraft designer and builder. In 1919 Junkers established an airplane factory at Dessau. Five years later he added a motor works. Junkers built the first successful all-metal aircraft and established one of the earliest mail and passenger airlines in Europe. In 1934 Junkers constructed a four-engined G38 commercial transport that carried 34 passengers and a crew of seven. In this revolutionary airplane the engines were "buried." Junkers developed the dreaded dive-bomber, the Stuka (Junkers 87) that Hitler used in his *Blitzkrieg* warfare. The Stuka carried three machine guns and, if desired, 1100 pounds of bombs. In a strafing attack it was an awesome weapon, with its gull wings, square-cut tail, and humped canopy. It looked like a flying vulture and when diving gave a terrifying whine. First tested with the Legion Condor in the Spanish Civil War in 1936, the Stuka was employed by Goering in the Polish campaign to destroy enemy tanks and airplanes on the ground. Goering boasted that the Stuka was invincible, but during the Battle of Britain in August 1940, the skilled pilots of the Royal Air Force found it an easy prey. Junkers died on February 3, 1935 in Gauting.

Signed photograph of Hugo Junkers.

SIEGFRIED KASCHE (1903-1947). Born on June 18, 1903, Kasche was a lieutenant general in the SA. In 1932 Kasche commanded SA Group Ostmark. After the Blood Purge of 1934, when many of the SA leaders were murdered, Kasche faced execution, but he talked Goering into releasing him. He was leader of SA Group Hansa from 1937-1941, and from 1941-1945 was the German ambassador to Croatia. He was executed in Yugoslavia in 1947.

Siegfried Kasche
SA = Obergruppenführer

Hannover, 1936/37.

Die besten Wünsche für frohe Weihnachtstage und für ein glückliches und erfolgreiches neues Jahr.

Heil Hitler!

Printed New Year's greetings, Hannover, 1936/37, signed by SA Lieutenant General Siegfried Kasche.

A. Southard

Siegfried Kasche

KARL KAUFMANN (1900-1969). Gauleiter of Hamburg. Born in Krefeld on October 10, 1900, Kaufmann served in World War I. In 1921 he was a co-founder of the Nazi party in the Ruhr. In 1930 he was elected delegate to the Reichstag. Accusations that Kaufmann had embezzled party funds and wore an Iron Cross never awarded to him resulted in his dismissal from all party appointments. In 1933 he was reinstated as Gauleiter. He retained this position until 1945. In 1941 he was promoted to *Obergruppenfuehrer* (lieutenant general) in the SS and the following year he was awarded the post of Reich Commissioner for Overseas Shipping. In 1948 he was sentenced to 18 months in a British-administered prison. He was released early because of ill health. Subsequently Kaufmann was twice arrested but both times was cleared and released after a brief imprisonment. He died on December 4, 1969 in Hamburg.

Der Reichsstatthalter in Hamburg

Heil Hitler!

Jhr

Official letterhead and signature of Karl Kaufmann.

Karl Kaufmann

WILHELM KEPPLER (1882-1960). Nazi industrialist. Born at Heidelberg on December 14, 1882, Keppler was an early member of the Nazi party and a zealous supporter of Hitler. He founded a society of businessmen which was, among other endeavors, devoted to assisting Himmler in his anti-Semitic crusade. Known as the Circle of Friends of the Reichsfuehrer (Himmler), the group raised huge sums to subsidize research into Aryan superiority. Keppler's Circle also obtained money for Hitler's coffers from non-Nazi businessmen. He was rewarded with the post of Reich Commissioner of Economic Affairs when Hitler became Chancellor. Keppler aided Hermann Goering in developing the Four-Year Plan (1936), an elaborate scheme to establish Germany's self-sufficiency and do away with all dependency on foreign nations. He played a major role in the *Anschluss* of Austria and was appointed Reich Commissioner in Austria. During World War II Keppler served in the Ministry of Foreign Affairs as a state secretary.

At the war's end Keppler was indicted by the Allies for war crimes and sentenced to ten years in prison. He was released on February 1, 1951 as a result of a clemency request by the American High Commissioner. Keppler died on June 13, 1960 in Kressbronn.

Heil Hitler!

(Keppler)

Signature of Wilhelm Keppler.

**Wilhelm
Keppler**

FELIX KERSTEN (1898-1960). Kersten was born in Latvia and studied agriculture in Holstein. In 1919 he joined the Finnish army and fought for the liberation of Finland in the war with Russia. In 1922 Kersten went to Berlin to study physiotherapy. He received a degree and started a lucrative practice. In 1939 he treated Heinrich Himmler for recurrent stomach spasms. His success with Himmler brought him other Nazi clients. He cured Rudolf Hess of his gall bladder trouble. He treated Dr. Robert Ley for a severe liver complaint.

Handwritten note by Felix Kersten, Stockholm, March 26, 1960.

Joachim von Ribbentrop came to him seeking a cure for severe headaches and vertigo.

Dr. Kersten never joined the Nazi party and did much to assist the Jews and other oppressed persons. The World Jewish Congress credited Kersten with the rescue of 60,000 Jews. In his memoirs, Kersten claimed that Himmler had revealed to him Germany's postwar plans. All American Jews would be surrendered to Nazi Germany for extermination; the German language would be the official tongue of Europe; the Pope would be hanged to insure the fall of Catholicism; and the old Nordic pagan faith would be revived.

Kersten died of a heart attack in Hamm, Germany, on April 16, 1960.

Felix Kersten

Signed portrait of
Manfred Freiherr von Killinger.

MANFRED FREIHERR VON KILLINGER (1886-1944). Lieutenant general in the SA (SA-Obergruppenfuehrer). Killinger joined the NSDAP in 1927 and rose quickly through the ranks of the SA. In 1935 he entered the diplomatic service and was, from 1936 to 1938, the German representative in San Francisco. His final appointment was as German ambassador to Rumania. Moments before the Russians captured the German embassy in Bucharest, he took his own life on September 3, 1944.

ADOLF KOB. Born on June 7, 1885 in Prague, Kob was a lieutenant general in the SA (Storm Troopers). On July 10, 1934 he was appointed leader of SA Group Mitte and he held this post almost until the end of the war in 1945.

Magdeburg, Neujahr 1937

Der Gruppenführer und die Männer der SA.-
Gruppe Mitte wünschen Ihnen ein erfolgreiches
Kampfjahr 1937.

Heil Hitler!

SA.-Gruppenführer

A. Southard

Printed New Year's greetings, Magdeburg, 1937, signed by SA Lieutenant General Adolf Kob.

ALFRIED KRUPP VON BOHLEN AND HALBACH (1907-1967). German industrialist. The son of Gustav Krupp von Bohlen and Halbach, Krupp was born in Essen on August 13, 1907. In 1943 he took over the management of the vast Krupp works in Essen, manufacturers of tanks, munitions, and armaments. Krupp employed Jewish concentration camp inmates from Auschwitz at his factories under conditions little better than those in the Polish extermination camps. At the urging of Albert Speer, the Nazi minister for armaments and war production, Krupp also used as slave labor 45,000 Russian civilians and 120,000 prisoners of war.

Captured by the Canadian forces in the spring of 1945, Krupp was tried by the Nuremberg Military Tribunal and on July 31, 1948 was sentenced to 12 years' imprisonment as a major war criminal. He was released on February 4, 1951 after a general amnesty issued for convicted industrialists. His confiscated property was returned to him and his steel works were soon again the leading producers in Europe. Shortly before his death the banks saved his over-extended firm from financial collapse. Krupp died of heart failure on July 30, 1967.

Signature of Alfried Krupp von Bohlen and Halbach

(Above) Alfried Krupp von Bohlen and Halbach on trial at Nuremberg. (Left) Photo and signature of Alfried's father, Gustav.

WILHELM KUBE (1887-1943). From 1928 to 1933 Kube served as Gauleiter of the Ostmark, and from 1933 until 1936 as Gauleiter of Kurmark. Subsequently he became president of Brandenburg-Berlin and Posen-West Prussia. In 1941 he was appointed governor of Belorussia where his ruthless administration aroused the ire of the Soviets. He was killed by partisans in September 1943.

Wilhelm Kube

Handwritten letter signed by Wilhelm Kube to Wilhelm Frick, July 31, 1941, sending condolences on the death of Frick's son.

Variant signature
of Wilhelm Kube

DR. HANS HEINRICH LAMMERS (1879-1962). Head of the Reich chancellery. Born at Lublinitz, Upper Silesia, on May 27, 1879, Lammers was a clever lawyer who specialized in interpreting legal tangles for the Nazis. From 1933 to 1945, he served as State Secretary and, eventually, as Minister and head of the chancellery. One of Hitler's last acts (April 23, 1945) was to order Dr. Lammers' arrest for high treason but the war ended before the order could be carried out.

Lammers was seized by the Allies and in 1949 pleaded that he knew nothing about "the Final Solution to the Jewish problem." He was sentenced to twenty years in prison and released from Landsberg on December 15, 1951. He died at Duesseldorf on January 4, 1962.

Signed photograph of Dr. Hans Lammers.

Der Reichsminister und Chef der Reichskanzlei

Berlin W. 8, den 31. Januar 1940
Voßstraße 6

Rk. 64 B g Rs.

Gehei[...]ichsache!

9 II

W.F.A.

An

den Chef des Oberkommandos der Wehrmacht
Herrn Generaloberst K e i t e l

Sehr verehrter Herr Generaloberst!

Die beiliegende Photokopie des Ihnen bekannten, vom Führer am 29. Januar d.J. vollzogenen Erlasses beehre ich mich, Ihnen mit der Bitte um Kenntnisnahme zu überreichen.

Heil Hitler!
Ihr sehr ergebener

Lammers

3/2.

3/2.

L soll eine kurze Mitteilung über diesen Führer-Erlaß an die ... vorhandenen ... zu vermeiden!

K

14. 11.

43.

OKW/628

Letter signed by Dr. Hans Lammers, January 31, 1940, to Wilhelm Keitel, sending a photocopy of an order signed by Hitler. Keitel has placed his ubiquitous initial at the top right of the message and written a three-line comment beneath, noting some slight differences in the order.

Keitel and Lammers

WILLY LIEBEL (1897-1945). Lord Mayor of Nuremberg. Liebel was born in Nuremberg on August 31, 1897 and served in the First World War. In 1925 he joined the Nazi party. He entered city government and represented Nazi interests in Nuremberg so well that he became Lord Mayor of the city on March 15, 1933, after the Nazi assumption of power.

Liebel was an ambitious man, who, unfortunately for him, had to contend with Julius Streicher. He and Streicher were bitter enemies and Liebel was one of the people most responsible for Streicher's dismissal as Gauleiter in 1940. Liebel apparently wanted the position for himself, but this was not to be. During the war, he grew increasingly close to Albert Speer, and became chief of the central office in Speer's ministry. In the closing days of the war he returned to Nuremberg, to act as mayor during the city's most perilous hour. What occurred next is somewhat unclear, but according to his friend Speer, this is what happened. One day, during the Nuremberg Trials, Streicher turned to Speer and with a sneer said, "I had that swine, your friend Liebel, shot a few hours before the Americans arrived." Another account states that Karl Holz, acting on Streicher's orders, personally shot Liebel, and then killed himself. Old scores were not forgotten in Streicher's Gau. It is also reported that Liebel committed suicide on April 20, 1945 in his Nuremberg headquarters.

Signature of Willy Liebel

A. Southard

Willy Liebel

DR. JULIUS LIPPERT (1895-1956).   From 1936 to 1940 he was Mayor of Berlin (Oberbuergermeister). An early member of the Nazi party and editor of *Der Angriff* (The Assault),   a party newspaper founded by Goebbels,   Dr. Lippert admired the Fuehrer for his political acumen but looked askance on his architectural plans. When Hitler redesigned the center of Berlin to include a new avenue 130 feet wide, Dr. Lippert insisted upon a width of only 100 feet. Explanations and recriminations from Hitler did not budge the mayor. Finally, after four years of repeated clashes with Dr. Lippert, Hitler burst into a tirade: "Lippert's an incompetent, an idiot, a failure, a zero." He then ordered Goebbels to sack the truculent mayor. Lippert spent the war years in the army, and was, from 1946 to 1952, in a Belgian prison as a war criminal. He died on June 30, 1956.

A. Southard

Signature of Dr. Julius Lippert

Dr. Julius Lippert

HINRICH LOHSE (1896-1964). Reich Commissioner for the "Ostland," the conquered Baltic States and White Russia. Born on September 2, 1896 in Muehlenbarbek, Lohse was appointed Gauleiter of Scheswig-Holstein in 1925 and President in 1933. In February 1934 he was promoted to SA-Gruppenfuehrer. From 1941 until 1944 Lohse was the Reich Commissioner, with headquarters at Riga, during the period when the "Final Solution" was being carried out with intensity and brutality in the Baltic States and White Russia. The Jews were subjected to mass-shootings in the Vilna ghetto and elsewhere, and Lohse made an effort to stop the slaughter. He inquired of his superiors in the Ministry of Eastern Territories whether "all Jews, regardless of age or sex, or their usefulness to the economy, were to be liquidated." The answer was that Lohse should "ignore the demands of the economy." Lohse did not challenge Himmler's orders. After the war Lohse was tried by a British court and in January 1948 was sentenced to 10 years' penal servitude. He was freed two years later because of ill health and died on February 25, 1964 in Muehlenbarbek bei Steinburg in Schleswig-Holstein.

Signed photograph of Hinrich Lohse

WERNER LORENZ (1891-1974). SS lieutenant general; head of the Reference Office for Racial Germans, or VOMI. Born in Gruenhof on October 2,1891, Lorenz was a cadet officer and air corps pilot in World War I. He owned an estate in Danzig. An early adherent of the Nazi party, Lorenz joined the SS in 1931 where he quickly earned a reputation for being a *bon vivant*. From 1937 until 1945 General Lorenz headed the VOMI, an office charged with defending the welfare of German nationals in other countries. Lorenz was the motivating force in Himmler's drive to absorb "racial" Germans into the Reich

Signature of Werner Lorenz

and thus extend Nazi power in occupied nations. Promoted to lieutenant general (Obergruppenfuehrer) in 1943, Lorenz showed great zeal and skill in his duties, yet never resorted to brutality. On March 10, 1948 he was sentenced to twenty years' imprisonment as a war criminal. He was released early in 1955 and died on May 13, 1974.

Werner Lorenz

Angolia

Werner Lorenz, shortly after his capture at Flensburg on May 10, 1945.

KURT G. LUEDECKE (1890-   ). SA leader; early friend of Hitler. Luedecke saw and heard Hitler for the first time at a mass meeting of Storm Troopers in the great central square *(Koenigsplatz)* of Munich on August 16, 1922. There was a crowd of about 40,000. Years later, in 1938, Luedecke wrote in his memoirs, *I Knew Hitler:* "I studied this slight, pale man, his brown hair parted on one side, falling again and again over his sweating brow. Threatening and beseeching, with small pleading hands and flaming steel-blue eyes, he had the look of a fanatic.

"Presently my critical faculty was swept away. Leaning from the tribune as if he were trying to impel his inner self into the consciousness of all those thousands, he was holding the masses, and me with them, under a hypnotic spell by the sheer force of his conviction..."

That evening Luedecke, an ardent nationalist only 32 years old, heard Hitler speak again. Once more he was a captive to Hitler's magic. After the speech he met Hitler, who was dissheveled and perspiring, with a dirty trench coat flung over his shoulder. The next day Luedecke offered himself to the cause. He and Hitler talked for four hours, then clasped hands. "I had given him my soul," wrote Luedecke.

Luedecke became a messenger and an envoy for Hitler. He visited Mussolini and told him about the rising Nazi leader in Germany. He traveled to the United States seeking support and financial aid for the new party led by Hitler. His efforts were met with ridicule. Eventually Luedecke clashed with Hitler. On May 9, 1933, Luedecke was arrested in Berlin. His inside knowledge of Hitler's operations had excited Goering's fears. Although immediately released, with Goering's apologies. Luedecke was re-arrested and ultimately put into the Oranienburg concentration camp. His old friend, Ernst Roehm, arranged for Luedecke's escape through Czechoslovakia to Switzerland and thence to New York. He lived in East Hempstead, Long Island, until after World War II, eventually returning to Bavaria where he wrote occasional articles.

Curt Georg Ludecke
Unterschondorf 189
Ammersee (8)
Germany   June 8, 1954

Dear Mr. Bumball:

Many thanks for your kind letter of May 30, but I am afraid my answers to your questions won't help you very much. As you probably have a copy of your letter I'll answer in the sequence of your questions.

1. Dr. Goebbels was, I think, fond of music but never played an organ as far as I know.

2. Especially in the turbulent times before the Beerhall Putsch in 1923 Hitler was referred to as "Wolf" (over the telefone, for instance), for the sake of camouflage but not as a petname as your question seems to suggest.

3. I only met Frau Hochstein once in a party in 1924, I believe.

4. Also Frau Schulze-Naumburg I have known but very slightly seeing her once or twice with other people.

5. I have seen Eva Braun but only remember vaguely an insignificant face, when selecting photos in the Munich shop of Heinrich Hoffmann, who then was not yet "Herr Professor", nor she the dulcinea of Hitler.

Of course, you are welcome should you visit Germany this summer, and I suggest for a meeting Unter-schondorf here on the Ammersee, prettily sited amid gardens, less crowded than the more famous but by no means more beautiful Starnberger See, thus providing a more natural setting for the splendid view of the chain of Alps, a lovely old village worthwhile seeing, only 24 miles from Munich. Don't hesitate to call on me, I shall very glad to see you.

Meanwhile, hoping to hear soon from you that you are on your way, I am with my very best wishes,

sincerely yours,

Letter in English signed by Kurt Luedecke, written to Stephen W. Bumball

A. Southard

Hitler and Kurt Luedecke, about 1930

Kurt Luedecke with Stephen W. Bumball, about 1954

ERICH FRIEDRICH WILHELM LUDENDORFF (1865-1937). German general and politician. Shortly after the outbreak of World War I, Ludendorff was appointed a quartermaster general of the German army. With Hindenburg he planned and executed the brilliant military strategy that defeated

Signed photogr⟨⟩ of General Erich Ludendor⟨⟩

Ludendorff

Russia and very nearly crushed the Allies. After the war Ludendorff fled to Sweden. On his return to Germany he lived in Munich and joined Hitler in the unsuccessful Beer-Hall Putsch. His last years were spent in promulgating wild, visionary schemes. Among the eccentric ideas he espoused were a crusade against Jews, Catholics, and Protestants, a return to the worship of the old Nordic gods, and a box-like invention to manufacture paper money with which to pay Germany's war reparations. Ludendorff became an extreme pacifist and argued bitterly with his earlier associates, Hindenburg and Hitler. He died in Bavaria on December 20, 1937, and was given a state funeral.

Handwritten letter signed by General Erich Ludendorff, Munich, June 9, 1922. "Bring up our youth with military potential and thoughts of greatness. We must become a hard and hardened race. . . ."

DR. MATHILDE SPIESS LUDENDORFF (1877-1966). Expert in mental diseases; second wife of General Erich Ludendorff. Mathilde inspired her celebrated husband, a World War I hero, to embark on a struggle against "powers above the State"--Jews, Jesuits, Communists, and Freemasons. In 1926 she and the general founded the Tannenberg Bund, a rabidly nationalistic association dedicated to subduing or destroying Jews and Communists. The Bund was never very successful and eventually was absorbed by the Nazi party.

Dr. Mathilde Ludendorff abhorred Christianity and urged a return to the ancient Nordic Pagan gods. She was an early admirer of Hitler. General Ludendorff joined the Nazis in the Munich Beer-Hall Putsch on November 9, 1923, and in 1924 became a Nazi delegate to the Reichstag. Despite Mathilde's expertise in mental aberrations she was unable to rescue her senile husband from his bellicose eccentricities. She and Ludendorff eventually quarrelled with Hitler and became bitter opponents of his policies. Egged on by Mathilde, Ludendorff in 1933 warned President von Hindenburg that "this sinister individual [Hitler] will lead our country into the abyss and our nation to an unprecedented disaster." In 1939 the worship of the pagan Norse gods urged by Mathilde was recognized by the Nazis.

After the war, Frau Mathilde Ludendorff continued her anti-Semitic attacks, even claiming that Wall Street bankers had backed Hitler in his electoral campaigns. In November 1949 Mathilde was summoned before a de-Nazification court in Munich and found guilty as a "Major Offender." She was sentenced to two years of "directed labor."

Signature of Frau Dr. Mathilde Speiss Ludendorff

HANNS LUDIN (1905-1947). Lieutenant general in the SA (SA-Obergruppenfuehrer). Born on June 10, 1905 in Freiburg, Ludin was appointed in April 1933 the leader of the SA Group Southwest. After a period of military service, he became German ambassador to Slovakia in January 1941. A secret enemy of Himmler, Ludin and his colleague,Dietrich von Jagow, sabotaged the Waffen-SS recruiting efforts in the Balkans. He was executed in Czechoslovakia on December 9, 1947.

Der SA.-Gruppenführer Südwest

Signature of Hanns Ludin with his letterhead as Group Leader of the SA for the Southwest.

Hanns Ludin

HANS LUTHER (1879-1962). Nazi ambassador to the United States. Dr. Luther served (1925-1926) as German Chancellor. He was forced to resign in a cabinet crisis over the colors of the German flag. From 1930 to 1933 he was president of the Reichsbank. In 1933 Hitler relieved him from this post, and dispatched him to Washington as ambassador. Luther aided in the seizure of the Rhineland by cabling secret information to Hitler about British and American leniency toward Germany. Luther was replaced in 1937, and completed his career working on agrarian finance matters. He died on May 11, 1962 in Duesseldorf.

Dr. Hans Luther   Washington D.C., 3.April 1937.

     Mit besten Empfehlungen an Frau Goetz und auf

Wiedersehen

                Ihr

Letter signed by Dr. Hans Luther as ambassador to the United States   311

VIKTOR LUTZE (1890-1943). Chief of Staff of the SA (1934-1943); Reichsleiter. Born in Bevergern on December 28, 1890, Lutze served in the army during World War I and in 1922 joined the Nazi party. He rose rapidly through the ranks of the SA, becoming an SA lieutenant general (SA-Obergruppenfuehrer) in 1933. Later that year he became president of the province of Hannover, and Police President of the city. After the murder of Ernst Roehm in the Blood Purge of 1934, Lutze was appointed Roehm's successor as SA Chief of Staff. An uninteresting and colorless leader, Lutze died in an automobile accident on May 3, 1943.

Viktor
Lutze

Berlin, Weihnachten 1936.

Der Stabschef

m. lb. Brückner!

Meine besten Wünsche für ein frohes Weihnachtsfest verbinde ich mit ebensolchen für das Jahr 1937, das uns, wie bisher, im alten Geist im Kampfe für den Führer und das nationalsozialistische Deutschland finden wird.

Heil Hitler!

Fr Lutze

Note signed "Your Lutze" by Viktor Lutze, sending Christmas wishes to Hitler's adjutant Wilhelm Brueckner.

A. Southard

**Viktor
Lutze**

Sehr geehrter Herr General !

Sie waren so liebenswürdig, mir meinen Adjutanten,
den SA-Obersturmbannführer Leutnant d.R. Hans-Peter
H e r m e l zu Beginn des Krieges zur Dienstleistung zu-
zuteilen.

Ich habe nunmehr dem Wunsche Hermels, wieder Dienst in
der Luftwaffe tun zu dürfen, entsprechen können und bitte
Sie, davon Kenntnis zu nehmen, dass ich mit der Beendigung
seiner Kommandierung zur Dienstleistung bei mir einverstan-
den bin.

Indem ich Ihnen nochmals meinen besten Dank für Ihre
Mühewaltung sage, verbleibe ich mit

H e i l   H i t l e r !
Ihr

**Letter signed by Viktor Lutze, Berlin, May 14, 1940, sending a new assistant back
to the Luftwaffe.**

313

Signature of Viktor Lutze

GEORG MAGNUS. German surgeon. An expert at the famed clinic in the Niessbaumstrasse in Munich. Professor Magnus was selected by Hitler to examine and treat Unity Mitford after she attempted to kill herself with a small-caliber revolver. Magnus decided it was too dangerous to attempt the removal of the bullet. He released Unity from the clinic and the Fuehrer sent her home to England.

Professor Magnus

München 27
Schönbergstraße 9
Tel. 481405

Lieber Herr Brückner,

     lassen Sie sich sehr herzlich danken für Ihre freundlichen Glückwünsche, und lassen auch Sie sich von Herzen sehr viel Gutes für das neue Jahr wünschen.

     Mit herzlichen Grüssen und Heil Hitler.

     Wie immer

       Ihr

     Letter signed by Dr. Georg Magnus, noted surgeon

DR. BENNO MARTIN (1893-1975). Police President of Nuremberg, 1934-1942. Dr. Martin studied law in Munich and passed his examination as assessor in 1922. In 1923 he became active with the Nuremberg police. He joined the Nazi party in the summer of 1933 and became a member of the SS in the following year. In 1934 Dr. Martin was appointed chief of police in Nuremberg. In 1942 he took over the duties of Higher SS and Police Leader for the 13th Service Command at Nuremberg. In this post he had supervisory authority over all police forces in Bavaria. He was arrested and detained by American troops at the war's end. Martin was imprisoned for three years but acquitted of any criminal charges. It should be noted that the Pope intervened on his behalf several times, since Martin had saved the Bamberg Cathedral from destruction. He died on July 2, 1975.

Official identification card of Dr. Benno Martin, bearing his photograph and signature

OTTO MEISSNER (1880-1953). From 1924 to 1945, Meissner was State Secretary/Minister in the Presidential Chancellery. When Hitler became Reich Chancellor in 1933, he kept Meissner on in this position. In 1937 he was given the title of Reichsminister. Meissner was tried for war crimes at Nuremberg on April 11, 1949 and acquitted. He died at Munich on May 27, 1953.

Facsimile signature of Meissner that appeared on countless routine awards.

Der Führer und Reichskanzler

hat aus Anlaß der Wiedervereinigung der sudetendeutschen Gebiete mit dem Deutschen Reich

dem Reichsminister

Dr. Wilhelm F r i c k

in Berlin

die

Medaille zur Erinnerung an den 1. Oktober 1938

verliehen.

Berlin, den 4. Mai 1939.

Der Staatsminister und Chef der Präsidialkanzlei des Führers und Reichskanzlers

Meissner

Award of the Medal of Remembrance for October 1, 1938 (occupation of the Sudetenland) to Wilhelm Frick, signed with a facsimile signature of Otto Meissner.

Signed photograph of Otto Meissner.

O. Spronk

Otto Meissner at his desk.

WILLY MESSERSCHMITT (1898-1978). Aircraft designer. Born in Frankfurt am Main on June 26, 1898, Messerschmitt created an all-metal fighting aircraft in 1935, the famous Messerschmitt-109, which dominated the skies over Europe until it ran into the Spitfire in the Battle of Britain.

At the end of the war in 1945 Messerschmitt devoted his creative genius to designing pre-fabricated houses and jet aircraft. He died on September 15, 1978 in Munich.

Close of a handwritten letter signed by Willy Messerschmitt

317

BARON CONSTANTIN VON NEURATH (1873-1956). German diplomat and Minister of Foreign Affairs (1932-1938). Born in 1873, von Neurath came from a distinguished family. He entered the diplomatic corps in 1901. Except for a brief period when he served in World War I, he continued in the diplomatic service until 1938 when he was forced to resign as Hitler's Foreign Minister.

Von Neurath had refused to join the Nazi party and was appalled by the Fuehrer's war plans. In 1939 he was appointed Protector for Bohemia and Moravia but was, however, only a figurehead. Reinhard Heydrich and Karl-Hermann Frank in reality ran the protectorate. Refusing to cooperate with Heydrich, von Neurath went on extended leave in 1943.

Despite his aversion to Nazi tactics, von Neurath was tried at Nuremberg and found guilty on four counts of crimes against humanity. He was sentenced to fifteen years' imprisonment. In 1954 he was released from Spandau Prison and died on August 14, 1956 on the family estate Leinfelderhof.

Signature of Baron Constantin von Neurath

Signed photo of
Baron Constantin von Neurath

Hess, von Neurath, and Hitler
at the Reichstag.

HANNS OBERLINDOBER (1896-1949). General (Obergruppenfuehrer) in the SA (Storm Troopers). Oberlindober was the leader of the organization of wounded war veterans (NSKOV) from November 1930 and an administrator of the Academy on German Law. He died in Polish captivity on April 6, 1949 in Warsaw.

Signed photograph of
Hanns Oberlindober

WILHELM OHNESORGE (1872-1962). Reich Post Minister from February 1937-1945. Ohnesorge was State Secretary in the Reich Post Ministry from March 1, 1933 and Reich Minister of Post from February 2, 1937. He was convicted as a major offender after the war but his sentence was commuted because of age and health. He died on February 1, 1962.

Der Staatsſekretär
im
Reichspoſtminiſterium

Berlin W 66, den ___24.12.36___
Leipziger Straße 15

Sehr   geehrter Herr Brückner!

Zum Weihnachtsfest und zum Neuen Jahr spreche ich Ihnen meine herzlichsten Wünsche aus und danke Ihnen gleichzeitig vielmals für das freundliche Gedenken.

Heil Hitler!

(Above) Wilhelm Ohnesorge. (Right) Heinz Tietjen, Dr. Ley, Ohnesorge, von Tschammer und Osten, and General Reinecke at the festivities commemorating the ninth anniversary of the "Kraft durch Freude" organization (November 27, 1941).

Letter signed by Wilhelm Ohnesorge, December 24, 1936.

FRANZ VON PAPEN, Nazi diplomat. Ambitious and conniving, von Papen (born in 1879) played both sides against the middle during his long career as a soldier, chancellor and diplomat. A vain and pompous man who frequently blundered in his schemes, von Papen somehow managed to come out of every scrape on top.

As ambassador to Austria (1936-1938) and Turkey (1939-1944), he enormously aided in the consolidation of Nazi power, but when on trial for war crimes at Nuremberg, von Papen claimed that he had always despised Hitler and his party. As usual, his duplicity proved successful and he was acquitted. In following trials, however, he was sentenced and released from captivity on January 26, 1949. He died on May 2, 1969.

**Franz
von Papen**

Ihr aufrichtig ergebener

Signature of Franz von Papen.

24/

VIII. Mein bester Franzi, Mütterchen schrieb gestern über ihre glückliche An-

kunft und auch von Deinem seelischen Befinden. Ich fühle so ganz mit Dir,

mein armer Bub, und will Dir gleich schreiben. Du weißt wie glücklich ich Mai 44

war – aber vielleicht nicht, wie sehr mir Dein Kummer später zu Herzen ging. Doch

sagte mir die Erfahrung, daß schließlich in Deinen Jahren das Wesentliche ein

irdisches Glück zu begründen weniger das Gefühl, als die seelische u. intellek-

tuelle Übereinstimmung zweier Menschen sei. Vielleicht war ich ein wenig ego-

istisch: Väter hoffen dem einzigen Sohn das Glück, das sie selbst fanden, zu

schaffen. Aber immer nur in dem Sinn, daß nur Dein Glück das unsrige sein sol-

le! Wenn also die Voraussetzung der seelischen u. intellekt. Übereinstimmung

nicht vorhanden ist – dann wäre es gewiß ein Unrecht den Schritt zu tun.

Dann rate ich Dir alsbald klare Verhältnisse zu schaffen. Es wird Dir helfen

wieder gesund zu werden. Komm zu mir, laß uns den Prozeß gewinnen, dann

bauen wir ein neues Leben auf. Nicht für mich, der ich schon mit einem Fuß

im Jenseits stehe – aber für Deine Zukunft! Alles weitere wird die Vor-

sehung entscheiden – und ich bete, daß sie Dich glücklich machen möge.

Für die Welt mag genügen, daß man – mittellos – nicht die Verantwortung

tragen will für Frau u. Kinder. Hoffe so von Herzen, Franzi, daß Alles bald ins

Gleichgewicht kommt, umarme Dich u. grüße unser Wallergänges. Papi

Handwritten letter from Franz von Papen to his son, apologizing for not being more understanding. "Come to me and help me win the trial...."

322

ERICH REIMANN. SA (Storm Troopers) brigadier general. A tough, front-line soldier, Reimann was adjutant to the chief of staff of the Storm Troopers. He was also commander of the elite SA Standarte "Feldherrnhalle."

Erich Reimann
SA.=Brigadeführer
1. Adjutant des Stabschefs
Führer der Wachstandarte „Feldherrnhalle"

Berlin, am 31. Dezember 1936

Die besten Wünsche zum Jahreswechsel und Sieg=Heil für 1937!

Heil Hitler!

(Above) New Year's greetings from Erich Reimann.

**SA-Gruppenfuehrer
Erich Reimann**

Reimann, as adjutant to SA-Stabschef Lutze.

FRITZ REINHARDT (1895-1969). Lieutenant general in the SA (SA-Obergruppenfuehrer). Born at Ilmenau on April 3, 1895, Reinhardt began his career as a schoolmaster. In 1928 he was appointed Gauleiter for Upper Bavaria. At the same time he was given the post of chief of the Nazi party's training school for orators. He served in the Reichstag as a delegate from Upper Bavaria and in 1933 was selected as State Secretary in the Reich Ministry of Finance. Reinhardt helped to finance the Wehrmacht and authored the "Reinhardt Program" that sponsored a tax to benefit workers. Reinhardt was imprisoned in 1945 and released four years later. A Munich de-Nazification court reclassified him as a "Major Offender" in 1950.

Signed photograph of Fritz Reinhardt.

ERNST ROEHM (1887-1934). SA Chief of Staff, 1930-1934. A heavy-set, ruthless professional soldier, Roehm was badly wounded in World War I. A homosexual who was inspired by a vision of a greater Germany, Roehm worked closely with Hitler and took part in the Beer-Hall Putsch (1923). He helped to organize the SA and the SS and commanded the Brown Shirts from 1930 to 1934.

Roehm's courage and organizational skill helped make possible Hitler's rise to power; but in an effort to placate the German army, which feared the growing power of the Brown Shirts, Hitler accused Roehm of conspiracy and moral delinquency and ordered him shot. About 150 SA leaders were rounded up and executed gangster-style on the same day, June 30, 1934. Roehm was shot at midday, July 1, 1934, in Stadelheim prison by Eiche.

Ernst Roehm, at home with his mother and their two dogs.

Signed photograph of Ernst Roehm, September 12, 1924, inscribed to a "true and faithful comrade."

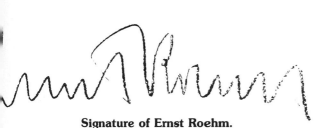

Signature of Ernst Roehm.

**Ernst
Roehm**

FRITZ SAUCKEL (1894-1946). Gauleiter of Thuringia from 1927 until 1945 and commissioner general of manpower in Nazi occupied territories. Born on October 27, 1894 in Lower Franconia, Fritz Sauckel became a seaman in 1910. In 1914 he was interned by the French and was not released until 1919. (Sauckel was extremely sensitive about his lack of military service and actually tried to stow away on a U-boat to make up for it during World War II.) After being released from French captivity he worked in a factory while attending an engineering school. In 1923 he joined the Nazi party. Four years later, after holding a variety of party posts, he was appointed Gauleiter of Thuringia. He held this post until the collapse of Nazi Germany in 1945.

Sauckel led the life of an ordinary high ranking Nazi political functionary until 1942 when Hitler picked him to become plenipotentiary general for labor mobilization. Ultimately, this position was to cost him his life. Although Goebbels called him "the dullest of the dull," the quasi-literate Sauckel became the most notorious slave-driver in history. This prosaic little man, who in another time and place would have been a complete cypher, was entrusted with labor recruiting in the nations seized by Germany. By false arrests and outright seizure, or by getting his victims drunk before signing them up, Sauckel "recruited" more than five million workers, thousands of whom died of malnutrition or disease in the labor camps and factories where they were subjected to brutal treatment.

Found guilty of war crimes and crimes against humanity at Nuremberg, Sauckel broke down and cried, still professing his innocence. He was hanged on October 16, 1946. The man who set the quotas which Sauckel had to fill, Albert Speer, was not executed.

327

A. Southard

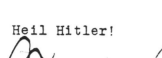

Signature of Fritz Sauckel in Roman script

Heil Hitler!

Gauleiter und Reichsstatthalter.

Signature of Fritz Sauckel in German script

Hiermit bitte ich Sie
mich heute nochmals
rufen zu lassen. Ich
möchte Ihnen einige
wichtige Punkte angeben
Mit Dank
und ergebenst
Sauckel

Handwritten letter signed by Fritz Sauckel, Nuremberg, July 13, 1946, asking his lawyer to call.

Fritz Sauckel

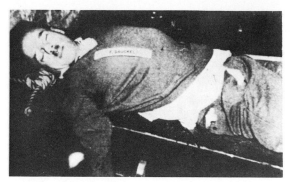

Fritz Sauckel after his execution, October 16, 1946.

FERDINAND SAUERBRUCH (1875-1951). German surgeon. Born in Barmen on July 3, 1875, Sauerbruch studied medicine and after a distinguished career was appointed chief surgeon of the German army with the rank of lieutenant general and was director of the Charité Hospital in Berlin. His name was one of the most prominent among the 960 professors and intellectual leaders who in 1933 took a public vow to support Hitler and the Nazi party. During the Third Reich Sauerbruch was recognized as Germany's greatest surgeon. He made many significant innovations in bone surgery. In August 1934 he was the attending surgeon during President Paul von Hindenburg's final illness. He operated on Joseph Goebbels and in 1940 removed a

---

CHIRURGISCHE UNIVERSITÄTSKLINIK DER CHARITÉ

SCHUMANNSTRASSE 20-21

BERLIN NW 7, DEN 27. 5. 35.

Herrn Professor R i n g l e b
B e r l i n.

Lieber Herr Kollege Ringleb !

Vorgestern habe ich vom Herrn Minister Ihre Ernennung erhalten und ich erlaube mir, das Schriftstück mit herzlichen Glückwünschen Ihnen zu übersenden.

Ihr

Signed letter of Dr. Ferdinand Sauerbruch, Berlin, 1935

growth from Hitler's throat. When Claus von Stauffenberg was gravely wounded in an air attack in North Africa, losing his left eye, right hand, and part of a leg, it was the great skill of Dr. Sauerbruch which saved his life.

A close friend of General Ludwig Beck, a leader in the anti-Hitler movement, Sauerbruch eventually joined the Resistance. After the unsuccessful bomb attempt on Hitler's life (July 20, 1944), Dr. Sauerbruch was interrogated by the Gestapo but not arrested. He was cleared by a de-Nazification court at the end of World War II. However, the East German government dismissed him from all his posts. He died in Berlin on July 2, 1951.

HJALMAR (HORACE GREELEY) SCHACHT(1877-1970). President of the Reichsbank (1923-1930; 1933-1939). A most interesting fact about this prosaic financier was his improbable middle names, given to him by a father who had lived in the United States and was an admirer of the great New York journalist. Born in 1877, Schacht was involved in a currency forgery scandal during World War I. He almost single-handedly brought about Germany's economic recovery in the 1920s. He played a key role in the Third Reich's economic revival as well. From 1934 to 1937 he was Minister of Economics, and from 1937 to 1943 was a minister without portfolio. In 1939 he was replaced as President of the Reichsbank. During the war, his open hostility to Hitler resulted in his arrest on July 29, 1944. He spent the remainder of the war in a concentration camp. Schacht was tried at Nuremberg but acquitted of all offences. He began a new career in finance, specializing in the emerging Third World, and died a wealthy man in Munich, on June 3, 1970.

Hjalmar Schacht

A. Southard

Handwritten proverb signed by Hjalmar Schacht. "If you choose to be a sailor, pick the commercial service."

PAUL SCHARFE. SS judge and head of the SS Court. As chief of the SS Legal Services, Scharfe took the position that because the SS man "naturally occupies a special place, primarily because it is his duty to protect the Movement and its Fuehrer, if necessary at the sacrifice of his life," he was not subject to judgment by any other court, civil or military.

Pooler

Signature of SS Judge Paul Scharfe

Paul Scharfe

ℍ-Brigadeführer Paul Scharfe, Chef des ℍ-Gerichts, zum ℍ-Gruppenführer

PRINCE FRIEDRICH CHRISTIAN SCHAUMBURG-LIPPE (1906-). From 1933 to 1935, Schaumburg-Lippe served as von Ribbentrop's chief personal adjutant, and from 1935 to 1943 was attached to the Propaganda Ministry. In 1943 he fought with the "Feldherrnhalle" division, but from 1944 to the end of the war was under house arrest in Austria. Schaumburg-Lippe wrote a book of recollections on the Nazis entitled *Between Crown and Dungeon* (Weisbaden, 1952).

Signature of Prince Schaumburg-Lippe, Berlin, 1940.

WILHELM SCHEPMANN (1894-   ). Chief of Staff of the SA. Schepmann was born on June 17, 1894, in Hattingen. He was a teacher until the First World War interrupted his career. After the war he returned to teaching, and by 1922 had joined the Nazi party. Schepmann began his career in the SA in the 1920s. He held several positions in the early 1930s including Police President of Dortmund in 1933 and commander of SA Group Saxony in 1934. He held this post until the death of Viktor Lutze in 1943, at which time he was immediately charged with carrying out the tasks of the SA Chief of Staff. In 1944 he was also made responsible for the military training of the Volkssturm (People's Army).

Although Schepmann was not on the "Major Offenders" list, he went underground after the war and did not surface until 1949. De-Nazification proceedings against him were dismissed in 1952, the same year he ran for office in the Lower Saxon local elections and was elected a member of the town council in Gifhorn, his home town.

Peter Theodore

Wilhelm Schepmann

Signature of Wilhelm Schepmann

Hitler greets Schepmann, the Reichsleiters, and the Gauleiters on August 8, 1944. Note that because of injuries incurred in the July 20 bomb blast, Hitler shakes hands with his left hand instead of his right.

BALDUR VON SCHIRACH (1907-1974). Reich Youth Leader, 1931-1940. Born in Berlin on March 9, 1907, von Schirach claimed descent from two signers of the Declaration of Independence. In 1924 he joined the Nazi party. His enthusiasm and ambition soon attracted Hitler's attention. At 24 he was appointed leader of Germany's youth. He later married Henriette Hoffmann, daughter of Hitler's official photographer.

From 1940 to 1945 von Schirach was Gauleiter of Vienna. Von Schirach was tried at Nuremberg. He admitted that he had concurred with the "resettle-ment" of the Jews but denied all knowledge of genocide. He denounced Hitler from the dock as a "millionfold murderer" and called Auschwitz "the most devilish mass murder in history." He was sentenced on October 1, 1946 to 20 years' imprisonment for crimes against humanity. He served his time at Spandau with Albert Speer and Rudolf Hess. In his memoirs, published a year after his release from prison on September 30, 1966, von Schirach wrote of the fatal fascination that Hitler had exerted on him and blamed himself for not working harder to prevent the concentration camps. Von Schirach spent his final years in seclusion in West Germany and died in his sleep at a small hotel in Korev an der Mosel on August 8, 1974.

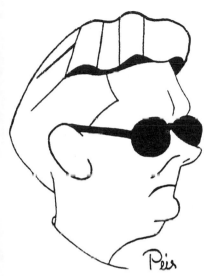

Caricature of Baldur von Schirach by Peis, done at Nuremberg, about 1946.

Bernard Harris, Jr.

Reichsjugendführer

Signed photo of Baldur von Schirach

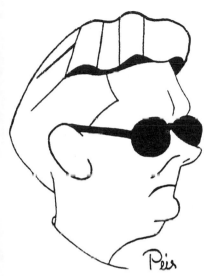

Signature of Baldur von Schirach.

DIE ZEHNTE WIEDERKEHR DES TAGES, DA SICH VOLK UND REICH ZU NEUER GRÖSSE ENTSCHLOSSEN INDEM SIE SICH IN DIE HAND DES FÜHRERS GABEN, FEIERT WIEN IN DEM BEWUSSTSEIN, DASS AN DIESEM TAGE DIE GRUNDLAGEN FÜR SEINE WIEDERKEHR IN DAS GEEINTE VATERLAND GESCHAFFEN WURDEN · ERFÜLLT VON DIESER ERHEBENDEN UND GLÜCKVERBÜRGENDEN ERINNERUNG, ENTBIETET DIE STADT WIEN DEM FÜHRER IHREN DANKBAREN GRUSS UND ERNEUERT DAS GELÖBNIS UNERSCHÜTTERLICHER TREUE ZU IHM UND GROSSDEUTSCHLAND SEINEM WERK·

Baldur von Schirach

Proclamation signed by Baldur von Schirach, commemorating the tenth anniversary of the Nazi seizure of power.

Baldur von Schirach at Nuremberg, about 1946.

für das neue Jahr

1937 New Year's greetings from von Schirach

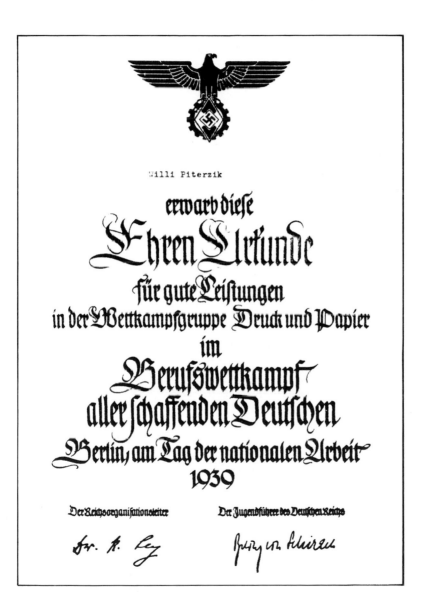

Honor award for achievement in printing and writing, signed in facsimile by Dr. Robert Ley and Baldur von Schirach.

MAX SCHMELING. Heavyweight champion and symbol of Nordic superiority. Even his never-used middle name, Siegfried, suggested to the Germans the invincible Teutonic power that lurked in his muscles. Schmeling was born in Klein Luckow, Uckermark on September 28, 1905. On June 30, 1930, at 24, he won the world's heavyweight championship from Jack Sharkey. But his greatest victory came after he had lost the championship back to Sharkey in a disputed "We wuz robbed" decision. On June 19, 1936 Schmeling knocked out Joe Louis, the Brown Bomber, who had never lost a fight. It was a stunning victory that delighted Hitler and provided ammunition for the Nazi beliefs in a superior race. Louis went on to win the world's championship but longed for a return bout with Schmeling. "I can never really be champion until I beat him," he said. Louis got the return bout and in two minutes and four seconds of the first round battered his German opponent into unconsciousness.

Schmeling enlisted in the German air force on the outbreak of World War II. On May 20, 1941 he was one of the daring parachutists who participated in the campaign for Crete, in which he was seriously wounded. After the war Schmeling won great popularity as an amiable retired athlete in both Germany and the United States.

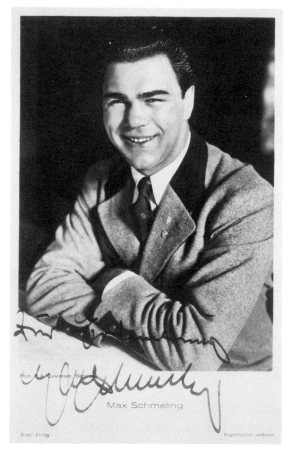

Max Schmeling

Signed photograph of Max Schmeling.

HEINRICH SCHOENE (1889-   ). A lieutenant general in the SA (SA-Obergruppenfuehrer), Schoene was born on November 25, 1889 in Berlin. From 1931 to 1934 he headed the SA in Schleswig-Holstein and took over command of SA Obergruppe 1 in 1934. He became Commissar General in the Ukraine in September 1941. In 1943 Schoene was appointed Inspector of the Marine-SA.

Heinrich Schoene

Der Führer der
SA-Gruppe Ostland

Heil Hitler!

Obergruppenführer

Printed letterhead, complimentary close of a letter and signature of SA Lieutenant General Heinrich Schoene

ERWIN SCHULZ. Brigadier general of the SS and Police. Schulz was an officer in the *Einsatzkommando,* a special task force devoted to killing Jews and other "undesireables" in Russia and Poland. Although a tough officer, General Schulz was revolted by the wanton butchery of Jews. He applied for a transfer. Other commando leaders, disgusted at the brutal work delegated to them, were haunted by nightmares, went AWOL, turned to alcohol, or became raving lunatics. Some shot themselves rather than continue to kill helpless civilians.

Official identification card of General Erwin Schulz, bearing his photograph and signature.

FRANZ XAVER SCHWARZ (1875-1947). National treasurer of the Nazi party. A fist-grasping administrator, Schwarz was born in Guenzburg on November 27, 1875. He served in the German army in World War I and joined the Nazi party in 1922. From his job as accountant in the Munich city hall, Schwarz stepped into the post of treasurer of the Nazi party. His ability to disguise the income of the party from all but the top leaders made him an invaluable aide to Hitler. Schwarz also numbered the members of the Nazi party consecutively to hide membership losses. It was he who raised the money to publish *Mein Kampf.* No doubt Schwarz's avarice and accounting skills also brought Hitler his first, shiny chauffeur-driven limousine.

Schwarz remained the party treasurer until 1945. As a reward for his services he was named a Reich Leader *(Reichsleiter)*. In 1943 Hitler appointed him a full general in the SS (SS-Oberst-Gruppenfuehrer). While he and Bormann ran the NSDAP during the war, only Schwarz controlled the pursestrings of the party and its formations. Schwarz died in an internment camp near Regensburg on December 2, 1947. A Munich de-Nazification court posthumously classified him as a "Major Offender."

Signed photograph of Franz Xaver Schwarz

Signature of Franz Xaver Schwarz

Hitler presents Schwarz with a gift on his 65th birthday (November 27, 1940).

LUTZ GRAF SCHWERIN VON KROSIGK (1887-1977). Minister of Finance. Born in Rathmannsdorf, Anhalt on August 22, 1887, von Krosigk was a Rhodes scholar at Oxford. He passed the bar examination in 1909. During World War I he served as a field officer, was wounded, and awarded the Iron Cross (First and Second Classes). From 1920 to 1932 he held various posts in the Ministry of Fianance.

Named Minister of Finance by Chancellor Franz von Papen in 1932, von Krosigk retained the post until the collapse of the Third Reich in 1945. Von Krosigk supported Hitler's anti-Semitic policy, observing, "We must do all we can to shove Jews into other countries." He was also Foreign Minister in Doenitz's short-lived government.

At the war's end, von Krosigk was brought to trial at Nuremberg, found guilty of war crimes, and sentenced to ten years' imprisonment. He was released in 1951 and died on March 4, 1977 in Essen.

Lutz Graf Schwerin von Krosigk

Signature of Schwerin von Krosigk

Signed photograph of Schwerin von Krosigk.

FRANZ SELDTE (1882-1947). Reich Minister of Labor from 1933-1945. Born in Magdeburg on June 29, 1882, Seldte studied chemistry at Braunschweig. He served as a captain in World War I, lost an arm in combat, and was awarded the Iron Cross (First and Second Classes). After the war, Seldte founded the Stahlhelm, the most important veterans' group. In 1934 he became head of the NSDFB, the omnibus Nazi organization which included all veterans' groups.

In 1933 Seldte was appointed Minister of Labor by Hitler. He remained in this post until the war ended. Seldte was indicted at Nuremburg but died on April 1, 1947 at a U.S. hospital in Nuremburg before he could be brought to trial.

Signed photograph of Franz Seldte.

Franz Seldte   Berlin, den 30. Januar 1935

Hochzuverehrender Herr Reichskanzler !
Mein F ü h r e r !

        Bei der mir bekannten überaus grossen Fülle
Ihrer Arbeit habe ich Ihnen am heutigen Tage meinen Besuch
nicht machen wollen.

        In Erinnerung an den grossen Tag, den 30.
Januar 1933, jedoch habe ich die Gedanken eines alten
Frontsoldaten, der seit 1918 Mitstreiter für das gleiche
Ziel und seit heute vor zwei Jahren Ihr Minister ist, in
einem Artikel, abgedruckt in beiliegender Kreuz – Zeitung,
niedergelegt.

        Das Gedankengut selbst der im NS Deutschen
Frontkämpfer- Bund (Stahlhelm) von mir gesammelten und
zusammengeschlossenen, für Sie und das neue Reich zu jeder
Stunde bereitstehenden Frontsoldaten ist in einem kleinen
Buche zusammengefasst worden, das ich mir erlaube, zu
Ihrem Tage, dem 30. Januar, Ihnen zu überreichen.

        In Verehrung und soldatischer Treue

                Ihr sehr ergebener

                        Franz Seldte

Letter from Franz Seldte to Hitler, Berlin, 1935, reminiscing about Hitler becoming Chancellor and sending a book on the NSDFB and the "front soldiers' spirit."

OTTO SKORZENY (1908-1975). A colonel in the SS (SS-Standartenfuehrer). A special agent under Himmler's direct orders, Skorzeny was born in Vienna on June 12, 1908 and joined the Nazi party in 1930. A tough, fearless Austrian, he was six feet, four inches tall. Skorzeny was widely respected during the war years when his daring exploits captured the world's attention. On September 12, 1943, acting on Hitler's personal orders, Skorzeny rescued Mussolini from his Italian captors in a dare-devil raid. Landing his special troops in a glider only a few hundred feet from where Il Duce was held prisoner, Skorzeny terrified the Italian guards who fled to the hills. Skorzeny bundled Mussolini into a tiny plane and got him safely to Nazi-occupied territory.

After the bomb attempt on Hitler's life on July 20, 1944 Skorzeny helped to quell a possible mutiny among the tank troops in Berlin and also put a stop to the indiscriminate executions of suspected conspirators.

In October 1944 Skorzeny performed another dashing feat by kidnapping the son of the Hungarian regent, Admiral Horthy, thus forestalling Hungary's defection from the Axis.

During the Battle of the Bulge in mid-December 1944, Skorzeny organized a special brigade of English-speaking German soldiers, put them in American uniforms, and infiltrated them in captured American tanks behind the American lines to misdirect traffic (as phony MPs), capture bridges for the advancing Nazis, and generally create mayhem among the American forces. At the time I was not far from the front. I had heard that Skorzeny was using many diabolical devices, such as stringing a heavy wire across a road by night to behead dispatch riders on motorcycles and stopping jeeps to throw tiny vials of acid into the eyes of the American occupants.

On December 24, 1944 (my thirty-first birthday), I was charge-of-quarters at our headquarters in Rheims where Skorzeny was reported to be directing the activities of Nazi infiltrators. I sat all night with my revolver out of the holster and inches away from my hand on the desk in front of me, listening to the sporadic gunfire in the streets outside and prepared to blow a hole through the first Teutonic face that appeared.

Many of the German infiltrators were subsequently captured and executed as spies. Skorzeny was tried by an American tribunal at Dachau in 1947 and acquitted. He moved to Spain where he established a prosperous cement business. He owned a country estate in County Kildare, Ireland, and a house on Mallorca. Skorzeny died in Madrid on July 5, 1975.

Signature of Colonel Otto Skorzeny, about 1974.

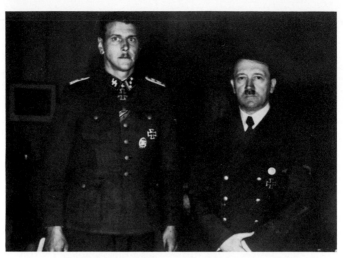

Otto Skorzeny with Hitler, September 1943.

O.U.,20 Mai 1945

Ich bestätige hiermit daß ich ausser Kleidungsstücke und Papiere nur die folgenden Wertgegenstände an die amerikanische Militärbehörde abgeliefert habe:

£ 130 (einhundertdreissig englische Pfunden)
RM 5000 (Reichsmark fünftausend)
L 10 (Lire zehn)

1 Füllfederhalter
1 Zigarettenetui
1 Feuerzeug,gold
1 " ,silber
1 Armbanduhr,Wintex 227852
1 Ring,gold mit Stein blau
1 Ehering,gold
1 Eisernes Kreuz
1 Ritterkreuz mit Eichenlaub
1 Ehrenblatt des deutschen Heeres
1 Bleistift "Temposparstift"
1 Zigarettenspitze,Horn
1 Goldmünze - 2o Kronen
2 Achselstücke,Oberstleutnant
1 Deutsches Kreuz in Gold (
1 Brieftasche,braun
1 " " ,schwarz

Es fehlen 1 Doxa Armbanduhr (Nickel)
70 engl. Pfund Papier
50 Goldmünzen in Zigarettenetui m. gold. Deck.

OTTO SKORZENY
Skorzeny

Document signed by Colonel Otto Skorzeny, with three lines in his hand, May 20, 1945, listing the articles turned over to his American captors. Included are his medals and various foreign monies, including Italian and British, that suggest his occupation as a secret agent.

Signed photograph of Otto Skorzeny.

GREGOR STRASSER (1892-1934). Close associate of Hitler; head of the Nazi Political Organization. Born on May 31, 1892 in Geisenfeld, Lower Bavaria, Strasser became a druggist. Like Hitler, he won the Iron Cross, First Class in World War I. Strasser joined the Nazi party in 1920 and by his indefatigable energy, organizational skill, and rabble-rousing oratory rose rapidly in the ranks. From 1926 to 1927 he was the propaganda chief of the NSDAP, and in 1928 became Reich Organization Leader. He often disagreed with other party leaders and eventually became estranged from Hitler.

After a stormy interview with Hitler in late 1932, Strasser resigned from the Nazi party. Less than two years later, in the bloody purge of June 30, 1934, Strasser was arrested at his Berlin home and murdered by the Gestapo.

Signature of Gregor Strasser

GREGOR STRASSER

Signed photograph
of Gregor Strasser.

OTTO STRASSER (1897-1974). A member of the Nazi party from 1925 to 1930, Strasser was a publisher whose ideology was far more liberal than Hitler's. Denounced by Hitler as a "parlor Bolshevik," Strasser was expelled from the Nazi party in 1930. Hitler bought stock in Strasser's publishing company and dissolved the firm. Strasser formed a splinter party known as the Black Front but was unable to command any voting strength. He then left Germany and eventually settled in Canada. He wrote a book on the Blood Purge of 1934 in which his brother, Gregor, was slain. In 1955 Strasser returned to Germany. He died in Munich on August 27, 1974.

Photograph of Otto Strasser, inscribed to Stephen Bumball.

DR. WILHELM STUCKART (1902-1953). Lieutenant general in the SS (SS-Obergruppenfuehrer); from 1935 to 1945 he was State Secretary in the Reich Ministry of the Interior. Born at Wiesbaden on November 16, 1902, Stuckart was a devoted supporter of Hitler. He was nevertheless appalled by the "Final Solution," Hitler's effort to exterminate the Jews. Stuckart tried to persuade Eichmann to spare the fringe categories of Jews - half-castes and those born of mixed marriages. When Eichmann was unmoved, Dr. Stuckart made a final desperate proposal directly to Himmler, suggesting sterilization. (However, Dr. Stuckart had first secretly ascertained from Dr. Conti, State Secretary for Health, that sterilization was impractical). Himmler was convinced by Stuckart's appeal and issued an order that saved the lives of 28,000 Jews born of mixed marriages.

Later, after the unsuccessful bomb attempt on Hitler's life (July 20, 1944), Gestapo Major General Paul Kanstein, one of the leaders of the anti-Hitler conspirators, was interrogated and released by Dr. Stuckart. Kaltenbrunner, convinced that Kanstein was guilty, was furious at Stuckart for his meddling and leniency and never forgave him.

The humane acts of Dr. Stuckart, carried out during the war at considerable personal risk, saved his life when he was tried. In the "Wilhelmstrasse" case of 1949, Stuckart was sentenced to three years and ten months imprisonment but was released the day after his sentence. He was killed in a car accident near Hannover in December 1953.

Dr. Wilhelm Stuckart

Signature of Dr. Wilhelm Stuckart.

HANS THOMSEN. Nazi charge d'affaires in Washington, D.C. A skilled and very knowledgeable diplomat, Thomsen was keenly aware of America's military might. He used all his means, financial and cultural, to promote sympathy for Germany and to discourage the United States from entering the war on the side of the Allies. He constantly urged the Nazis not to resort to sabotage or espionage in the United States "for there is no surer way of driving America into the war." Thomsen supported and encouraged the American

Autograph note signed by Hans Thomsen, 1956.

isolationist movement led by Charles A. Lindbergh. It is quite possible that, had Japan not struck at the United States, Thomsen could have kept America out of the European conflict and saved Hitler from the ultimate disaster. The Fuehrer, however, was determined to back his Oriental allies. Above all, in a clash with the United States, he wanted to be the first to declare war. On December 9, two days after the surprise Japanese assault on Pearl Harbor, Thomsen was instructed to burn his secret codes and confidential papers. On December 11, 1941, at 2:30 in the afternoon, as ordered by Hitler, Thomsen handed the American secretary of state, Cordell Hull, a declaration of war and asked for his passport. He died in 1968.

**Hans
Thomsen**

FRITZ THYSSEN (1873-1951). Industrial millionaire and early supporter of Hitler. In 1928, with his father, Thyssen founded the United Steel Works and in the same year became chairman of the International Steel Society. He met Hitler in 1923 and was carried away by his eloquence. Through Ludendorff he made an initial gift of 100,000 gold marks ($25,000) to the then-obscure Nazi cause. In 1931 he joined the Nazi party. In 1932 he wrote: "I am convinced that Hitler is the only man who can and will rescue Germany from ruin and disgrace." Hitler, in turn, looked upon Thyssen as one of Germany's leading economic experts.

Gradually Thyssen turned against the Fuehrer. In 1938 he resigned from the Prussian Council of State to protest the Nazi persecution of Jews. He denounced Robert Ley, a well-known alcoholic and head of the German Labor Front as "a stammering drunkard." In 1939 he criticized the coming of war. Thyssen fled to Switzerland and on December 28, 1939 wrote a long letter to Hitler in which, after telling of his former high regard for the Nazis, he stated:

"When on November 9, 1938, the Jews were robbed and tortured in the most cowardly and brutal manner, and the synagogues destroyed all over Germany, I protested. . .All my protests obtained no answer and no remedy. . . ." Hitler's only reply to this letter was to confiscate Thyssen's property and, as soon as chance afforded, to arrest him and his wife in France. Both were held in a concentration camp until the end of the war. On his liberation by Allied troops, Thyssen went to Argentina. He died in Buenos Aires on February 8, 1951.

HAUS THYSSEN
MÜLHEIM-RUHR-SPELDORF

Handwritten letter signed by Fritz Thyssen to Herr Goetz, a fellow banker, congratulating Goetz on the bank's report and Goetz's success.

352

[handwritten French text]

Last paragraph of a handwritten letter signed in French, with a variant signature, by Fritz Thyssen. Writing from Cannes on July 7, 1940, Thyssen explains that he has tried "to save Europe from the great danger that menaces it." Thyssen points out that "my case is a political case of great importance. . .I have never altered my opinion and neither my wife nor I will ever fall alive into the hands of my Nazi enemies who have abused me in every way and will also abuse France. . . ."

Fritz Thyssen

FRITZ TODT (1891-1942). Nazi military engineer. Born in Pforzheim, Baden on September 4, 1891, Dr. Todt served as a flying observer in World War I and joined the Nazi party in 1922. In July 1933 he became inspector general of roads in Hitler's cabinet and was responsible for building a vast network of high speed highways suitable for military transportation. He also supervised the construction of the Siegfried Wall, a line of defenses around western Germany, and a chain of submarine bases along the north French coast (1942). He was appointed Minister of Armaments and Munitions on March 17, 1940 and inspector general for water and energy on August 6, 1941. Todt was killed in an airplane crash leaving Hitler's headquarters in Rastenburg on February 8, 1942.

H e i l   H i t l e r   !

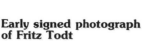

Signature of Fritz Todt from a letter.

Early signed photograph of Fritz Todt

ERNST FREIHERR VON WEISZÄCKER (1882-1951). Nazi diplomat. Born in Stuttgart on May 12, 1882, Weiszäcker joined the Imperial Navy in 1910, served throughout World War I, and entered the Foreign Office in 1920. He held many official posts under the Nazi administration. In 1943 he was appointed Ambassador to the Holy See and at the war's end in 1945 was given sanctuary. Arrested by Allied authorities as a war criminal, von Weiszäcker was tried at Nuremberg and sentenced to seven years' imprisonment. The sentence was later reduced, and in 1950 he was released under a general amnesty. Von Weiszäcker insisted that he had always opposed Hitler's foreign policy and had often tried in vain to resign from the diplomatic service. He died on August 4, 1951. His memoirs were published the same year.

Ernst Freiherr von Weiszäcker

Herrn Admiral a.D.
Leopold Bürkner

Frankfurt/Main
Mainzerlandstr. 424

Sehr verehrter Herr Bürkner,

    Ihre guten Wünsche aus Anlass meiner Rückkehr in die Freiheit habe ich mit herzlichem Dank erhalten. Etwas verspätet kommt mein Dank, Sie werden sich aber vorstellen können, dass nach Rückkehr von einer quasi Nordpolexpedition nun alles mögliche wieder auftaucht, was der Behandlung harrt.

    Hoffentlich werden Sie meine "Erinnerungen" nicht langweilen. Ich hätte in manchem ausführlicher sein müssen, aber man muss die Leute ja jetzt nicht mit Retrospektivem füttern, sondern das Gesicht nach der Zukunft richten.

    Alle guten Wünsche und beste Grüsse von Haus zu Haus

immer Ihr

Letter signed by Ernst Freiherr von Weiszäcker, 1950. Thanks for good wishes on his return from a "semi North Pole expedition."

Von Weiszäcker (right) in his diplomatic evening dress uniform, conferring with Dr. Wilhelm Stuckart.

FRITZ WENDEL. Test pilot and flight captain. A daring aviator and a jet plane expert, Wendel worked for Messerschmitt. He tested the new Me-262, the world's first jet fighter, on July 18, 1942. Earlier, on April 27, 1939, Wendel had set a world's speed record of 469 miles per hour in an Me-109R, a plane equipped for airfield landings. For this feat he received a telegram of congratulations from Hitler. Wendel continued to test aircraft for Messerschmitt until the war ended in 1945. He then became a brewer in Augsburg. In later years Wendel suffered acutely from a circulatory ailment. He finally shot himself with a hunting rifle at his home in Augsburg.

Captain Fritz Wendel in the cockpit of a test model Messerschmitt.

HORST WESSEL (1907-1930). Song writer. Born at Bielefeld on September 9, 1907, Wessel was the son of a Protestant clergyman. He abandoned his law studies to live with a former prostitute in the slums of Berlin. Wessel joined the Nazi party at nineteen and became the leader of a troop of Brown Shirts (Storm Troopers). He wrote the lyrics for the celebrated "Horst Wessel Song" (originally titled by Wessel "Raise High the Flag") that became the official anthem of the Nazis. Wessel was murdered on February 23, 1930 by a gang of Communists that burst into his room. His untimely death transformed him into a heroic symbol, an idealist who had given his life for the Nazi cause. Goebbels called him "a Socialist Christ."

Horst
Wessel

The first stanza of the famous "Horst Wessel" song written out and signed by
Wessel for a comrade. The first three lines read:
   "Die Fahne hoch!
   Die Reihen dicht geschlossen!
   SA marschiert mit ruhig festem Schritt. . ."
   "Hold the flag high!
   Close up the battered ranks!
   SA marches forward with calm firm stride. . ."

Horst Wessel (left foreground, with upraised right hand) leading his Brown Shirts,
Nuremberg, 1929.

AUGUST WILHELM, PRINCE OF PRUSSIA (1867-1949). Nazi SA general. Born at the palace in Potsdam on January 29, 1887, Prince August Wilhelm was the fourth son of Kaiser Wilhelm II. He served as a colonel in World War I and subsequently held many administrative posts in Prussia. In 1929 he joined the Nazi party and toured Germany lecturing on behalf of Hitler. Although badly beaten in a police raid at Koenigsburg in 1931, he kept up his association with the Nazis, especially the SA (Storm Troopers). Hitler appointed Prince August Wilhelm a member of the Prussian State Council in 1933. The prince rose swiftly in the SA ranks. He became a brigadier general in 1933 and was named a full general in 1943. The prince was always in awe of Hitler and remained a dedicated Nazi throughout the war, thus forfeiting his opportunity to lead the monarchists who opposed the Fuehrer. August Wilhelm died in Stuttgart on March 25, 1949.

Signature and title of August Wilhelm, Prince of Prussia, June 1947.

WILHELM II (1859-1941). Kaiser of Germany. A firm believer in the divine mission of his royal family, the Hohenzollerns, Wilhelm II was a powerful, brilliant administrator who played a major role in European politics. At the start of World War I the Kaiser was the dominant force among the Central Powers. After the defeat of Germany he was forced to abdicate (November 28, 1918). He settled at Doorn, Holland. Hitler occasionally derided the Kaiser as a weakling, but when the Fuehrer defeated the Allies in the Battle of France the exiled Kaiser congratulated him on his triumph.

Wilhelm's second wife, Hermine, whom he married in 1922, was closely associated with the Kaiser in all his later activities. She was an enthusiastic supporter of Hitler. Wilhelm died on June 4, 1941 in Doorn.

Kaiser Wilhelm II

Development of the signature of Kaiser Wilhelm II

1867, age 18, a modest prince

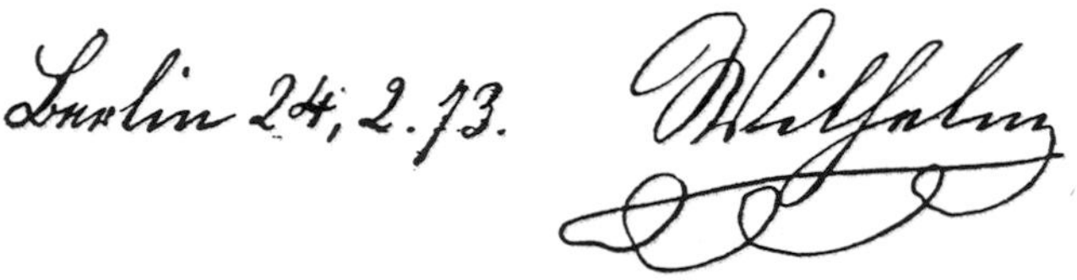

1873, age 24

1875, age 26

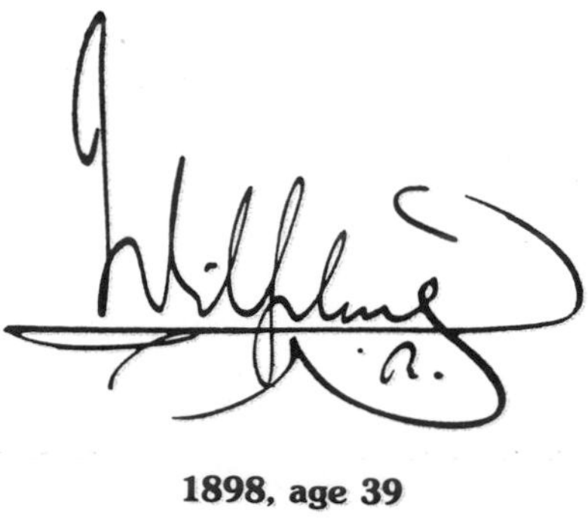

1898, age 39

1914, age 55, the most powerful monarch in the world

Lieber Herr Viereck !

        Ihr Freund und Biograph hat mir einen sehr liebens-
wuerdigen Brief geschrieben, in dem er mich bittet, einen Beitrag
fuer das Sammelwerk ueber Sie zu geben. Abgesehen davon, dass ich mir
nicht schmeichle, eine biographische Skizze ueber Sie gut machen zu
koennen, halte ich es in der heutigen Zeit, wo alle Laender gegen
Deutschland stehen, fuer angebracht, dass wir Exilierte uns moeg -
lichst zurueckhalten und nicht durch Wort oder Schrift hervortreten .
Ich glaube, das werden Sie verstehen und meine Gruende wuerdigen,
diese auch Ihrem Freunde mit bestem Dank fuer die freundliche Absicht
mitteilen. In Stresa ist ja Amerika nicht vertreten, kein toter Wilson ist dorthin abgesandt worden- es sieht ja sehr dreuend in der
Welt aus. Der Einzige, der, wenn auch nicht auf Kosten von Deutschlands Ehre und Freiheit, unbedingt den Frieden erhalten will und
zwar nicht bloss fuer Deutschland, sondern zum Besten der Welt, ist
Adolf Hitler ! Merkwuerdig, dass so viele ihn nicht verstehen und
verstehen wollen; gewiss ist die Lage sehr schwierig und ernst fuer
Deutschland und es drueckt auf einem, aber ich vertraue, dass Hitler
sich durchsetzt und glaube auch an seinen Stern.
        Die Nachricht ueber eine Erkrankung des Kaisers war
zum Glueck erfunden, Er ist selten so wohl gewesen wie die letzten
Monate, gruesst bestens mit mir.
        Ihnen Allen alles Gute wuenschend,

                    Ihre ergebene

Letter signed by Hermine, wife of Kaiser Wilhelm II, to George Sylvester Viereck (April 26, 1935). The empress expresses her faith in Hitler and adds that she "follows his star."

CROWN PRINCE WILHELM (1882-1951). Eldest son of Kaiser Wilhelm II and heir to the German throne. A weak and vacillating youth, the crown prince served as an army commander in World War I and at the end of the conflict fled to the Netherlands with his father. The kaiser kept his son in a subordinate position and treated him almost with contempt. After the death of the Kaiser, the prince hinted frequently that he was available for almost any high political post. He supported Hitler in 1932. Although Wilhelm never became an active member of the Nazi party, he swore allegiance to Hitler and on several occasions donned a swastika badge. The Fuehrer had no intention of restoring the Hohenzollern dynasty, however, and never gave the prince any post in the Nazi government. He died on July 21, 1951 in Hechingen.

Signed photograph of Crown Prince Wilhelm.

KARL WOLFF (1900-1984). Head of Himmler's personal staff; military governor of Northern Italy. Born in Darmstadt on May 13, 1900, Karl Wolff served in World War I, winning both classes of the Iron Cross. After the war he became a member of the Hessian Freikorps. In 1931 he joined the NSDAP and the SS. Wolff rose quickly in the SS, serving briefly in 1933 as Ritter von Epp's personal adjutant. He came to Himmler's attention while in this post, and the Reichsfuehrer-SS soon took the young officer as his own adjutant. Un-

Wolff and Himmler

Karl Wolff as military governor of Italy

Pooler

til 1943 Wolff served also as head of Himmler's personal staff and liaison officer for the Reichsfuehrer with Hitler. In 1942 he was promoted to lieutenant general in the SS (SS-Obergruppenfuehrer). Wolff was dismissed as Himmler's personal adjutant in 1943 because he insisted on divorcing his wife, which was against Himmler's wishes.

Wolff was sent to Italy in 1943 as military governor of Northern Italy. He was also Plenipotentiary General of the Wehrmacht in Italy. In effect, Wolff controlled German-occupied Italy for the last two years of the war. By February 1945 he was convinced that the war was lost, and he opened negotiations with the Allies in Switzerland which resulted in an early surrender in Italy. This step, which could have cost him his life, would serve him well in the postwar years.

Because of his record in Italy, Wolff was hardly bothered by the Allies after the war. Sentenced by a de-Nazification court to four years, he served one

Handwritten organizational plan of Buchenwald Concentration Camp by Karl Wolff, whose signature appears in the lower left.

Der Reichsführer-SS
Der Chef des Persönlichen Stabes

H e i l   H i t l e r   !

Letterhead and signature of Karl Wolff

week of his sentence before being released. He later became a successful advertising executive.

In the aftermath of the Eichmann case, however, he was arrested and charged with complicity in the "Final Solution" by the West German government. In 1964 he was sentenced to a prison term of fifteen years and was not released until 1971.

UDO VON WOYRSCH. Lieutenant general in SS; leader of an *Einsatzgruppe,* a special task force organized to liquidate the Jews in occupied areas. Von Woyrsch served as a first lieutenant in World War I and later as an officer in the Frontier Protection Service. Under Himmler's direction he organized the SS in Silesia. During the Night of the Long Knives (June 30, 1934), when Roehm and other SA leaders were rounded up and executed, Woyrsch took command in Silesia and at Goering's orders arrested a number

Udo von Woyrsch

of SA leaders, disarmed all SA headquarters guards, and occupied the police headquarters in Breslau. Some of the SA officers were slaughtered in a private feud by von Woyrsch's men. In September 1939 Woyrsch took charge of an *Einsatzgruppe,* or "murder squad," assigned the task of exterminating Jews and Poles in the Katowice area. The plan was to deport 50,000 Jews from Danzig and West Prussia into the interior of Poland. So brutal were Woyrsch's troops and so frequent were the mass murders that Nazi officers in the area objected strongly and insisted that Himmler withdraw Woyrsch's special "task force." When the Nazi officers also recommended that von Woyrsch's men be sent to the front instead of killing defenseless civilians, Himmler gave in and called a halt to the massacres. He was Higher SS and Police Leader in military district IV and district leader in Dresden from April 20, 1940 to February 12, 1944.

Signature of SS Lieutenant General Udo von Woyrsch

George Petersen

Reich- and Gauleiters meet Hitler at the Fuehrerhauptquartier in early August 1944.

The Gauleiters

THE GAULEITERS

The highest subdivision of the NSDAP (Nazi party) was the Gau (district). The chief of each district was the Gauleiter (Gau leader). Many Gauleiters simultaneously held the position of provincial president (Reichsstatthalter) and during the war were charged with civil defense responsibilities. The number of districts fluctuated and by the war's end there were forty-three. The Gauleiters were appointed by the Fuehrer, and ostensibly responsible only to him, but during the war they took their orders from Martin Bormann.

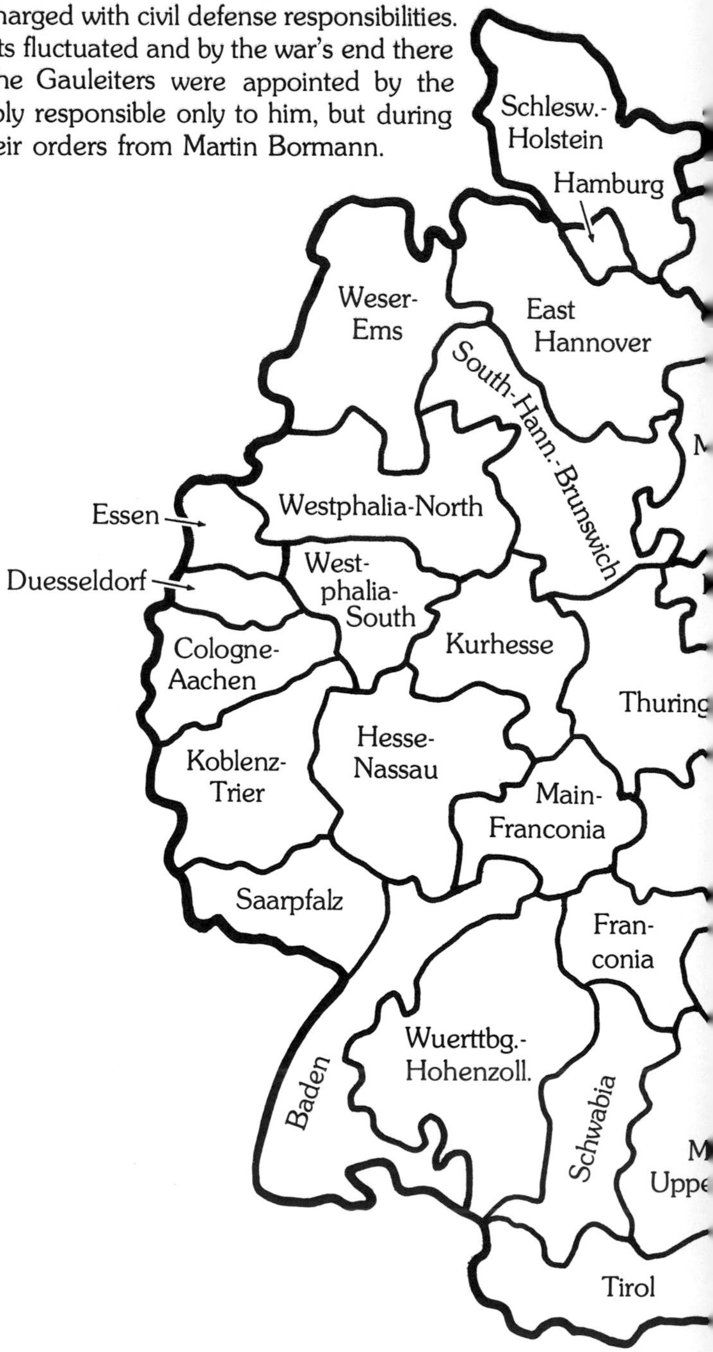

Schlesw.-Holstein

Hamburg

Weser-Ems

East Hannover

South-Hann.-Brunswich

Essen

Westphalia-North

Duesseldorf

West-phalia-South

Cologne-Aachen

Kurhesse

Thuring

Koblenz-Trier

Hesse-Nassau

Main-Franconia

Saarpfalz

Fran-conia

Baden

Wuerttbg.-Hohenzoll.

Schwabia

M
Uppe

Tirol

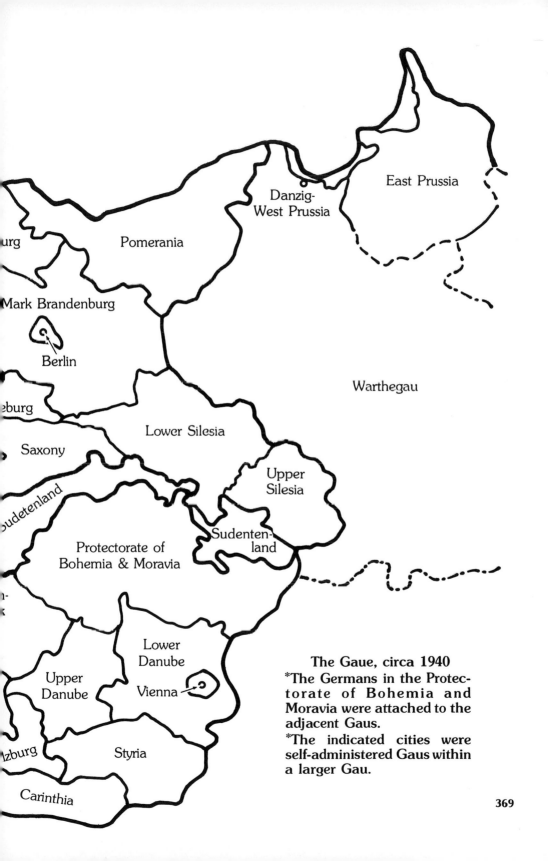

East Prussia

Danzig-
West Prussia

Pomerania

urg

Mark Brandenburg

Berlin

eburg

Warthegau

Saxony

Lower Silesia

udetenland

Upper
Silesia

Protectorate of
Bohemia & Moravia

Sudenten-
land

n-

k

Lower
Danube

Upper
Danube

Vienna

The Gaue, circa 1940
*The Germans in the Protec-
torate of Bohemia and
Moravia were attached to the
adjacent Gaus.
*The indicated cities were
self-administered Gaus within
a larger Gau.

zburg

Styria

Carinthia

ERNST WILHELM BOHLE (1903-1960). Gauleiter of the Auslandsorganisation (Foreign Organization). Born on July 28, 1903 in Bradford, England, Bohle was unique among Gauleiters since he did not run one particular district, but oversaw the affairs of all Germans living outside the Reich. Bohle did not join the Nazi party until March of 1932, but in slightly more than one year he was placed in charge of the A.O. (Foreign Organization), with the title of Gauleiter. He remained in charge of the A.O. until the end of the war.

Stab des Stellvertreters

des Führers

Der Leiter
der Auslands-Organisation

Letterhead and signature of Ernst Wilhelm Bohle.

Heil Hitler!

Ihr

Gauleiter

Ernst Wilhelm Bohle (Auslands-Organisation in Berlin, supervising Germans living abroad).

In 1937 he entered the foreign service as head of the Foreign Organization. In the diplomatic corps he held the rank of state secretary. Appointed a lieutenant general in the SS (SS-Obergruppenfuehrer), Bohle would probably have been administrator of Great Britain in the event of a successful invasion.

He was sentenced to five years' imprisonment by an Allied court in April 1949 but was released at the end of that year. Bohle died in November 1960 in Duesseldorf.

FRITZ BRACHT (1899-1945). Gauleiter of Upper Silesia from 1941 until 1945. One of the more obscure Gauleiters, Bracht was born on January 18, 1899 in Heiden. In 1940 he was appointed Gauleiter of Upper Silesia. He held this post until the end of the war. Rather than be imprisoned and tried, he took a fatal dose of poison. It should be noted that the Auschwitz extermination camp was situated in his Gau and that he visited it at least twice. On his second visit (July 1942), he, Himmler, and Higher SS and Police Leader Schmauser observed the whole extermination process.

Signature of Fritz Bracht

JOSEF BUERCKEL (1895-1944). Gauleiter of Rheinpfalz from 1926 until 1933. From 1933 until 1935 he was in charge of organizing the Nazi party in the Saarland. He was temporarily Gauleiter of Vienna from 1939-1940. (See additional biographical information in the Personalities chapter.)

Jo{ef Bürckel
Gauleiter

Meinen Mitarbeitern
zur Jahreswende !

Josef Buerckel

JOACHIM ALBRECHT EGGELING (1884-1945). Deputy Gauleiter of Magdeburg-Anhalt from 1935 until 1937, and Gauleiter of Halle-Merseburg from 1937 until 1945. Born on November 30, 1884, Eggeling became a farmer. His early career in the Nazi party was largely devoted to agricultural matters. He was appointed to run Magdeburg-Anhalt after the death of Gauleiter Loeper in 1935. In 1938 he was appointed Gauleiter of Halle-Merseburg. He held this post until April 1945 when, unlike many of his colleagues, he chose to stay in his home city and fight in its defense. He was killed in action shortly before the fall of Halle in April 1945.

Signed photograph of Joachim Albrecht Eggeling

August Eigruber

A. Southard

AUGUST EIGRUBER (1907-1947). Gauleiter of Upper Danube from 1938 until 1945. Born in Steyr, Austria, in 1907, August Eigruber held a variety of posts in the pre-1938 Austrian Nazi party. As Gauleiter of Upper Austria, he was responsible for the founding in 1936 of the *Austrian Observer (Oesterreichische Beobachter)* newspaper. After the *Anschluss* of 1938, he became Gauleiter of Upper Danube, a position he held until the end of the war.

On May 28, 1947 Eigruber was executed by the Americans at Landsberg Prison, presumably because of his association with the notorious Mauthausen concentration camp in his district.

Heil Hitler!

Gauleiter und Reichsstatthalter

373

FRIEDRICH KARL FLORIAN (1894-1975). Gauleiter of Duesseldorf from 1929 until 1945. Born in Essen on February 4, 1894, Friedrich Karl Florian served as an aviator in World War I. After Germany's defeat he joined the Freikorps movement. By 1929 he was Gauleiter of Duesseldorf. He held this office until the end of the war.

Florian was sentenced by a de-Nazification court to six years' imprisonment in September 1949 but was released in May 1951. He died in Unterbach on October 25, 1975.

Friedrich Karl Florian

Friedrich Karl Florian   Düsseldorf, im Dezember 1936
          Gauleiter

Mit herzlichen Grüßen zum Weihnachtsfest verbinde ich zum bevorstehenden Jahreswechsel meine besten Wünsche für ein neues Jahr voll Schaffenskraft und Arbeitsfreude zur steten Mitarbeit am Aufbauwerk des Führers.

Heil Hitler!

A. Southard

ALBERT FORSTER (1902-1954). Gauleiter of Danzig-West Prussia from 1930 until 1945. (See additional biographical information in the Personalities chapter.)

Albert Forster

Signature of Albert Forster

PAUL GIESLER (1895-1945). Gauleiter of Westphalia-South from 1941 until 1943, and of Munich-Upper Bavaria from 1944 until 1945. Giesler was an architect but spent most of his life in party duties. He held posts in the SA (in 1938 he was in command of SA Group Alpenland) before switching over to the party. By 1941 he was Deputy Gauleiter of Westphalia-South. Later that year he was promoted to Gauleiter.

He had barely settled into this post when he was dispatched to Munich-Upper Bavaria to replace the ailing Gauleiter Adolf Wagner. Much to Giesler's consternation, the invalided Wagner refused to surrender his post to him. Until Wagner finally died in April 1944, Munich had two men running the "capital of the movement." From 1944 until 1945 Giesler governed the district. Shortly after his brutal suppression of the Bavarian uprising of April 1945, Giesler and his wife committed suicide in Berchtesgarden.

Paul
Giesler

ODILO GLOBOCNIK (1904-1945). Gauleiter of Vienna from 1938 until 1939. Globocnik was born in Trieste (Italy) on April 21, 1904. In 1918 he emigrated to Austria where he joined the Nazi party in 1922. He held a number of posts in the Austrian Nazi party and in 1933 joined the SS. Later that year he was appointed Deputy Gauleiter for all Austria. Globocnik helped greatly in the Austrian *Anschluss,* after which he was made a state secretary. On May 24, 1938 he was appointed Gauleiter of Vienna. He was removed from office in January 1939 because of personal corruption and was replaced by Josef Buerckel.

This effectively marked the end of Globocnik's career in the Nazi party, but not in the SS. In September 1939 he became SS and Police Leader in Lublin. He was then selected by Himmler to play a key role in the destruction of the Polish Jews. Although successful in his task of liquidating the Jews, Globocnik had plundered his victims so openly that Himmler banished him to Trieste, where he became SS and Police Leader for the Adriatic coastland. He committed suicide on May 31, 1945, shortly after being taken prisoner by the British, by Weissensee in Carinthia.

**Der ⚡⚡- und Polizeiführer
im Distrikt Lublin**

Odilo Globocnik

DR. JOSEPH GOEBBELS (1897-1945). Led Gau Ruhr, together with Kaufmann and von Pfeffer, from March 7 to June 20, 1926; Berlin-Brandenburg from November 9, 1926 until his death (redesignated Gau Greater Berlin on October 1, 1928). (See additional biographical information in the Inner Circle chapter.)

Dr. Joseph Goebbels

Signature of Dr. Goebbels

ARTHUR GREISER (1897-1946). Gauleiter of Warthegau in 1939; renamed Wartheland in 1940. (See additional biographical information in the Personalities chapter.)

Der Gauleiter und Reichsstatthalter im Reichsgau Wartheland

Heil Hitler!

Ihr Ihnen stets ergebener

ℋ-Gruppenführer.

Letterhead and signature of Arthur Greiser

WILHELM GRIMM (1889-1944). Gauleiter of Middle Franconia from 1928 until his district was dissolved in 1929. Wilhelm Grimm was born on December 31, 1889 in Hof. From 1906 until 1919 he served in the army. He was mustered out with the rank of lieutenant. His political career began in 1920 as an associate of Julius Streicher. In 1922 he joined the Nazi party and was appointed Gauleiter of Middle Franconia in 1928. A year later this district was merged with Julius Streicher's Nuremberg-Fuerth to become Franconia. Grimm then became Deputy Gauleiter under Streicher, a post he held until 1932. In 1932 Hitler appointed him an associate judge on the party supreme court. He was then promoted to the position of Reichsleiter, in charge of the second chamber of the party court (Walter Buch presided over the first chamber). In August 1941 he entered military service and in 1943 received the honorary rank of lieutenant general in the SS (SS-Obergruppenfuehrer). He died while on an official trip in July 1944.

München
Oberstes Parteigericht

Heil Hitler!

Letterhead and signature of Wilhelm Grimm

A. Southard

Wilhelm Grimm

Josef Grohé

Hoover Institution

JOSEF GROHÉ. Gauleiter of Cologne-Aachen from 1931 until 1945. Born on November 6, 1902, Grohé joined the Nazi party in 1922. When the French occupied the Rheinland, he was with a Nazi resistance group and was forced to flee to Munich. Grohé returned to Cologne in late 1923. He held a number of posts in the party there before becoming the editor of the *West German Observer (Westdeutscher Beobachter)* in 1926. He was editor until 1931 when he became Gauleiter of Cologne-Aachen. He was also Reich Commissar for occupied Belgium and Northern France (1944).

Grohé spent five years in prison after the war. After his release in September 1950 he returned to Cologne and, it is reported, entered the film industry.

H e i l   H i t l e r

Ihr sehr ergebener

JOSEF GROHÉ
GAULEITER DER NSDAP GAU KÖLN-AACHEN
PREUSSISCHER STAATSRAT
M. D. R.

Letterhead and signature of Josef Grohé   A. Southard   379

KARL HANKE (1903-1945). Gauleiter of Lower Silesia from 1940 until 1945. Hanke had a long and colorful career in the Nazi party. His first key post was as Joseph Goebbels' personal adjutant in the propaganda ministry. While Dr. Goebbels was involved with the Czech film star, Lida Baarova, his youthful adjutant was giving much attention to the propaganda minister's wife. Their affair was broken off at the Fuehrer's insistence (as was the Goebbels-Baarova liaison). Hanke, by now a state secretary in the propaganda ministry, entered the army. In the French campaign of 1940, he was attached to Erwin Rommel's staff. Although not a professional soldier, Hanke fought courageously. Rommel recommended him for the Knight's Cross but the recommendation was later withdrawn, by Rommel, because of some unpleasant remarks made by Hanke. At the end of 1940 Hanke was released from military service. Still not in favor in Berlin, he was appointed Gauleiter of Niederschlesien (Lower Silesia).

In Hitler's last testament, Hanke was named as Himmler's successor as Reichsfuehrer-SS. Shortly before the fall of Breslau, Hanke abandoned his post and flew off in one of the few helicopters then in operation. This cowardly act did not help him, for he was beaten to death by Czechs in the early summer of 1945.

Signature of Karl Hanke

Deeter

OTTO HELLMUTH (1896-1968). Gauleiter of Main-Franconia from 1928 until 1945. Born on July 22, 1896, Hellmuth was a dentist by profession. He served in World War I and joined the Nazi party in 1925. In 1928 he was appointed Gauleiter of Lower-Franconia (renamed Main-Franconia in 1933). He held this post until the end of the war.

Dr. Hellmuth disappeared from view after the German defeat in 1945 but was captured in Bremen in 1947. An American court sentenced him to death, but the sentence was later commuted to life imprisonment. He was released in 1955 and died in April 1968 in Reutlingen.

Heil Hitler!

Gauleiter.

A. Southard

Signature of Otto Hellmuth

Otto Helmuth

KONRAD HENLEIN (1898-1945). Gauleiter of the Sudetenland from 1938 until 1945. (See additional biographical information in the Personalities chapter.)

Gauleiter Hanke with men of the Volksturm while inspecting barricades in "Fortress Breslau."

FRIEDRICH HILDEBRANDT (1898-1948). Gauleiter of Mecklenburg from 1925 until 1945. Born on September 19, 1898, Hildebrandt was wounded several times during World War I. In 1920 he joined a branch of the security police in Halle. He was quickly dismissed, however, because of excessive brutality. By 1923 he had joined the Nazi party. In 1925 he laid the foundations for the party organization in Mecklenburg. From 1925 until 1945 he was

Friedrich Hildebrandt

Reichsstatthalter und Gauleiter
in Mecklenburg und Lübeck

Heil Hitler !

Ihr

**Letterhead and signature
of Friedrich Hildebrandt**

Mecklenburg's Gauleiter. Hildebrandt was executed by the Americans at Landesberg Prison on November 5, 1948.

FRANZ HOFER. Gauleiter of Tirol from 1938 until 1945. Born at Bad Gastein on November 27, 1902, Hofer joined the Nazi party in 1931. In 1932 he was appointed Gauleiter of Tirol. In 1933 the Austrian authorities arrested and imprisoned him. Three months later his Nazi comrades helped him to break out of jail. During the escape he was seriously wounded. He fled to Germany, where he remained until the *Anschluss* in 1938. He was then reappointed to his old post which he held until the end of the war. He was arrested by American troops but escaped in 1948. He settled down in Muelheim/Ruhr under a false name. He later lived under his real name and died on February 18, 1975 in Muelheim.

Signed photograph of Franz Hofer

KARL HOLZ (1895-1945). Acting Gauleiter of Franconia from 1942 until 1945. (See additional biographical information in the Personalities chapter.)

Signature of Karl Holz

Karl
Holz

Signed photograph of
Rudolf Jordan

Rudolf Jordan
Gauleiter und
Preußischer Staatsrat

Ein recht frohes Julfest
und ein glückliches Neues Jahr
wünscht

Halle, im Dezember 1936

A. Southard

Signed New Year's greetings from Rudolf Jordan, 1936 (Magdeburg-Anhalt).

RUDOLF JORDAN. Gauleiter of Halle-Merseburg from 1931 until 1937, and Magdeburg-Anhalt from 1937 until 1945. Born on June 21, 1902, Jordan joined the Nazi party in 1925. In 1931 he was appointed Gauleiter of Halle-Merseburg. He retained this post until 1937, when he was sent to run the district of Magdeburg-Anhalt. Jordan was also an SA lieutenant general (SA-Obergruppenfuehrer). He was captured by the Russians and released in 1955.

HUGO JURY (1887-1945). Gauleiter of Lower Danube from 1938 until 1945. Born on July 13, 1887, Hugo Jury was one of the key personalities in the Austrian Nazi party and in the *Anschluss* of 1938. By profession a doctor (specializing in tuberculosis), he became deputy leader (under Seyss-Inquart) of the Nazi movement in Austria. He was appointed minister of social administration in the extremely short-lived Seyss-Inquart government. His last position was that of Gauleiter of the Lower Danube. On the day Germany surrendered, Dr. Hugo Jury committed suicide.

Signed photograph of Hugo Jury

Karl Kaufmann

KARL KAUFMANN (1900-1969). Gauleiter of Rheinland-North from September 27, 1925 to March 7, 1926; Gauleiter of the Ruhr, together with Goebbels and von Pfeffer, from March 7, 1926 to June 20, 1926; Gauleiter of the Ruhr (alone) from June 20, 1926 to October 1, 1928; and Gauleiter of Hamburg from April 15, 1929 to the end of the war.

Heil Hitler!

Jhr

Der Reichsstatthalter in Hamburg

Letterhead and signature of Karl Kaufmann

ERICH KOCH. Gauleiter of East Prussia from 1928 until 1945; High Commissioner for the Ukraine. Koch was born on June 19, 1896 in Elberfeld. He chose the railway service as a career, but this was interrupted by his military service in 1915. He joined the Nazi party in 1922 and took part in the resistance movement against the French in the Rheinland. By 1927 he was Deputy Gauleiter for the Ruhr. The next year he was made Gauleiter of East Prussia, a post he retained until the end of the war.

In 1941, after a brief period as administrator of occupied Bialystok, he was made Reich Commissar for the Ukraine. Koch's policies were so harsh that within a year he managed to create a pro-Russian Ukraine. He stated in a speech at Kiev on March 5, 1943: "I will draw the very last out of this country. I did not come to spread bliss. . .we are the master race, which must remember that the lowliest German worker is racially and biologically a thousand times more valuable than the population here."

Following the loss of the Ukraine to advancing Russian forces, Koch went back to East Prussia. Soon after the Russian offensive of January 1945 had overrun much of his district, he abandoned his post, commandeered an icebreaker, and sailed for Denmark. He remained in hiding until May 1949 when he was arrested by the British in Hamburg. Extradited in 1950 to Warsaw, he was accused of complicity or responsibility in the gas-chamber and concentration camp deaths of four million Russians, one hundred and sixty thousand Jews, and seventy-two thousand Poles. He spent nearly ten years in prison and was eventually tried for war crimes. A broken, old man, emaciated and coughing, Koch defended himself by declaring that the Polish Com-

Signature of Erich Koch

Erich
Koch

munists were guilty of much worse crimes than he was charged with. His long, impassioned harangues to a court whose authority he denied were not successful. Koch was pulled to his feet to hear a double verdict. The judge ordered him to pay one symbolic zloty (four cents) to a Polish Jew named Hersz Pianko whose entire family of sixty-three persons was wiped out under Koch's brutal administration. The second verdict: death for Koch. The sentence was later commuted to life imprisonment for reasons of ill health (Polish law prevents seriously ill prisoners from being executed). He is still imprisoned in Barczewo in northern Poland.

WILHELM KUBE (1887-1943). Gauleiter of Ostmark from 1928 until 1933, and Kurmark from 1933 until 1936. (Ostmark and Brandenburg were joined in 1933 to form Kurmark.) Wilhelm Kube was born on November 13, 1887 in Glogau. He became general secretary of the Conservative party in Silesia before World War I. In 1928 he joined the Nazi party. He brought his political followers with him and as a reward was made Gauleiter of Ostmark in 1928 and Kurmark in 1933.

In 1936 Kube was stripped of his offices, although still permitted to use the title "Gauleiter." He had apparently attributed Jewish ancestry to Major Walter Buch, but his undoubted corruption was the real basis for his dismissal.

On July 16, 1941 Hitler proposed Kube for the post of Commissar of Moscow. This move was opposed by Goering and Rosenberg, and Kube had to settle for the Generalkommissariat of Belorussia. Kube's regime in his new territory introduced corruption and graft on a high scale. Although not hostile to the people in his domain, and although he protested against anti-Jewish measures, he offered no real resistance to the atrocities, even taking credit for the death of 50,000 Jews in 1942.

Kube urged that the Belorussians be treated better and that they be allowed some form of self-government. But on September 22, 1943 a servant girl planted a bomb under his bed and blew him to bits.

A. Southard

Signature of Wilhelm Kube

Wilhelm Kube

387

HARTMANN LAUTERBACHER. Gauleiter of South-Hannover-Brunswick from 1940 until 1945. Youngest of all the Gauleiters, Lauterbacher was born in 1909 and joined a Nazi youth group in 1922. Until 1940 his career was largely with the Hitler Youth. From 1933 until 1940 he was Baldur von Schirach's chief of staff and personal representative. In August 1940 he was appointed Gauleiter of South-Hannover-Brunswick, replacing Bernhard Rust. Interned after the war, he escaped from a prison camp on February 5, 1948 and fled to Italy. In 1950 the Italians arrested him and returned him to Germany. He apparently escaped again, this time to Argentina.

Photograph and signature of Hartmann Lauterbacher

DR. ROBERT LEY (1890-1945). Gauleiter of Rheinland-South from 1925 until 1931. (See additional biographical information in the Builders chapter.)

Signature of Dr. Robert Ley

Dr. Robert Ley

HINRICH LOHSE (1896-1964). Gauleiter of Schleswig-Holstein from 1925 until 1945. (See additional biographical information in the Personalities chapter.)

Signed photograph of Hinrich Lohse

Signed photograph of Wilhelm Friedrich Loeper

WILHELM FRIEDRICH LOEPER (1883-1935). Gauleiter of Magdeburg-Anhalt from 1928 until 1935. Loeper was a professional soldier who served throughout World War I as an army officer. He reentered the army in 1920. For his part in the Beer-Hall Putsch he was dismissed from the military in 1924. On April 1, 1927 he was made Gauleiter of Anhalt/Province North Saxony (renamed Magdeburg-Anhalt on October 1, 1928). He held this post until his death on October 23, 1935 after a long illness.

DR. ALFRED MEYER (1891-1945). Gauleiter of Westphalia-North from 1931 until 1945. Born on October 5, 1891 in Goettingen, Alfred Meyer chose to be a professional soldier. He was wounded several times during World War I and was captured by the French in 1917. After his return home, he worked briefly in a mine, then studied economics. In 1926 he joined the Nazi party. In 1931 he was appointed Gauleiter of Westphalia-North. He held this post until the end of the war. In 1941 he was also made state secretary in the East Ministry and served as Alfred Rosenberg's deputy. Dr. Meyer killed himself in April 1945 by the Weser River.

Münster (Westf.), 31. Dezember 1936

Zum Jahreswechsel

sende ich herzlichste Heilgrüße und Wünsche!

Heil Hitler!

Gauleiter und Reichsstatthalter

New Year's greetings from Alfred Meyer

WILHELM MURR (1888-1945). Gauleiter of Wuerttemberg-Hohenzollern from 1928 until 1945. Wilhelm Murr served throughout World War I in the army. In 1921 he joined the Nazi party and in 1928 became Gauleiter of Wuerttemberg-Hohenzollern. He committed suicide on May 14, 1945 in Egg/Bregenz.

Signature of Wilhelm Murr

Wilhelm Murr

MARTIN MUTSCHMANN (1879-1948). Gauleiter of Saxony from 1925 until 1945. A successful factory owner in Plauen, Mutschmann was seriously wounded in World War I and released from military service in 1916. In 1922 he joined the Nazi party and in 1925 was made Gauleiter of Saxony. In 1935 he became the Prime Minister of Saxony as well. Mutschmann was captured by the Russians in 1945. The most accurate accounts available state that he died in Dresden in June 1948 as a Russian POW.

Martin Mutschmann

Der Reichsstatthalter
in Sachsen

Heil Hitler

Ihr sehr ergebener

Martin Mutschmann

391

DR. FRIEDRICH RAINER (1903-1947). Gauleiter of Salzburg from 1938 until 1941, and of Carinthia from 1942 until 1945. Born on July 28, 1903, Dr. Rainer was an early adherent of the Nazi movement in his native Carinthia and held a series of posts in the party offices there. After the *Anschluss* in 1938 he was made Gauleiter of Salzburg and in 1941 was transferred back to his home district as Gauleiter of Carinthia. He was also administrator of occupied Yugoslav territory adjacent to his district. After the war he was extradited by the Americans to Yugoslavia where, on August 18, 1947, he was executed for war crimes.

Dr. Friedrich Rainer

DER GAULEITER UND
REICHSSTATTHALTER
IN KÄRNTEN

Signed photograph of Fritz Reinhardt

FRITZ REINHARDT (1895-1969). Gauleiter of Upper Bavaria-Schwabia from 1929 until 1931 (redesignated Upper Bavaria on October 1, 1928). (See additional biographical information in Personalities chapter.)

KARL ROEVER (1889-1942). Gauleiter of Weser-Ems from 1929 until 1942. Roever served in World War I from 1914 to 1916 as an infantryman. He was then transferred to the propaganda section of the German High Command. In 1923 he joined the Nazi party and in 1928 became Gauleiter of Weser-Ems. On the night of May 13, 1942 Roever startled the party hierarchy when he announced that he was going to see the Fuehrer on the next day and then proceed to meet Winston Churchill, in order to make peace. Coming virtually on the first anniversary of Rudolf Hess' flight to Scotland, the matter was immediately brought to Martin Bormann's attention. An SS physician diagnosed the last stages of syphilis in Roever, and he was rushed to an isolated area. Two agents were sent by Bormann to examine Roever, and they reported on May 15 that the sick man had succumbed to heart failure. The whole matter was hushed up and soon forgotten in the course of the war.

Signed photo of Karl Roever

BERNHARD RUST (1883-1945). Gauleiter of Hannover-North from 1925 until 1928 and of South-Hannover-Brunswick from 1928 until 1940. He was furloughed from this post in 1933 but not replaced as Gauleiter until 1940. (See additional biographical information in Cultural Leaders chapter, volume 2.)

O. Spronk

Bernhard Rust

Signature of Bernhard Rust

FRITZ SAUCKEL (1894-1946). Gauleiter of Thuringia from 1927 until 1945. (See additional biographical information in the Personalities chapter.)

Signature of Fritz Sauckel

Fritz Sauckel

DR. GUSTAV ADOLF SCHEEL (1907-1979). Gauleiter of Salzburg from 1941 until 1945. Born on November 22, 1907, Scheel chose medicine as his profession. Beginning in 1930 he held various posts in Nazi student groups and in 1936 became Reich Student Leader. He was simultaneously in charge of the National Socialist Students' Bund, the organization of Nazi university students.

In November 1941 he was appointed Gauleiter of Salzburg while continuing to retain his previous posts. He was given the rank of SS-Obergruppenfuehrer on August 1, 1944 and appointed Minister of Culture in Hitler's will. After the war he was sentenced to five years' imprisonment by a de-Nazification court. After his early release he established a medical practice. He died on March 25, 1979 in Hamburg.

Dr. Gustav Adolf Scheel

DER GAULEITER UND REICHSSTATTHALTER
IN SALZBURG

Heil Hitler!

Ihr

Letterhead and signature of Dr. Scheel

HANS SCHEMM (1891-1935). Gauleiter of Bavarian-Ostmark from 1928 until 1935. Schemm served as a medic in World War I. Following Germany's defeat, he became a teacher and joined the Nazi party. In October 1928 he was made Gauleiter for Upper-Franconia (name changed to Bavarian-Ostmark in 1933). In addition to his post as Gauleiter, Hans Schemm founded and led the Nazi Teachers' League. After Hitler's assumption of power, Schemm also became Bavarian Minister of Culture. On March 5, 1935 he was killed in an air crash.

Signed photograph of Hans Schemm

Hans Schemm lying in state

BALDUR VON SCHIRACH (1907-1974). Gauleiter of Vienna from 1940 until 1945. (See additional biographical information in the Personalities chapter.)

Signed photograph of Baldur von Schirach

Artur Axmann (left) and Baldur von Schirach (right) wearing army uniforms in late 1940.

National Archives

FRANZ SCHWEDE-COBURG (1888-1966). Gauleiter of Pomerania from 1935 until 1945. Born on March 5, 1888, Schwede became so closely identified with the Nazi movement in Coburg that he added the name of the city to his own name. He was a professional soldier, but after World War I became an official in the Coburg city government. In 1922 he joined the Nazi party. In 1933 he became mayor of Coburg, a post he held until June 30, 1934. In July 1934 he was appointed Gauleiter of Pomerania. On May 15, 1935 the city of Coburg allowed him to change his name to Schwede-Coburg.

After World War II, Schwede was classified as a "Major Offender" by the Munich de-Nazification court. He was released from custody in 1955. He died on October 19, 1966 in Coburg.

Der Gauleiter und Oberpräsident
von Pommern

Heil Hitler !

Ihr

**Letterhead and signature of
Franz Schwede-Coburg**

GUSTAV SIMON (1900-1945). Gauleiter of Koblenz-Trier from 1931 until 1945 (renamed Moselland in 1941). Born on August 2, 1900, Simon joined the Nazi party in 1925. In 1928, at the request of Dr. Robert Ley, he became a

Heil Hitler
Ihr

Signature of Gustav Simon

professional party activist. In 1931 he was appointed Gauleiter of Koblenz-Trier. Simon also became chief of the civil government for Luxembourg in 1940. Sentenced to death after the war by a Luxembourg court, Simon committed suicide in his prison cell on December 28, 1945.

Gustav Simon

JAKOB SPRENGER (1884-1945). Gauleiter of Hesse-Nassau-South from 1927 until 1933, and of Hesse-Nassau from 1933 until 1945. Born in Oberhausen on July 24, 1884, Sprenger was a postal official until World War I

Jakob Sprenger

broke out. He served as an army lieutenant during the war. In 1922 he joined the Nazi party. In 1927 he became Gauleiter of Hesse-Nassau-South. The district was later expanded and renamed Hesse-Nassau. Sprenger killed himself on April 8, 1945 in Koessen/Tirol.

Signature of Jakob Sprenger

JULIUS STREICHER (1885-1946). Gauleiter of Nuremberg-Fuerth from 1928 until 1929, and of Franconia from 1929 until 1940. (See additional biographical information in the Builders chapter.)

Julius Streicher

Signature of Julius Streicher

EMIL STUERTZ (1892-   ). Gauleiter of Mark Brandenburg from 1936 until 1945 (Kurmark was renamed Mark Brandenburg in 1940). Originally a seaman, Stuertz was an early member of the Nazi party, becoming Deputy Gauleiter of Westphalia-South in 1930. In 1936 he was appointed Gauleiter of Kurmark, succeeding Kube. He was taken prisoner by the Russians in May 1945 and was never heard from again.

Signature of Emil Stuertz

Signature of Otto Telschow

OTTO TELSCHOW (1876-1945). Gauleiter of East-Hannover from 1925 until 1945. Except for military service in World War I, Otto Telschow was a police official from 1901 to 1924 in Hamburg. He joined an anti-Semitic party in 1905 and was an early member of the Nazi party. In 1925 Telschow was made Gauleiter of Lueneburg-Stade (renamed East-Hannover in 1928). He retained this position until the end of the war. He died on May 31, 1945 of heart failure in a hospital in Lueneburg after attempting suicide by slashing both wrists and taking poison.

JOSEF TERBOVEN (1898-1945). Gauleiter of Essen from 1928 until 1945 and Reich Commissioner for Norway. After service in World War I, Terboven became a bank official in Essen. He joined the Nazi party in 1925 and became Gauleiter in 1928. After the invasion of Norway on April 9, 1940, the

Josef
Terboven

Josef Terboven   Essen, den .....11. Dezember..... 193 7.
Hohe Buchen 2

Lieber Brückner !

Zu Deinem heutigen Geburtstag übermittele ich
Dir gleichzeitig im Namen meiner Frau herz-
liche Glückwünsche.

Ich hoffe, dass Du Dich bald einmal wieder im
Westen sehen lässt, sodass wir Gelegenheit
haben, den Geburtstag wenn auch nachträglich
so doch nicht weniger nachdrücklich zu feiern.

       Heil Hitler !

    Dein

Letter signed by Josef Terboven, sending birthday greetings to Hitler's adjutant, Wilhelm Brueckner.

Ich hoffe, dass Du gesundheitlich alles einiger
massen gut überstanden hast und sich auch der Junior auf
dem Wege der anhaltenden Besserung befindet.

Herzlichen Gruss und Heil Hitler!
Dein

Letterhead and conclusion of a friendly letter signed "Josef" by Josef Terboven.

Pooler

Quisling and Terboven in Norway

Fuehrer was not satisfied with Quisling's leadership and named Terboven to the post of Reich Commissioner for Norway. He remained in Norway until the end of the war, but did not relinquish his Gauleiter post.

It was not an office that called for ruthlessness, but Terboven made it his business to bully and harass the Norwegians, especially the Jews. His administration was not unlike that of Heydrich in Czechoslovakia.

At first Terboven made a pretense of amiability toward the Norwegian Jews. But within a year he began deporting the Semitic population of northern Norway to Germany. Some of the Jews in Trondheim he rounded up and executed. He left the Jews in Oslo alone, except for compelling them to wear a Jewish star and carry identification marked with a large "J."

On May 11, 1945 Terboven killed himself dramatically with a blast of dynamite. In an elaborate underground fortress he had constructed beneath Castle Skaugum in Oslo, Terboven ignited a stick of dynamite and, according to a servant, "blew himself to bits."

DR. SIEGFRIED UIBERREITHER. Gauleiter of Styria from 1938 until 1945. Dr. Uiberreither was born on March 29, 1908 in Salzburg. A lawyer by profession, he was heavily involved with the Austrian Nazi movement. After the *Anschluss* he was appointed police president of Graz and shortly thereafter, Gauleiter of Styria. Except for a brief period in the army, he governed the district until the end of the war. He was also chief of the civil administration in occupied Lower Styria.

DER GAULEITER UND REICHSSTATTHALTER
IN DER STEIERMARK

Heil Hitler !

**Letterhead and signature
of Dr. Uiberreither**

Interned by the Allies, Dr. Uiberreither escaped in 1947 with his family and made his way to Argentina.

Gauleiter Uiberreither as a mountain trooper in Norway, 1940

FRITZ WAECHTLER (1891-1945). Gauleiter of Bayreuth from 1935 until 1945 (Bavarian Ostmark was renamed Bayreuth in 1942). Waechtler was an early party member and held numerous posts in the Thuringian Nazi organization in the 1920s. He was appointed Deputy Gauleiter in 1929. In 1933 he was made Minister of the Interior for Thuringia. Two years later he was sent to the Bavarian Ostmark. From December 5, 1935 to April 19, 1945 he held this post. As a former teacher, he was also head of the NS-Lehrerbund, the Nazi Teacher's Organization.

A heavy drinker, Waechtler ran afoul of Martin Bormann in the last days of the war. On April 19, 1945 he was executed on a charge of defeatism by an SS unit commanded by Deputy Gauleiter Ludwig Ruckdeschel. Ruckdeschel ran the district during the brief period before the Nazi surrender.

Fritz Wächtler
Gauleiter der Bayer. Ostmark
Reichswalter des NS.-Lehrerbundes

Heil Hitler!

**Letterhead and signature
of Fritz Waechtler**

ADOLF WAGNER (1890-1944). Gauleiter of Greater Munich from 1929 until 1931, and of Munich-Upper Bavaria from 1932 until 1944. Born in Lorraine on October 1, 1890, Wagner studied mining at a technical school before World War I. During the war he was severely wounded and lost most of his right leg. After he was discharged, he entered the mining business. In 1922 he joined the Nazi party. For his part in the Beer-Hall Putsch he was briefly imprisoned. In 1928 he was made administrator of Upper Pfalz. One year later he also became Gauleiter of Munich (Upper Pfalz and Munich combined on November 1, 1930 to form Gau Munich-Upper Bavaria). He held this post until his death in 1944.

After the Nazis assumed power, Wagner was appointed Bavarian Minister of the Interior and Deputy Prime Minister of Bavaria. In 1936 he also became Bavarian Minister of Education and Culture. He held the rank of lieutenant general in the SA (SA-Obergruppenfuehrer).

Intelligent and feisty, Wagner was one of the few people who addressed Hitler by his first name. In many ways he was a radical Nazi. He was fervently anti-Semitic and anti-Catholic. In June 1942 Wagner was delivering a speech very hostile to the Catholic church. He concluded with the remark: "If everything I have said is not true, may the Lord God strike me down!" Moments later he suffered a massive stroke. Although he could not move or speak, he gradually recovered to a degree sufficient to enrage Martin Bormann and Wagner's appointed successor, Paul Giesler.

Wagner refused to give up his position and issued orders as if nothing had happened. The Fuehrer stood by his old friend and allowed him to retain the title of Gauleiter until his death on April 12, 1944, but insisted that Giesler carry out the affairs of the district. Bormann ordered that all of Wagner's orders be totally ignored. After Wagner's death, he was accorded an enormous state funeral.

Signature of Adolf Wagner

Adolf Wagner

JOSEF WAGNER (1899-1945). Gauleiter of Westphalia-South from 1928 until 1941, and Silesia from December 1934 until January 1941. Wagner was born on January 12, 1899 in Lorraine. He was a very early member of the Nazi party, joining in 1922. For two years (1929-1931) he headed the Nazi organization in the Ruhr. From 1928 until 1941 he was Gauleiter of

Westphalia-South. After the dismissal of Helmuth Brueckner in 1935, he was also made Gauleiter of Silesia. Thus he ran two districts simultaneously. Wagner was also in charge of introducing price controls to combat inflation, and apparently had the Fuehrer's respect, admiration, and support.

Signature of Josef Wagner

Josef
Wagner

Wagner, however, was a devout Catholic and thus incurred Martin Bormann's hostility. Bormann began to plot against him. Wagner's post as Gauleiter of Silesia was taken from him in 1940 and given to Karl Hanke and Fritz Bracht. In 1941 Wagner's daughter fell in love with a Waffen-SS officer. When the young couple asked for permission to marry, Gauleiter Wagner and his wife refused to allow it. The young man did not have a good reputation and, worse, was not a Catholic. A letter from Frau Wagner to her daughter fell into Bormann's hands and was added to other "evidence" of Wagner's "crimes."

The drama reached its climax on the afternoon of November 9, 1941. In front of the assembled Reichsleiters and Gauleiters, Bormann read the offending letter. Hitler announced that he "would not stand for this sort of thing." Wagner tried to defend himself, but Hitler publicly proclaimed his expulsion from the party leadership corps.

The case was then handed over to Walter Buch, the party's supreme judge. Although confronted with much "damning" evidence, Wagner defended himself so valiantly that Buch and the six Gauleiters on the jury reversed Hitler's decision and ordered Wagner be reinstated to his posts. Hitler refused to support the court's decision.

Wagner's ultimate fate is unclear. He was expelled from the party and arrested in the aftermath of July 20, 1944. Most reports indicate that he was executed by the SS in a concentration camp on April 22, 1945.

ROBERT WAGNER (1895-1946). Gauleiter of Baden from 1925 until 1945. Born on October 13, 1895 in Lindach, Wagner served in an infantry regiment during World War I and remained in the army until 1924. He was one of the earliest followers of Hitler and took part in the unsuccessful Beer-Hall Putsch in 1923. Wagner was imprisoned six times for political "rowdyism." He organized the Nazi party in Baden and was chairman of the local Nordic Society. Between 1940 and 1945 he was Chief of the Civil Administration in Alsace and implemented the arrest and deportation of 6,500 Jews, with no previous warning, to unoccupied France. He was imprisoned in 1945 and sentenced to death by a French military court. He was executed at Strasbourg on August 14, 1946.

Robert Wagner
Gauleiter und Reichsstatthalter
in Baden

Meine besten Glückwünsche zum Neuen Jahr

Heil Hitler!

New Year's wishes signed by Robert Wagner

KARL WAHL (1892-1981). Gauleiter of Schwabia from 1928 until 1945. Wahl was born on September 24, 1892. From 1910 until 1921 he was in the army. In 1921 he joined the Nazi party and the Brownshirts (SA). In 1928 he was made Gauleiter of Schwabia, a post he held until the Nazi defeat in 1945. Although a determined opponent of Martin Bormann, he successfully resisted all of Bormann's attempts to replace him.

After the war Wahl served light sentences imposed by de-Nazification courts. He went into the textile business. He wrote his memoirs and died on February 18, 1981 in Augsburg.

Signature of Karl Wahl

PAUL WEGENER. Gauleiter of Weser-Ems from 1942 until 1945. Wegener was born on October 1, 1908 in Varel. He was appointed Gauleiter of Weser-Ems in May 1942 after Karl Roever's death. Originally a businessman, Wegener held a variety of posts in the party, including a post on Rudolf Hess' staff. In 1936 he was made Deputy Gauleiter of Mark-Brandenburg and in early 1940 served as a Luftwaffe war correspondent.

Wegener was classified as a "Major Offender" after the war, and was sentenced by a de-Nazification court to a prison term of six years.

```
H e i l   H i t l e r !
        Ihr.
```

Signature of Paul Wegener

Paul Wegener

KARL WEINRICH (1887-1973). Gauleiter of Hesse-Nassau-North from 1928 until 1934, (the district was then restructured as Kurhesse from 1934-1944). Karl Weinrich was born on December 2, 1887. In 1906 he decided upon a military career. He served until the end of World War I. In 1922 he joined the Nazi party in Pfalz. In 1925 he held his first post in the Kassel Nazi party. In 1928 he became Gauleiter of Hesse-Nassau-North.

In the fall of 1943 Weinrich's capital city, Kassel, was heavily bombed. Weinrich at the time was in the countryside and did not rush back to the city until the danger was past. When he did return, however, his first concern was his private property. This was too much for Bormann, who promptly put him on extended sick leave. He was replaced by the Deputy Gauleiter of the Lower Danube, Karl Gerland. Weinrich was taken prisoner at the end of the war. A de-Nazification court sentenced him to six years' imprisonment in 1949, but he was released in November 1950. He died on July 22, 1973 in Hausen/Hessen.

Signed photograph
Karl Weinrich

Gauleiter WEINRICH

413

Prominent Refugees from the Third Reich

Albert Einstein at Princeton, about 1945

The rapid rise to power of Hitler and the Nazis took the German Jews and liberal intellectuals totally by surprise. The Jews had, to a large measure, been assimilated with the Nordic Germans and were playing a vital role in the development of science and art in Germany. However, as soon as Hitler became chancellor in 1933 he dissolved all rival political parties and labor organizations. He passed decrees excluding Jews from civil, political, and economic posts. The Nordic Germans who opposed Hitler's policies were treated much the same as the Jews. In 1935 the Nuremberg race laws took away the German citizenship of the Jews and authorized the confiscation of Jewish-owned property. The Fuehrer embarked on a wide program of anti-Semitism. Jews were rounded up, beaten, and sent to concentration camps. Jewish books were pitched into bonfires. On various pretexts synagogues were looted and burned.

The result was a mass exodus of Jews and non-Jewish intellectuals from Germany, the most colossal brain-drain since the Spanish inquisition.

KARL BARTH (1886-1968). Protestant leader and opponent of Nazism. Born at Basel on May 10, 1886, Barth held professorships at Goettingen, Muenster, and Bonn. Barth's New Testament philosophy held that man could not solve his own problems but was dependent upon revelation provided by God. In 1935 Barth was ordered by the Gestapo to begin his lectures on God with a salute and the Nazi greeting: "Heil Hitler!" He denounced this procedure as blasphemy and also refused to take an oath of allegiance to Hitler. He was removed from his post at Bonn and finished his academic career at the University of Basel. Barth died in Basel on December 10, 1968.

Signature of Karl Barth

EDUARD BENEŠ (1884-1948). Czech statesman. Born in Kožlany, Bohemia on May 28, 1884, the son of a peasant, Beneš became a lecturer in economics at the University of Prague before entering politics. In 1935 he succeeded Masaryk as President of Czechoslovakia. In 1938 Hitler, eager to seize Czechoslovakia, declared: "The oppression of the Sudeten Germans and the terror exercised by Beneš admits no delay." Against the threats of Hitler Beneš fought gallantly but the appeasement policies of Britain and France cost the Czechs their independence. In October 1938, after the signing of the Munich pact, Beneš resigned as President and the Nazis annexed much of Czechoslovakia. Beneš fled to London and headed the Czech government in exile. After the defeat of Germany in 1945 he returned and resumed his former post as president. In February 1948 the Communists seized power in Czechoslovakia and Beneš resigned. He died in Bohemia on September 3, 1948.

Eduard Beneš

de sympathie exprimés dans votre lettre, je vous prie d'agréer mes respectueux compliments

Eduard Beneš

Conclusion of a handwritten letter signed in French by Eduard Beneš

ELIZABETH BERGNER. Actress. Born in Poland on August 22, 1897, Bergner was educated at the Vienna Conservatory and made her stage debut in Zurich in 1919. She appeared in Berlin and on Broadway in plays directed by Max Reinhardt. Her husband, Dr. Paul Czinner, directed most of her films. She became a great star in German movies. With Hitler's ascent to power, she and her husband moved to England in 1933. Bergner was nominated for an Oscar for her performance in *Escape Me Never* (1935). Since 1938 she has been a British citizen.

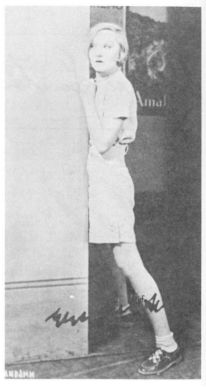

Signed photograph of Elizabeth Bergner

CURT BOIS. German actor. Born in Berlin in 1901, Bois made his screen debut at eight. He began his serious acting career as a cabaret performer. With the advent of the Third Reich in 1933 he emigrated to America where he played character roles in many films. Some of the movies in which he appeared were *Tovarich* (1937), *The Great Waltz* (1938), and *Casablanca* (1942). In 1950 he returned to Germany.

Signature of Curt Bois

MAX BORN (1882-1970). German physicist. Born at Breslau on December 11, 1882, Born became a lecturer in physics at Berlin (1915) and Frankfurt am Main (1919), then Director of the Institute of Theoretical Physics at Goettingen in 1921. A brilliant physicist and expert in quantum mechanics, Born was an intimate friend of Albert Einstein. In April 1933 he was "placed on leave" by the Nazi Ministry of Education because of his Jewish ancestry. Born left Germany and accepted a new post at Cambridge University. In 1954 he was awarded the Nobel Prize for his work on the statistical foundations of quantum mechanics. From 1936 until 1954 Born was professor of natural philosophy at Edinburgh University. He spent his final years in Germany and died on January 5, 1970 in Goettingen.

First page of a handwritten letter on technical matters written by Max Born 419

Signature of Max Born

WILLY BRANDT. German Social Democratic Chancellor of Germany. Born in Luebeck on December 18, 1913, the illegitimate son of an unknown father, Willy Brandt grew up in poverty. As a youth he joined in street fighting against the Nazis. In 1933 Brandt left Germany to continue from abroad the battle against Hitler. He lost his German citizenship and became a Norwegian. Several times he ventured into Germany in a Norwegian uniform, risking capture and execution. Once he hid in a prisoner-of-war camp to escape the Gestapo.

After the war Brandt returned to his homeland. From 1957 until 1966 he was Mayor of Berlin. He was named chancellor in 1969. Brandt helped to put Germany on a strong democratic basis and followed a firm policy of non-aggression. In 1971 he won the Nobel Peace Prize. He resigned as chancellor in 1974 when it was disclosed that one of his aides was an agent for East Germany.

Willy Brandt

A. Southard

Signature of Willy Brandt

BERTOLT BRECHT (1898-1956). German dramatist and poet. Born in Augsburg, Bavaria on February 10, 1898 of mixed Catholic and Protestant ancestry, Brecht served briefly in the German army during World War I. Although celebrated for his revolutionary lyric poems and ballads, his greatest success was scored as the librettist for Kurt Weill's *The Threepenny Opera* (1928). As a Communist, Brecht was a natural target for the Nazis. He escaped to Denmark in 1933 where he remained for six years. In 1941 he emigrated to the United States. His dramas, written in America, emphasize the conflict between the individual man and a corrupt society. He wrote anti-Nazi plays and a one-act drama about the Spanish Civil War. In 1954 the Soviets awarded him the Stalin Peace Prize. Brecht died in East Berlin on August 14, 1956.

Handwritten manuscript poem written and signed in Gothic script by Bertolt Brecht

Bertolt Brecht

Bertolt Brecht's portrait on a stamp issued by the German Democratic Republic

Handwritten note by Brecht signed "Eugen Brecht".

Variant signatures by Bertolt Brecht. *Top:* **Brecht's full signature in Roman script;** *bottom:* **signature in Gothic script**

MARTIN BUBER. Jewish philosopher and scholar. Born in Vienna on February 8, 1878, Buber attended the Unversities of Leipzig, Berlin, and Zurich. He worked zealously for the development of Hasidism and urged in his writings the wider recognition of the cultural significance of Judaism. Buber was the editor of several Jewish periodicals and a professor of comparative religion at Frankfurt University from 1924 until the advent of the Third Reich in 1933. Forced to flee from Germany, Buber eventually went to Palestine and settled in Talbieh, Jerusalem. The most celebrated Jewish scholar of modern times, he wrote or edited scores of books, founded the Zionist Society (1898), and was a guest lecturer at leading universities throughout the world. He died on June 13, 1968 in Jerusalem.

Signature of Martin Buber

MADY CHRISTIANS (1900-1951). German-American actress. In 1912 Mady made a film in America for the German-American theater. She returned to Europe to study under Max Reinhardt and in the 1920s starred in many German stage productions. In 1933, with the advent of the Third Reich, she left Germany for good. Her most famous film role was as the title character in _I Remember Mama_ (1944). Not long before her death she was blacklisted by Hollywood for alleged Communist activities.

Signature of Mady Christians

PAUL CZINNER (1890-1972). Hungarian-German director. Born in Budapest, Czinner became a child violin prodigy. He went to Vienna at 14 and later acquired a doctorate in philosophy and literature. Czinner wrote a play, then turned his attention to directing in 1919 in Vienna. In 1924 he met and married Elizabeth Bergner. She starred in most of his subsequent movies. In 1933, when the Nazis took over Germany, Czinner emigrated with his wife to England. In 1940 they came to the United States where Miss Bergner starred in several films while her husband produced and directed Broadway plays. Later they returned to England where Czinner developed multiple-camera techniques to record opera and ballet performances for the screen. He died on June 22, 1972 in London.

Signature of Paul Czinner

HELMUT DANTINE. Austrian-American actor. Born on October 7, 1917 in Vienna, Dantine fled to the United States in the late 1930s to escape the Nazi *Anschluss* in Austria. His impenetrable, handsome features won him many Nazi roles at Warner Brothers during World War II. After a film career he turned to producing and in 1970 became president of Schenck Enterprises.

Signed photograph of Helmut Dantine

Helmut Dantine, as a German officer in *Edge of Darkness*.

MARLENE DIETRICH. German-American actress. Born in Berlin on December 27, 1901, Dietrich studied with Reinhardt and began her acting career in 1922. She achieved international fame with her performance in Emil Jannings' *The Blue Angel* (1930). Dietrich adamantly refused to live in Germany during the Nazi regime. After 1937 she worked mainly in American films where her distinctive voice and theatrical mannerisms won her many interesting roles. While in England in 1937 filming *Knight Without Armor* she was approached by the German Ambassador to Great Britain, Joachim von Ribbentrop, with a personal and generous offer from Hitler to return to Germany. She refused. As a result her films were banned in Germany. During World War II Dietrich entertained American troops and made anti-Nazi broadcasts in German. She was awarded the Medal of Freedom. In the 1950s she embarked with great success on a new career as cabaret singer.

Marlene Dietrich

Signature of Marlene Dietrich

ALBERT EINSTEIN (1879-1955). German physicist. Perhaps the most celebrated refugee to escape from Nazi Germany, Albert Einstein was born at Ulm, Wuerttemberg, on March 14, 1879, of Jewish parentage. A shy youth, he rebelled against formal instruction and was tutored at home. His favorite subjects were algebra and geometry. At 17 Einstein entered a polytechnic school in Zurich. While still a young man he began to turn out scientific papers of great importance on molecules, light, and moving bodies. His general theory of relativity superseded Newton's dynamics. In 1914 Einstein was appointed to the chair of physics at the University of Berlin. When Hitler came to power in 1933 Einstein was stripped of his post in Berlin and was fiercely attacked in the Nazi press. All his property in Germany was confiscated. Einstein fled to England, then came to the United States where he took a position at the Institute for Advanced Study at Princeton. He looked upon Nazism as a reversion to barbarism and devoted much of his time to aiding Jews who were trapped in Germany or in Nazi satellite nations. Often regarded as the greatest scientist of modern times, Einstein died at Princeton on April 18, 1955.

Albert Einstein in 1932

426   **Handwritten quotation signed by Einstein, 1922**

Ich bin 1879 in Ulm (als Deutscher) geboren. Meine Jugend bis zum 16. Jahre verbrachte ich in München, wo ich das Gymnasium besuchte. Nach kurzem Aufenthalt in Italien ging ich 1895 in die Schweiz. 1896–1900 studierte ich in Zürich (nachdem ich das Bürgerrecht der Stadt Zürich 1901) am Eidgenössischen Polytechnikum Mathematik und Physik. 1902–1909 war ich als Ingenieur am Schweizerischen Patentamt (in Bern) angestellt. 1909 wurde ich ausserordentlicher Professor an der Universität Zürich, 1911 ordentlicher Professor an der deutschen Universität Prag. 1912 wurde ich an das Polytechnikum nach Zürich als Lehrer der theoretischen Physik berufen. Seit Ostern 1914 bin ich in Berlin an der Akademie der Wissenschaften mit Lehrberechtigung aber ohne Lehrverpflichtung angestellt.

Die Daten meiner wichtigsten wissenschaftlichen Gedanken sind

1905. Spezielle Relativitätstheorie. Trägheit der Energie. Gesetz der Brown'schen Bewegung. Quantengesetz der Emission und Absorption des Lichtes

1907 Grundgedanke für die allgemeine Relativitätstheorie

1912 Erkenntnis der nicht-euklidischen Natur der Metrik und der physikalischen Bedingtheit derselben durch die Gravitation

1915. Feldgleichungen der Gravitation. Erklärung der Perihelbewegung des Merkur.

A. Einstein.

Handwritten autobiography signed by Albert Einstein

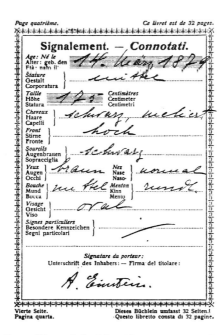

Page from Einstein's identification record, signed

LION FEUCHTWANGER (1884-1958). German author of Jewish historical novels. Born in Munich on July 7, 1884, Feuchtwanger studied philosophy at Berlin and Munich. In 1932 his *Josephus (Der juedische Krieg)* was widely acclaimed as a masterpiece. Because of his Jewish descent, Feuchtwanger was forced to flee Germany when the Nazis came into power. He embarked on a passionate crusade against Hitler and the Third Reich. In 1934 he published in London a statement entitled, "Murder in Hitler Germany." Feuchtwanger died in Los Angeles on December 21, 1958.

**Lion
Feuchtwanger**

Signature of Lion Feuchtwanger

JAMES FRANCK (1882-1964). German-American physicist. Born in Hamburg on August 26, 1882, Franck was educated at the University of Heidelberg and the University of Berlin, from which he received his PhD degree in 1906. From 1920 until 1933 he was director of the Physical Institution at the University of Goettingen. In 1926 he was awarded the Nobel Prize

Handwritten note signed by James Franck

in Physics. Seven years later Franck was forced to leave Germany when Hitler came into power. Subsequently he was a visiting professor and teacher at many universities, eventually winding up at Duke University in Durham, North Carolina. During World War II, Franck worked on the atomic bomb. In June 1945 he issued an impassioned appeal not to drop the bomb on Japan. Franck died on May 22, 1964 during a visit to Goettingen.

James Franck

SIGMUND FREUD (1856-1939). Austrian neurologist; founder of the science of psychoanalysis. Born in Freiberg, Moravia, Freud graduated with a medical degree in 1881 from the University of Vienna. From 1902 until 1938

Sigmund Freud

he was a professor of neuropathology at Vienna. Freud produced during the first three decades of the 20th century a plethora of distinguished books and monographs on psychoanalysis. He developed a method for treating hysteria by hypnosis. His theory that dreams are an unconscious representation of repressed desires, especially sexual desires, brought him world-wide fame. In 1938 Freud was forced by the Nazi administration to leave Vienna. He spent his last months in London where he died on September 23, 1939.

Development of Sigmund Freud's signature. *Top:* **1907, age 51;** *center:* **1911, age 55;** *bottom:* **1930, age 74**

Handwritten note signed by Sigmund Freud, Vienna, 1933.

Freud and his associates in Berlin, 1922.
Left to right: **Otto Rank, Sigmund Freud, Karl Abraham**

WALTER GROPIUS (1883-1969). German architect. Born in Berlin on May 18, 1883, Gropius studied architecture in Berlin and Munich. In 1919 he opened his own school of design and architecture in Weimar. The year after the Nazis came to power (1934), Gropius moved to London. Three years later he emigrated to the United States to become professor of architecture at Harvard University. One of his most celebrated creations is the Harvard Graduate Center (1950). A leading exponent of new techniques in building, Gropius introduced many innovations. He died in Boston on July 5, 1969.

Walter
Gropius

Variant signatures of Walter Gropius

FRITZ HABER (1868-1934). German chemist. Born in Breslau on December 9, 1868, Haber was largely self-taught in the field of chemistry. He probed deeply in his earlier years into the effect of electricity on various organic substances. In 1918 Haber was awarded the Nobel Prize for developing a successful synthesis of ammonia from hydrogen and nitrogen. By 1920 he was regarded as the world's greatest expert in physical chemistry. The advent of the Nazis in 1933 did not affect Haber personally, for although he was a Jew his great fame and prior army service as chief of chemical warfare from 1916 until 1918 brought him immunity. Haber was ordered in 1933 to dismiss all Jews from his staff. He resigned in protest. His health failed rapidly and he died from a heart attack in Basel, Switzerland on January 29, 1934. A memorial meeting, organized by Max Planck, was held in Haber's honor in defiance of orders from the Nazi Ministry of Education. It was the only public protest by scientists during the Third Reich.

Variant signatures of Fritz Haber

PAUL HINDEMITH (1895-1963). German composer. Born on November 16, 1895 in Hanau, Hindemith studied at the Frankfurt Conservatory and began his career as a viola player. His earliest compositions were for string quartets; they exhibited a daring new style. Later Hindemith composed in a wide variety of musical genres that revealed the influence of Stravinsky and Schoenberg. The songs he wrote for the Berlin cabaret, *News of the Day,* infuriated Joseph Goebbels, the Nazi propaganda minister. A lustful man who, by virtue of his position as head of the German film and stage community, had his choice of beautiful actresses, Goebbels feigned a moral attitude and criticized Hindemith as one of the "atonal musicians who out of sheer sensationalism stage scenes involving nude women in their bathtub in the most disgusting and obscene situations." From 1927 until 1937 Hindemith was a professor at the Berlin College of Music. In 1934 the Nazis banned his compositions as "degenerate music." Hindemith left Germany in 1938 and eventually came to the United States where he taught at Yale. He became an American citizen. In 1953 he returned to Europe to teach at the University of Zurich. He died in Frankfurt am Main on December 28, 1963.

Variant signatures of Paul Hindemith

**Paul
Hindemith**

OTTO KLEMPERER (1885-1973). German conductor. Born in Breslau into a Jewish family, Klemperer studied music in Frankfurt and Berlin, where at 21 he made his conducting debut. On Mahler's recommendation he was appointed assistant conductor of the German Opera House. By 1927 he was the director of the Kroll Opera in Berlin. With the advent of the Nazi regime in 1933 Klemperer was forced to leave Germany. In America he became the conductor of the Los Angeles Philharmonic Orchestra. His performances of the symphonies of Beethoven and Mahler won him enormous fame in the post-war years. He died on July 7, 1973 in Zurich.

Signature of Otto Klemperer

Otto
Klemperer

HEDY LAMARR, Actress. Born Hedwig Eva Maria Kiesler in Vienna on November 9, 1913, the daughter of a Jewish banker, Hedy was discovered by Max Reinhardt in 1930 and put into films as a bit player. She won instant fame when she appeared gloriously naked in a ten-minute sequence of a 1933 Czech production of *Ecstasy*. She then married munitions magnate Fritz Mandl who tried to buy up all the prints of the "scandalous" movie. After the advent of the Nazis Hedy was forced to leave Germany. She arrived in Hollywood billed as "the world's most beautiful woman." For once the press agents did not exaggerate. I saw Hedy at very close range several times. Her long wavy hair was raven black and had the irridescent sheen of a crow's plumage. Her skin was like Parian marble, yet seemed to have the translucence of mother-of-pearl. Her eyes were a deep cerulean blue. I looked into them and nearly lost my balance. After making a number of successful films, all illuminated by her radiance, Hedy was cast away by the moguls of Hollywood. At last report she was on relief.

Signature of Hedy Lamarr

Photograph of Hedy Lamarr signed with her real name, Hedy Kiesler.

Hedy Kiesler

Signed photograph of Hedy Lamarr

FRITZ LANG (1890-1976). Film director. Born on December 5, 1890 in Vienna, Lang studied to become an architect but at 20 ran away from home to lead the life of an artist in Munich and Paris. He then wandered through Africa, China, and Russia, supporting himself, as did his arch-enemy, Adolf Hitler, by painting and selling picture postcards. On the outbreak of World War I he was conscripted into the Austrian army. He was wounded four times and rose to the rank of lieutenant. While convalescing from his wounds he began to write film scripts. His success in this field led in 1919 to a job as director with the Decla company in Berlin. In 1924, during a brief visit to America, Lang was so impressed with the New York skyline and the wildly rushing crowds of people that he conceived the idea for his next film, *Metropolis* (1927), a landmark in

435

Scene from Fritz Lang's film *Metropolis* (1927), in which the unthinking lower classes are depicted as automatons, mere geometric patterns hypnotized and then manipulated by their masters. *Metropolis* was one of Hitler's favorite movies.

Scene from Leni Riefenstahl's Nazi ra film *Triumph of the Will* (1935). Huma are again, as in *Metropolis,* shown obedient pawns, nothing more than mob masses of architecture.

movie artistry. Four years later Lang created the famous masterpiece *M,* based on a true case of a child murderer in Duesseldorf.

Lang's next film was *The Last Will of Dr. Mabuse* (1933), in which Nazi slogans were constantly mouthed by the film's most evil characters. The film was banned by the Nazis and Lang, whose mother was Jewish, was summoned to the office of Dr. Joseph Goebbels, the propaganda minister. To Lang's utter astonishment, Goebbels apologized for the ban and informed Lang that the Fuehrer had personally requested the appointment of Lang to supervise and direct Nazi film productions. Fearing that Goebbels would discover his Jewish

Signature of Fritz Lang

Fritz Lang

background, Lang took the next train to Paris, leaving behind his possessions and bank savings.

Lang's extraordinary contributions to the movie industry continued when he emigrated to America where he received his citizenship papers in 1935. He made several powerful anti-Nazi films. Most of his movie themes were built around criminals and violence and the inexorability of fate. Lang spent his final years in retirement in his Beverly Hills home. He died on August 2, 1976.

STEFAN LORANT. Pictorial journalist. Born in Hungary, Lorant was editor of the *Munich Illustrated Press* until the day after Hitler took over the Bavarian government. Lorant was placed in "protective custody." For more than six months he was kept in a concentration camp. The Hungarian government finally obtained his release and Lorant went to London where he founded *The Picture Post*, an English weekly that reached a circulation of 1,500,-000. Lorant wrote an account of his concentration camp experiences, *I Was Hitler's Prisoner.* In 1940 he came to America where his pictorial life of Lincoln (1941) won him wide acclaim. He has since written other successful pictorial books.

Signature of Stefan Lorant

Stefan Lorant

PETER LORRE (1904-1964). Hungarian-German actor. Born Laszio Loewenstein on June 26, 1904 in Hungary, Lorre started his career as a bank clerk, then studied acting in Vienna and made his debut in Zurich. He was still an unknown when Fritz Lang cast him as a psychopathic child murderer in *M* (1931). Lorre's sinister, pathetic expression and mysterious, quietly menacing manner won him world-wide fame. He appeared in several other German films but when the Nazis took over Germany he fled to Paris, then to London and finally in 1935 to Hollywood. In America he continued his inscrutable roles, starring as "Mr. Moto." He appeared in several outstanding movies with Humphrey Bogart, including *Casablanca* and *The Maltese Falcon*. Lorre died at 60 of a heart attack on March 23, 1964.

Signed photograph of Peter Lorre

Signature of Peter Lorre

HEINRICH MANN (1871-1950). German novelist; eldest brother of Thomas Mann. Born in Luebeck on March 27, 1871, Mann became a distinguished editor in Berlin and was selected as president of the Prussian Academy of Arts (Poetry Division) in 1930. His novels portrayed with great skill the social life in Germany before and after World War I. When Hitler came to power in 1933, Mann was forced to resign his post in the Prussian Academy of Arts. He escaped to Paris by way of Prague and joined the literary war against Fascism and Nazism. Mann wrote many verbal assaults on the Nazi regime. He died in Santa Monica, California, on March 12, 1950.

Heinrich
Mann

Signature of Heinrich Mann

Handwritten note signed by Heinrich Mann

THOMAS MANN (1875-1955). German novelist. One of the greatest of modern authors, Mann was born on June 6, 1875 in Luebeck. When his family moved to Munich, Mann found a position in an insurance office and at the same time studied at the university before turning to journalism. His early psychological novels attracted wide attention. During World War I Mann was swept into the vortex of nationalistic hysteria and lauded German militarism as "inherent in the German soul, its ethical conservatism, its soldier-like morality. . ." Mann wrote a eulogistic essay on Frederick the Great. He viewed World War I as a clash between western civilization and German *Kultur*. Subsequently Mann repudiated this view and became a staunch defender of liberalism in all forms. In 1929 he was awarded the Nobel Prize for Literature. 439

His defense of the Weimar Republic, long the target of Hitler's oratorical wrath, aroused the enmity of the Nazis. Mann was in Switzerland when Hitler came into power and decided to stay there in exile. From his pen came fresh outpourings of condemnation for the Nazis.

Early in 1936 the Third Reich government stripped Mann of his German citizenship. On December 19, 1936 his honorary degree from the University of Bonn was rescinded. The letter to him from the dean of the philosophical faculty and Mann's scorching reply constituted a savage indictment of Nazism. In 1938 Mann emigrated to the United States where he taught for a while at Princeton. He continued his attacks on Hitler and the Nazis until the war's end. In 1954 Mann went back to Switzerland where he died on August 12, 1955.

**Thomas
Mann**

Thomas Mann's Swiss identification papers, with his photograph, physical description, and signature. Also with the photograph and signature of his wife, Katharina.

Variant signatures of Thomas Mann

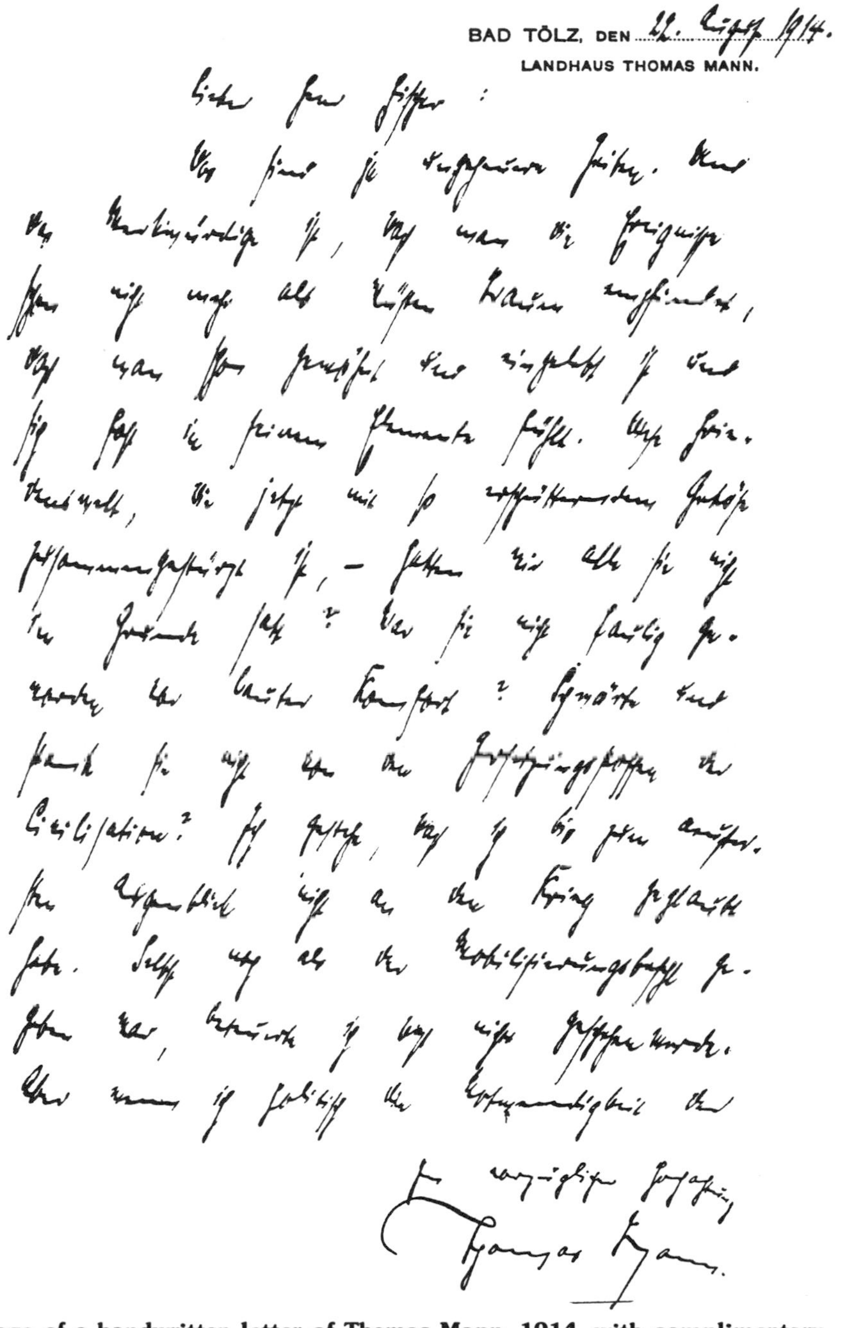

BAD TÖLZ, DEN 22. Sept. 1914.
LANDHAUS THOMAS MANN.

First page of a handwritten letter of Thomas Mann, 1914, with complimentary close and signature

OTTO PREMINGER. German-American director. Born on December 5, 1906 in Vienna, Preminger was the son of the attorney general of the Austrian Empire. He received a doctor of laws degree but at the same time studied with Max Reinhardt as actor and assistant. Preminger revealed his brilliance as a director almost at once and Reinhardt put him in charge of his theater in Vienna. Preminger always wore his hair cut short and looked so convincingly Prussian that although Jewish he was able to remain unmolested in Germany until 1935. In that year he went to Hollywood where, after a verbal clash with Darryl Zanuck, he was virtually blacklisted. He next played the role of a Nazi villain on Broadway in *Margin for Error* and scored a great hit. Back in Hollywood again he was reconciled with Zanuck and directed *Laura,* an immense financial and critical success. Preminger's triumphs continued and he directed *Anatomy of a Murder* in 1959. He is often seen in New York restaurants, notably Trader Vic's, pontificating and jesting with friends at dinner.

Signed photograph of Otto Preminger

Raymond Ward

A. Southard

Signature of Otto Preminger

Otto Preminger in The Pied Piper.

VERA HRUBA RALSTON. Czech-American actress. Born in Prague on June 12, 1921, Vera studied classical ballet and ice-skating. At thirteen she was the skating champion of Prague. After a superb performance in the Berlin Olympics of 1936, Vera was asked by Hitler to "skate for the swastika." She replied: "I'd rather skate on it."   When the Nazis invaded the Sudetenland, Vera was on the last airplane to fly out of Prague. After a two-year tour with the Ice Vanities in America, Vera landed a job as actress at Republic Pictures in Hollywood. She was billed as "the most beautiful woman in the world." Her film career was long and undistinguished, except for her intimate friendship with the studio president, Herbert J. Yates.

Vera Hruba, performing at the 1936 Berlin Olympics.

Signed photograph of Vera Ralston

443

MAX REINHARDT (1873-1943). Austrian-American theatrical director. Born Max Goldmann in Baden, near Vienna, on September 9, 1873, Reinhardt began his career as a bank clerk but in 1893 became an actor in Salzburg. He performed as a character actor until 1902. From 1903 until 1906 Reinhardt staged plays of Wilde and Gorky and other leading writers at the *Neues Theater* in Berlin. He introduced many innovations into the theater, including the apron stage designed to bring the actors close to the audience. By 1933 Reinhardt's unique productions of the world's great dramatists - Shakespeare, Ibsen, Shaw, and others - had won him international fame. Unable to remain in Nazi Germany, he presented his celebrated *Deutsches Theater* to the German people, then left for England. Later he came to the United States where he opened an acting school in Los Angeles. Reinhardt became an American citizen in 1940. He died in New York City on October 30, 1943.

Signature of Max Reinhardt

Max Reinhardt

ERICH MARIA REMARQUE (1898-1970). German novelist. Born in Osnabrueck on June 22, 1898, Erich Kramer later spelled his name backwards, getting the *nom de plume* he made famous. Remarque entered the German army at 17 and served from 1915 to 1918 during World War I. A decade later he wrote the compelling *All Quiet on the Western Front (Im Westen nichts Neues)*. Published in 1929, this realistic novel which deglamorized war and revealed the brutality and irrationality of mortal hatred won Remarque instant fame. The book was a best seller and was made into a highly successful motion picture.

A few years before his death I met Remarque and chatted with him for several hours about war novels and war. He told me: "I was stripped of my German citizenship by Hitler because of my pacifism. *All Quiet* was banned in Germany and copies were publicly burned. A few years later, when the United States entered World War II, the movie based on my novel was also banned in America because it opposes the whole idea of war and was sympathetic towards the German soldiers who were nothing but cannon fodder."

I asked Remarque about the characters in *All Quiet:* "Every character in the book," he said, "was a composite of several people I met when I was a soldier."

Remarque died at Ancona, Italy, on September 25, 1970.

Signature of Erich Maria Remarque

Erich Maria Remarque

LUDWIG RENN. Anti-Nazi author. Born Arnold Vieth von Golsenau in Dresden on April 22, 1889, Renn was an officer in World War I in the German army, successively the commander of a company and then a battalion. He studied a great variety of subjects after the war at the Universities of Goettingen and Munich. From 1928 until 1932 he served as secretary of the Alliance of Proletarian Writers. His novel *Der Krieg (War),* won him a wide audience. When the Reichstag was mysteriously burned on February 27, 1933, Renn was arrested for complicity and sentenced to 30 months in prison. He fled to Switzerland in 1936 and then joined the Loyalists in the Spanish Civil War as chief of staff of the International Brigade. From 1941 until 1946 he was the leader of the Free German movement. In 1947 he took up residence in the German Democratic Republic and became a professor of anthropology at the Technical College of Dresden. He died on July 21, 1978 in East Berlin.

Signature of Ludwig Renn

ARNOLD SCHOENBERG (1874-1951). Austrian-American composer. Often regarded as the father of twentieth-century music, Schoenberg learned as a youth to play several stringed instruments and began to compose while still in his teens. After a brief stint working in a bank, he turned to music for a living. From the age of 21 he was a choral master. Schoenberg's first great composition, *Transfigured Night* (1899), shows strongly the influence of Brahms and Wagner. At this time Schoenberg changed his religion from Jewish to Protestant and moved from Vienna to Berlin. Later he returned to Vienna where he worked as a teacher. One of his pupils was Alban Berg. Schoenberg's atonal music was so ultra-modern as to be almost cacophonous. He introduced a 12-tone scale and constantly broke the established rules of musical composition. In 1933 he escaped from the Nazi regime and came to the United States. From 1936 until 1944 he was a professor of music at U.C.L.A. where I was a student in the 1930s. I often observed his slender, solemn figure gliding across the campus between the library and Royce Hall. One of my closest friends, a music major and an admirer of Schoenberg, persuaded me to attend a string-sextet performance of Schoenberg's music in Royce Hall. I'd never heard anything by him. The most revolutionary music I'd ever listened to was by Stravinsky and I had no inkling of what to expect. I fidgeted about while the musicians appeared to tune their instruments. After about five minutes of gut-rubbing dissonance, I turned to my friend and whispered: "When are they going to start?"

"Shut up, you idiot," he whispered back. "They've been playing for five minutes!"

Schoenberg died on July 13, 1951 in Brentwood, California.

Arnold Schoenberg

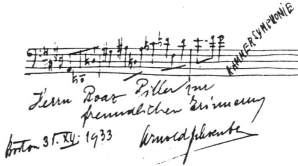

Handwritten musical excerpt signed by Arnold Schoenberg from his *Kammersymphonie*

ERNST TOLLER (1893-1939). German poet and dramatist. Born in Samotschin, Posen (now Poland) on December 1, 1893, Toller was the son of a Jewish merchant. He entered World War I as a volunteer but became disenchanted and later helped to organize strikes to stop the war. He joined the revolution in Bavaria and was elected President of the Bavarian Soviet Republic. When the revolution was put down, Toller was arrested and imprisoned for five years. His plays, always expressionistic in technique, explore the problems of the working classes and the horrors of war. Many of them were written during his prison years. When Hitler became Chancellor, Toller's books were burned in public and he was deprived of his German citizenship. He fled to America and became active in anti-Fascist movements. Apparently in despair over conditions in Germany, Toller committed suicide in New York on May 22, 1939.

Signature of Ernst Toller

Ernst
Toller

CONRAD VEIDT (1893-1943). German-British actor. Born at Potsdam near Berlin on January 22, 1893, Veidt was a student of Max Reinhardt and made his acting debut in Reinhardt's *Deutsches Theater* in Berlin. He established a reputation for demoniacal roles by playing Cesare, the somnambulist in *The Cabinet of Dr. Caligari* (1919). For a while in the mid-1920s he acted in Hollywood. In 1929 he went back to Germany where, as an internationally famous actor, he played sound parts with great skill. In 1933, after the Nazi takeover, he left for England with his Jewish wife. The following year he returned to Germany on a visit and was held by the Gestapo on the pretext that he was "too ill to travel." His employer, a British movie firm, sent private doctors to Germany to rescue him. One of Veidt's last roles was that of the tough and impeccably polite Nazi major in *Casablanca* (1942). He died the next year in Hollywood on April 3, 1943.

Signature of Conrad Veidt

Conrad Veidt in
Escape.

BRUNO WALTER (1876-1962). German orchestra conductor. Born Bruno Schlesinger in Berlin on September 15, 1876, Walter studied music at the Stern Conservatory. Early in his career he fell under the influence of Gustav Mahler. He became Mahler's assistant in Vienna, eventually succeeding him as director of the Vienna Opera in 1907. From 1913 until 1922 Walter was music director of the Munich State Opera and from 1936 until 1938 he held the same post in Vienna. His Jewish origin forced him to leave Austria in 1938. After a brief stay in France, Walter made his home in the United States. He was widely acclaimed for his masterful interpretations of Mahler, Mozart, Schubert, and Beethoven. He died in Beverly Hills, California, on February 17, 1962.

Bruno
Walter

Signature of Bruno Walter

KURT WEILL (1900-1950). German composer. Born in Dessau on March 2, 1900, Weill was descended from a long line of rabbis but was "the least pious Jew of the family." In 1918 he graduated from the celebrated "High School for Music" in Berlin and soon became a popular composer. With a text by Bertolt Brecht, the noted poet, he produced the delectable satire, *The Threepenny Opera,* a world-wide hit that featured the jazzy song, "Mack the Knife." Weill and Brecht collaborated on other dramatic operettas. Weill's last German work, *The Silverlake,* was presented in Magdeburg in 1932. Gangs of Nazis hooted and jeered during every performance. Weill's ridicule of middle-class values and his Jewish birth were offensive to the Nazis and he fled to France in 1933 with the Gestapo at his heels. In 1935 he emigrated to the U-nited States where he composed folk operas on American subjects. He died in New York on April 3, 1950.

Signature of Kurt Weill

Kurt Weill

FRANZ WERFEL (1890-1945). Austrian author. Born in Prague on September 10, 1890, Werfer attended the University of Prague. He married the widow of the noted composer, Gustav Mahler. In 1933 his novel, *The Forty*

Signature of Franz Werfel

Days of Musa Dagh, won him instant, international fame. After the Nazi occupation of Austria, Werfel fled to France. When France fell in 1940 he emigrated to the United States. He died in Beverly Hills, California, on August 26, 1945.

Franz Werfel

Handwritten manuscript poem in Roman script signed by Franz Werfel

STEFAN ZWEIG (1881-1942). Austrian biographer and novelist. Born in Vienna on November 28, 1881, Zweig came from a well-to-do Jewish family. An ardent pacifist, Zweig won global fame for his penetrating biographies of Erasmus; Mary, Queen of Scots; Balzac; and other great figures of history. In 1934 he escaped from the Nazi regime and went to London. In 1941, with his second wife, he emigrated to Brazil. They died in a suicide pact near Rio de Janiero on February 22, 1942.

Signature of Stefan Zweig

Nach welchem Namen ist America America benannt?
Diese Frage beantwortet schon jedes Schulkind stramm und unbe-
denklich: nach Amerigo Vespucci. Aber die zweite Frage werden selbst
die Erwachsenen schon zögernder und unsicherer finden, die Frage:
warum würde eigentlich dieser Weltteil gerade auf Amerigo Vespuccis Vornamen getauft? Weil Vespucci America entdeckte? Er hat es niemals
entdeckt? Oder vielleicht weil er als erster statt bloss der vor-
gelegenen Inseln das eigentliche Festland betreten? Und deshalb
nicht, denn nicht Vespucci hat als erster jede Continent betreten
sondern Columbus und Sebastian Cabot. Also dann vielleicht weil
er brieflich behauptet hat, als erster hier gelandet zu sein.
Vespucci hat nie diesen Rechtstitel bei irgend einer Instanz angemeldet. Oder weil er als Gelehrter
und Cartograf diesen seinen Namen vorgeschlagen? Auch
dies hat er niemals getan und wahrscheinlich zeit seines Lebens nie
von dieser Namensgebung erfahren. Aber warum, wenn er nicht
von all dem geleistet, warum fiel gerade ihm die Ehre zu,
seinen Namen für alle Zeiten zu verewigen? Warum heisst dann
America nicht Columbia sondern America?

Wie dies kam, ist eine kraue Geschichte voll von Zufällen
Irrtümern und Missverständnissen, eine richtige Komödie der
Irrungen, diese Geschichte eines Namens, dem auf Grund einer
Reise die er nie gemacht hat und die gemacht zu haben er selbst
nie behauptet hat, die ungeheure Kühne zugeteilt, seinen Vornamen
zum Namen des vierten Weltteils unserer Erde zu
erheben. Seit vier Jahrhunderten wird Amerigo Vespucci be-

Page of the original, handwritten manuscript of Stefan Zweig's Amerigo Vespucci, 1941

ACKNOWLEDGEMENTS

I am grateful to all the friends who have aided me and I wish particularly to thank LTC John R. Angolia and his publisher, Roger James Bender, for permission to use photographs and biographical data from their outstanding reference works, *For Fuehrer and Fatherland: Military Awards of the Third Reich* and *For Fuehrer and Fatherland: Political & Civil Awards of the Third Reich;* Mr. Richard Wolfe from the National Archives and Records Service, Washington, D.C., for many examples of the handwriting of Nazi personalities of the Third Reich; The Leopold Stocker Verlag, Graz, Styria Province, Austria, for the use of several very early examples of Hitler's handwriting; and George Petersen and A. Mollo, contributors of important documents to the excellent books of John R. Angolia.

My thanks are also due to the following for their great cooperation and assistance in obtaining autographs and signed photographs: Cosmopress, II, Chemin Falleti CH, 1208 Geneva, Switzerland. (Anne Frank material); Defense Audiovisual Agency, Dava Still Photo Depository Activity, Washington, D.C.; The Chief of Military History, Department of the Army, Washington, D.C.; Fran Elisabeth Kinder, Federal Archives, Koblenz, E. Rhine Province, Prussia, Germany; Christie Hannahs Collection for use of an Axmann document. My thanks also go to the following for permission to reproduce art works: The Staedtische Galerie in Lenbachhaus, Munich, for "The Wild Chase" by Franz von Stuck; *Philadelphia Museum of Art* for Grosz's *Self-portrait for Charlie Chaplin; Collection Crous, Krefeld for Dix's Frau Lange;* Collection Dr. H. M. Rolans, London, for Ermsts' *Bride of the Winds;* The Phillips Collection, Washington, for Kokoschka's *Portrait of Mms. Franzos;* The Detroit Institute of Arts for Pechstein's *Under the Trees;* Kunstmuseum, Basel, for Klee's *Villa R.;* Galerie Maeght, Paris, for Kandinsky's *Landscape with Tower.* My thanks also to the Hoover Institution Archives, Stanford, California, for permission to reproduce a note signed by Hitler's adjutant, Fritz Wiedemann, 1935, a note signed by Philipp, Prince of Hessen, 1935, and a document signed by Gauleiter Albert Forster, 1939.

My gratitude is due also to Andrew Southard for his many helpful comments and suggestions after going over the manuscript with great care and for important fresh information on the Gauleiters and other municipal leaders of Nazi Germany; Peter Stahl of Norden, California, who made a number of admirable suggestions during our telephone conversations; Ronald von Klaussen of New York, New York, who generously offered material from his splendid collection, including a remarkable document of Otto Skorzeny; to my old friend, Shea Tenenbaum of Long Island City, New York, for his help in obtaining a rare autograph of Anne Frank. My thanks also go to Frank D. Gish of

Englewood, Colorado, for his enthusiastic cooperation in supplying biographical data relating to Hitler's career as an artist and copies of several works of art by Hitler from Mr. Gish's own archive. Special thanks to James Camner of Plainsboro, New Jersey; Herman Darvick of Rockville Centre, New York; and George Del Collo. Thanks are due also to the Rendells of Newton, Massachusetts, Paul C. Richards of Templeton, Massachusetts, and the firm of J. A. Stargardt of Marburg, West Germany, for the use of facsimiles from their world-famous catalogs.

Particularly I am indebted to my friend, Dr. David S. Light of Miami Beach, Florida, who provided me with a photograph of a letter of Ilse Koch; K. Robert Wilhelm, Jackson Heights, New York, for his generous loan of the last page of an important handwritten document of Julius Streicher; my old friend, Robert F. Batchelder, the distinguished autograph expert of Ambler, Pennsylvania, for his loan of Nazi autographs, including a page from a rare handwritten letter of Hermann Goering; and Randall Sutherland of Pittsfield, Illinois, who lent me for reproduction a scarce letter of Hanna Reitsch. I am further greatly in debt to Jerry Granat Manuscripts, Hewlett, New York, for their generous cooperation in permitting my use of an Albert Speer holograph letter; David Staton of Delray Beach, and Hugh Trueman of Canada for their helpful assistance and permission to use a handwritten postcard of Geli Raubal; Edward A. Schaefer, Arlington, Virginia, a World War II researcher and consultant for his helpful aid; John H. Zollner of Riverdale, New York, for the loan of a rare Sepp Dietrich document, and my friend, R. C. "Duke" Schneider of Longboat Key, Florida, who offered many valuable suggestions and provided important and rare material. I am further obliged to my long-time friend, Keith Wilson of Independence, Missouri, who gave lavishly of his time and effort to make this a better, more useful book; Terence J. Dodson of Houston, Texas, for a rare, early handwritten letter of Adolf Hitler from his personal collection; Frank D. Thayer, Jr., of Silver City, New Mexico, for the use of rare autographs; C.E. Snyder of Bowie, Maryland, for permission to use rare photographs of Hitler, and my friend, the late Larry D. Lewis of Springfield, Massachusetts, for providing forgeries of Hitler letters as well as useful information about their source. I owe a large debt of gratitude to Ben E. Swearingen of Lewisville, Texas, who not only gave permission to reproduce rare letters from his personal collection but worked tirelessly to assist me; John Pechy of Los Angeles, California, for the loan of a Winifred Wagner letter; Neale Lanigan, Jr., my good friend and autograph expert of Fairview Village, Pennsylvania, for his assistance in obtaining a photograph of a letter of Ilse Koch; Dr. B.C. West of Elizabeth City, North Carolina, an old friend and one of the leading philographers in the South, who aided me frequently and who magnanimously placed at my disposal a large collection of signed photographs of Nazi leaders; Annie Utch, my friend and neighbor of New York City and Westhamptom Beach, for her invaluable assistance in translating hard-to-decipher Nazi letters and documents.

My thanks are due to Ian Sayer of Hounslow, Middlesex, England, for his magnanimity in placing his great collection of Third Reich letters and documents at my disposal. I am grateful for the pains he took in supplying me with excellent photographs of some of the remarkable items in his famous collection; Michael Levin of Tel Aviv, Israel, for going through much trouble to furnish me with useful facsimiles from his private collection and Israeli archives. My special gratitude is due to Marie Bernard of New York City, the world-famous graphologist, who provided some magnificent analyses of Nazi handwriting and thus added an additional and important dimension to this work; and to Thomas W. Pooler of Grass Valley, California, who generously supplied me with several fascinating documents from his splendid collection of Heinrich Himmler.

Richard Calow merits special mention because he placed at my disposal not only the important books in his library, but his superlatively fine collection of signed photographs and letters of aces and U-boat commanders of the Third Reich, probably the finest in the world. He went far out of his way to assist me. The chapters in the second volume of *Leaders of the Third Reich* that cover the fighting pilots and naval leaders are in a large measure due to his enthusiastic cooperation and generosity.

A World War II special agent with the U.S. Army's Counter Intelligence Corps and a noted expert on the Third Reich, Stephen W. Bumball, of Rahway, New Jersey, was ceaseless in his efforts to assist in my writing and research. He offered me constant encouragement during the most difficult times of creativity and organization. He patiently read the manuscript as portions of it were completed and corrected historical slips and spelling errors, as well as mistakes in translation. Frequently he translated difficult passages for me and thus eased my work. His comments and gentle criticism were of enormous value. In addition, Stephen Bumball supplied many dozens of important photographs and documents from his own magnificient collection of the Third Reich. His help truly added power and dimension to this book. Without his aid you would now be holding a slimmer and less interesting and accurate volume.

My publisher, Roger James Bender of San Jose, California, certainly established a historic record of help from publisher to author. Right from the beginning he worked on this book with the skill and zeal of a co-author. He spared no energy in searching out rare photographs and autographs. He contacted collectors and institutions in an effort to add to the completeness and interest of this work. His suggestions in organization of chapters and arrangement of the many noted personalities according to their historic significance and position greatly improved my original concept. If all authors had publishers like Roger Bender the chronicles of publishing would be far richer in great historic and literary works.

I am especially grateful to my executive assistant, Dianne Barbaro, for her secretarial adroitness and the use of her remarkable memory in recalling names, places, and events that frequently escaped me.

Above all, I am grateful to my wife, Diane, who constantly offered constructive suggestions and ideas which vastly improved this book and smoothed out some of the cobblestones in my prose.

PUBLISHER'S ACKNOWLEDGEMENTS

In the quest for additional historical documentation, signatures, and photographs, I wish to personally acknowledge the tremendous, unselfish work of Jeff Hanson of Elmwood, Massachusetts. At my request he gave me three full months of his precious time to scour through his vast archives of period Third Reich material to fill in those long-forgotten "gems" of knowledge which made our presentation of the personalities covered more detailed and interesting. Braving the U.S. mail, he sent a wealth of books, photos, and signatures to make the coverage more complete than believed possible. And to my old friend, Andy Southard of Salinas, California, I owe so much for his untiring efforts to find photos and signatures in his impressive library and historically-significant "Brueckner" collection, which you will find referenced throughout this work. And true to form, my friends and co-workers spared no effort to comply with my wishes for additional items when it was within their power to do so. I thank them one and all.

Individuals:

John R. Angolia
Chris Bruner
Don Frailey
Christie Hannahs
Bernard Harris, Jr.
Ken Lazier
Richard Mundhenk
Ole Hall Olsen
George Petersen
Tom Pooler

Richard Schulze-Kossens
Carlton Schwab
David Sims
Otto Spronk
Joe Stone
Hugh Page Taylor
Peter Theodore
Barny Tomberlin
Ed Voelker
Raymond Ward

Institutions:

Belgium Army Museum
Berlin Document Center
Hoover Institution
National Archives
U.S. Army Audio/Visual Dept.

SPECIAL THANKS

Although listed above as a contributor, I find it necessary to give special recognition to Ole Hall Olsen who, in the last weeks of this project, presented me with hundreds of up-dated facts and dates which make this work even more valuable. He was able to amass this information by persistently contacting numerous official agencies across Europe and making it available to me.

INDEX

Herzog, Otto, biography of, 282; letter signed by, 282; photograph of, 282

Hess, Rudolf, 9, 158, 217, 277, 294, 335, 393, 411; biography of, 111; handwriting of, positively identifies him as prisoner at Spandau, 115; photographs of, 41, 111, 113, 114, 244, with Hitler, 161; presents Hitler with a letter of Frederick the Great, 70; signatures and handwriting of, 112-114

Hewel, Walther, photograph of, with Hitler, 130

Heydrich, Lina, 123

Heydrich, Reinhard, 123, 241, 318, 405

Hierl, Konstantin, biography of, 227; letter signed by, 338, signed photograph of, 288

Hildebrandt, Friedrich, biography of, 382-383; letterhead and signature of, 382; photograph of, 382

Hilgenfeldt, Erich, biography of, 284; document signed by, 285; photograph of, 284

Himmler, Gudrun, 123

Himmler, Heinrich, 43, 48, 102, 138, 145, 157, 161, 222, 224, 236, 237, 250, 257, 262, 263, 294, 304, 310, 349, 363, 364, 365, 376; arrest report of (May 1945), 122; biography of, 115-116; Hitler's opinion of, 168; identity cards of, 115, 116; photographs of, 116, 119, 257, 363, in death, 122, with Hitler, 169; SS dagger award signed by, 118; signatures and handwriting of, 117-121; witnesses execution of Jews, 115

Himmler, Margarete Boden "Marga," (wife of Heinrich), biography of, 123; identification record of, with photograph and signature, 123; photograph of, 123

Hindenburg, Field Marshal Paul von, 32, 308, 310, 330; appoints Hitler chancellor, 9; biography of, 286; photograph of, 286; signatures of, 33, 286

Hindemith, Paul, biography of, 433; photograph of, 433; variant signatures of, 433

Hitler, Adolf, admires portrait of Frederick the Great, 70; analysis of his signature, 40-41, of his script, by Marie Bernard, 13; anti-Semitic decrees of, 416; appointed chancellor, 9; appraisal of his life, 5; assassination attempt on, 170, his premonition of, 174; authentic handwriting compared with diary forgeries, 59-60; awards and appointments of, 32-39; biography of, 8-10; body of, burned by Guensche, 148; bookplates of, 54, 208; career of, in World War I, 9; comparison of, with Attila, 9, with Demosthenes and Patrick Henry, 8, with Genghis Khan, 9, with Nero, 9-10; correspondence of, with "Maria," 210-213; declines offer to escape from bunker,

132-133; description of him by Mussolini, 8, by Albert Speer, 8, by George S. Viereck, 8; deterioration of his handwriting, 22-23; development of his handwriting, 10-31; diaries of, forged by Kujau, 57-60; dictates final will, 154; documents signed by, 33-34, 36-39, 147, 171; facsimile signatures of, 43-48, 50; final request of, 26; flamboyance of his award documents, 32; flogged by his father, 79; forgeries of, 51-60, diaries by Kujau, 57-60, inscriptions in Mein Kampf, 55, philatelic postcard signed, 53, signature on sketch of tank, 54; handwritten letters by, 14-19, handwritten notes by, for speeches, 12-13; his decline and fall traced through his signature, 40-41; influences on his mental development, 61-91, by Bismarck, 62, by Houston S. Chamberlain, 64, by Karl von Clausewitz, 65, by Charles Darwin, 66, by Dietrich Eckhart, 68, by Fichte, 69, by Stefan George, 73, by Frederick the Great, 70, by Hegel, 73-74, by Karl May, 69, by Nietzsche, 83, by Schopenhauer, 85, by Franz von Stuck, 87-88; inscriptions by, in Mein Kampf, 18, 27, 55; last page of his first will, signed (1938), 21; love affair with "Maria," 210-213; membership card in German Workers' Party, 220; models his appearance after von Stuck's "Wild Huntsman," 87-88; opinions of himself, 181, of Himmler, 168, of Ludwig III, 78, of Geli Raubal, 196, of Wagner, 89; personal habits of, described by Krause, 157-158; photographs of, 15, 27, 29, 30, 36, 41, 56, 57, 93, 101, 135, 142, 148, 153, 157, 159, 161, 167, 169, 170, 180, 181, 184, 192, 196, 205, 207, 226, 244, 259, 266, 275, 276, 308, 319, 334, 341, 346, after bombing attempt on his life, 137, by F. Bauer, 10-11, at his father's grave, 77, contemplating a bust of Nietzsche, 85, with Eva Braun, 186, with forged signatures, 53, 56, with his staff, 130, with Gauleiters, 336-337, with Mussolini, 80, 177, with Nazi leaders, 270; photographs signed by, 7, 173; political testament of, 21; portrait of, as a Wagnerian hero, 91; predicts a bloody war in Europe, 134; quoted on burning of Reichstag, 257; quotes Frederick the Great, 70; rarity of his early letters, 12; signatures of, 184, 259, after bombing attack on him, 23-26, 31, altered by Trevor-Roper on Hitler's political testament, 48-49, compared with his father's, 75, development of, 27-31, on marriage contract, 24-25, on last will and testament, 26; supported by Ludendorff, 9; women in his life, 187-213

Hitler, Alois (father of Adolf), biography of, 74-75; flogs his son Adolf, 75, 79;

inscriptions by Hitler in, 18, 27, 55; quoted, 219

Meissner, Otto, 43; biography of, 315; document signed with facsimile signature, 316; facsimile signature of, 315; photographs of, 165, 317; signed photograph of, 317

Meissner, Frau Otto, 100

Messerschmitt, Willy, biography of, 317; handwritten note signed by, 317; signed photograph of, 318

Metropolis (movie), compared with *Triumph of the Will*, 435-436

Meyer, Dr. Alfred, biography of, 390; document signed by, 390; photograph of, 390

Mitford, Jessica, 193

Mitford, Unity, 312; attempted suicide of, 194; biography of, 192-194; handwritten letter by, 193-194; her opinion of Hitler, 193; photograph of, with Hitler, 192

Model, Field Marshal Walther, 171

Morales, Dr. Constantin, meets von Braun, 252

Morrell, Dr. Theodor, 138, 192, 281; biography of, 162; letter signed by, 163; photograph of, 162, with Hitler, 130; shoots drugs into Hitler, 162

Moses, 68

Mosler, Sir Oswald, photograph of, with Hitler, 192

Mozart, Wolfgang A., 448

Mueller, Renate, biography of, 195; signed photograph of, 195

Munich Illustrated Press, 437

Munich pact, 416-417

"Murder in Hitler Germany" (Feuchtwanger), 428

The Murder of Rudolf Hess, 115

Murdoch, Rupert, publishes forged diaries of Hitler's, 57

Murr, Wilhelm, biography of, 390; photograph of, 391; signature of, 390

Mussolini, Benito, 83, 106, 307; analysis of his signature, 42; decline and fall of, traced through his signatures, 42; handwritten letter to Clara Petacci, 82; his opinion of Hitler, 8; imitated by Hitler; 80; photograph of, 41, with Hitler, 80, 177; rescued by Skorzeny, 345; signature of, 81; signed photograph of, 81

Mutschmann, Martin, biography of, 391; letterhead and signature of, 391; photograph of, 391

Myth of the Twentieth Century (Rosenberg), 235

Napoleon I, 65

National Socialist Students' Bund, 396

Nazi Teachers' League, 396

Negrelli, Leo, 104

Nehru, J., 198

Nero, compared with Hitler, 9-10

Neues Theater (Berlin), 444

Neurath, Baron Konstantin von, biography of, 318; photographs of, with Hitler, 226, 319; signature of, 319; signed photograph of, 319

New Jersey forger, 51

News of the Day (cabaret), 433

Nietzsche, Friedrich, 72, 77; bust of, contemplated by Hitler, 85; handwriting of, 85; handwriting of, when insane, 85; influence of, on Hitler, 83; philosophy of, 83; photograph of, 83, with his mother, 84; signatures of, 83, 84

Night of the Broken Glass, 258, 268

Night of the Long Knifes. See Blood Purge

Nuremberg (when scene of the war crimes trials), 94, 103, 111, 114, 124, 127, 138, 231, 236, 237, 249, 273, 296, 314, 318, 327, 331, 334, 342, 343, 350; autographs of war criminals forged, 51

Oberlindober, Hans, signed photograph of, 319

Oesterreichische Beobachter (Austrian Observer), 373

Ohnesorge, Wilhelm, biography of, 320; letter signed by, 320; photograph of, 320

"Old Fighters," photograph of, 214-215

Olympic Games (1936), 111, 201

On War (Clausewitz), 65

Order of the German Eagle, 50

Origin of Species (Darwin), 66

Papen, Franz von, 342; biography of, 321; handwritten letter signed by, 322; photograph of, 321; signature of, 321

Papen-Manstein, Heinrich von (pseudonym), peddles Hitler fakes, 52

Payne, Robert, 48-49

The Peasantry as a Life Source of the Nordic Race (Darré), 217

Peis, caricatures made by him at Nuremberg: of Goering, 108, of Alfred Rosenberg, 235, of Baldur von Schirach, 335, of Julius Streicher, 243

The People's Court, 273

Petacci, Clara, letter of Mussolini to, 82; photograph of, 82

Pfeiffer, Hans, biography of, 164; photograph of, 165; signature of, 164

Philipp (prince of Hessen), biography of, 283-285; letter signed by, 283; photograph of, 284

Pia, Sister, biography of, 203; handwritten letter signed by, 204; signed photograph of, 203

The Picture Post, 437

Strosstrupp Hitler (forefunner of SS), 168, 172, 178

Stuck, Franz von, influence of, on Hitler, 87-88; signature of, 87; wierd art of, illustrated and described, 87-88

Stuckart, Dr. Wilhelm, biography of, 349-350; photographs of, 350, 355; signature of, 350

Stuertz, Emil, biography of, 402; photograph of, 402; signature of, 402

Stuka dive-bomber, 291

Stumpfegger, Dr. Ludwig, 138

Sudeten Deutsche Partei, 280-281

Sutton, Arthur, forgeries of Hitler's signature by, 52, 54

Swastika, first German use of, 72

Swearingen, Ben, 155, 204

Tannhauser (Wagner), title page of, 91

Telschow, Otto, biography of, 402; photograph of, 402; signature of, 402

Terboven, Josef, biography of, 403-405; letters signed by, 403, 404; photographs of, 403, with Quisling, 404; suicide of, 405

Third Reich, popular interest in, 5

Thomsen, Hans, biography of, 350-351; handwritten note signed by, 350; photograph of, 351

The Threepenny Opera (Brecht and Weil), 421, 449

Thus Spake Zarathustra (Nietzsche), 83; handwritten page of, 84

Thyssen, Fritz, biography of, 351-352; handwritten letters signed by, 352, 353; opposes Hitler's anti-Semitism, 351-352

Tietjen, Heinz, photograph of, 320

Todt, Maj. Gen. Fritz, biography of, 353; photograph of, with Hitler, 259; signature of, 353; signed photograph of, 353

Toland, John, 204

Toller, Ernst, biography of, 446-447, photograph of, 447; signature of, 447

Tovarich (movie), 418

Transfigured Night (Schoenberg), 446

Treitschke, Heinrich von, 65

Trevor-Roper, H., alters a historic document, 48-49

The Triumph of the Will (Nazi propaganda film), 85, 201; compared with *Metropolis,* 436

Troost, Gerdy, biography of, 204-205; photograph of, with Hitler, 205; signature of, 205

Troost, Paul Ludwig, 204

Tschammer und Osten, von, photograph of, 320

Twain, Mark, opinion of the German language, 51

Uiberreither, Dr. Siegfried, biography of, 405-406; letterhead and signature of, 405;

photographs of, 405, 406

Veidt, Conrad, biography of, 447; photograph of, 448; signature of, 447

Versailles, Treaty of, 9, 19

Victor Emmanuel III (king of Italy), photograph of, 41

Vienna Academy of Arts, 8

Viereck, George Sylvester, 258, 361; description of Hitler by, 8

Virginia House of Burgesses, 8

Voelkischer Beobachter, 235

Volksturm (People's Army), 333

Voyage of the Beagle (Darwin), 66

V-2 rockets, 252

Wacherie, Professor, photograph of, 205

Waechtler, Fritz, biography of, 407; signature of, 407; photograph of, 407

Wagner, Adolf, 375; biography of, 407-409; photograph of, 408; signature of, 408

Wagner, Josef, biography of, 408-409; photograph of, 409; signature of, 409

Wagner, Richard, 83, 87, 205, 446; anti-Semitism of, 63; handwritten letter signed by, 90; handwritten music signed by, 90; Hitler's opinion of, quoted, 89; influence of, on Hitler, 89, 91; photograph of, 91; portrait of, 89; title page of *Tannhauser,* 91

Wagner, Robert, biography of, 410; document signed by, 410; photograph of, 410

Wagner, Siegfried, 205

Wagner, Walter (performed Hitler's marriage ceremony), 24

Wagner, Winifred, 89; admiration for Hitler, 206; biography of, 205-206; handwritten note signed by, 206; letter signed by, 207; photographs of, with Goebbels, 206, with Hitler, 207

Wahl, Karl, biography of, 410-411; photograph of, 411; signature of, 411

Waite, Robert G. L., 87

Waldorf-Astoria Hotel, 52

Walter, Bruno, biography of, 448; photograph of, 448; signature of, 448

Weber, Christian, biography of, 178; signed photograph of, 178

Weber, Dr. Friedrich, biography of, 185; photographs of, 184, 185, with Hitler, 161; signature of, 184

Weber, Frau Friedrich, photograph of, 184; signature of, 184

Wegener, Paul, biography of, 411; photograph of, 412; signature of, 411

Weill, Kurt, biography of, 449; photograph of, 449; signature of, 449

Weinrich, Karl, biography of, 412; signed photograph of, 413

Weiszacker, Ernst, biography of, 354; letter signed by, 354; photographs of, 354, 355

A GLANCE AT OTHER LEADING PERSONALITIES OF THE THIRD REICH

An upcoming companion volume to this book contains chapters on:
*Hitler as an Artist
*Cultural Leaders of the Third Reich
*The "Degenerate" Artists
*Those Held Accountable
*The Master Spies
*Cohorts and Allies of the Third Reich
*Men Against Hitler
*The Field Marshals & Grand Admirals
*Military Leaders and Heroes of the Reich

The companion volume matches this book in size, length, and format. In it are numerous biographies, all illustrated with portraits and autographs, plus a complete index for easy reference.

On the following pages are sample pages as they will appear in their appropriate chapters.

BERNHARD RUST (1883-1945). Reich minister for science, education and culture. Born on a farm in Hannover on September 30, 1883, Rust attended several universities where he studied philosophy, language, and art history. After college he taught school in Hannover. He served four years in World War I and was awarded the Iron Cross (First and Second Classes) and the Hohenzollern Order. After the war, Rust joined the Nazi party. He was elected Gauleiter from his district and in 1930 was a Nazi delegate to the Reichstag. In 1933 Hitler appointed him Prussian minister of culture and the following year he was named Reich minister for science, education, and culture. Rust elatedly reported that he had "liquidated the school as an institution of intellectual acrobatics." He continued to Nazify the schools and the textbooks and to misdirect the cultural course of Germany until his suicide in May 1945.

**Signature of
Bernhard Rust**

Bernhard Rust (center) in discussion with Dino Alfieri, Italian Ambassador to Germany, and Giuseppi Bottai, Italian Minister of Education (September 25, 1941).

GEORGE GROSZ (1893-1959). German artist; "degenerate." Born Georg Ehrenfried in Berlin on July 26, 1893, Grosz studied in Dresden and quickly developed a satiric style with which he scourged stuffy members of the establishment. Favorite butts of his acid paintings and drawings were the church, rich industrialists, and military bigwigs. His *Ecce Homo,* in which Christ was depicted wearing a gas mask and army boots, scandalized the devout. Grosz was tried for blasphemy. He won great fame for his vivid realism. By 1932 Grosz was alarmed at the rising tide of Nazism and emigrated to the U-nited States where he became a naturalized citizen. He died in Berlin on July 7, 1959.

Because of his savage attacks on goose-stepping Prussian Junkers, Grosz was a special target of Hitler's ire. Two hundred of his artistic creations were in the 1936 exhibition of degenerate art. They subsequently vanished, as did most of Grosz's earlier work in Germany, no doubt destroyed by the Nazis.

Self-portrait of George Grosz. Even in his own self-portraits, of which he painted and drew a great many, Grosz exhibited the scathing style that characterizes all his work.

Self-portrait for Charles Chaplin by George Grosz

Signature of George Grosz

469

DR. JOSEF MENGELE. Chief doctor at Auschwitz extermination camp. Born in Guenzburg, Bavaria, on March 16, 1911, Mengele was the son of a machinery manufacturer. As a young man he elected to study philosophy. However, while a student at Munich he encountered the Aryan racism of Alfred Rosenberg. Fascinated by what he believed to be a universal truth--that the Aryan race could and would develop a superman--Mengele turned to medicine so that he could test the theories of Rosenberg. After an exciting meeting with Hitler, he was determined to prove that humans could be bred exactly like animals, with full pedigrees. Mengele took his medical degree at the University of Frankfurt am Main. Soon afterward he got a job as research expert at Himmler's newly founded Institute of Hereditary Biology and Race Research. Mengele's specialty was twins and hereditary pedigrees. He was rabidly inspired by the hope of creating a race of handsome, blond, blue-eyed, brilliant, and physically powerful Nordic supermen. To this end he was soon to sacrifice every particle of morality and decency. He was to become a human monster.

In 1939 Mengele joined the Waffen-SS as a second lieutenant. He served as a medical officer in France and Russia. In 1943 he at last got the chance he was waiting for. He was appointed chief doctor at Auschwitz extermination camp with an unlimited supply of human guinea pigs at his disposal. He at once began a study of racial deformities. All prisoners who were in any way malformed were immediately butchered upon their arrival at Auschwitz so that Mengele and his assistants could examine the bodies in a special dissection ward. No twins escaped his scalpel. He even sewed twins together to create artificial Siamese twins.

Mengele personally made the selection of prisoners who were to be "spared" for hard labor and those who were to go to the gas chambers. According to eye-witnesses he would stand, thumb in pistol-belt, selecting the victims for execution. With a wave of his hand he would send a "squad" of Jews to the right (work force) or to the left (gas chambers). No pleas or outcries moved him. He was icily indifferent to women and children who threw themselves at his feet begging for mercy. They were beaten and kicked and sent off by the truckload to be slaughtered. Once, when an entire cell block of 750 Jewish women became lice-ridden, Mengele solved the problem by dispatching them all to the gas chambers.

When the war ended in May 1945, Mengele was in a British internment hospital. He contrived to escape. With a forged passport in the name of "Gregorio Gregori," he fled to Rome and thence to Buenos Aires. He has allegedly been spotted in Brazil, Argentina, and Paraguay. It is said that Paraguay made Mengele a citizen in the late 1950s. The Haifa Documentation Center has offered a reward of $50,000 for his capture. He remains at large, however; and, since the confirmation of Martin Bormann's death (May 1945), Mengele holds the unenviable distinction of being the world's most-wanted war criminal.

Josef Mengele. Signature of Josef Mengele

ELYESA BAZNA. Nazi spy in Turkey, known as "Cicero." An Albanian, Bazna started life as a juvenile delinquent, then worked as a fireman, locksmith, chauffeur, and finally as a valet. Fired by a German official who caught him reading his mail, Bazna eventually got a post as valet to the British ambassador in Turkey, an envoy with the preposterous name of Sir Hughe Knatchbull-Hugessen. Bazna had spent his life in taking advantage of every opportunity that came his way. A small man in his early forties, he had no intention of turning spy, but when the ambassador left the keys to his black dispatch box on his bedside table while taking a bath, Bazna could not resist the opportunity. He quickly made a wax impression of the keys.

A friend made the keys for Bazna. With access to the ambassador's black box and safe, the valet embarked on the greatest espionage feat of World War II--the mass photographing of top-secret British documents. He bought a camera with a 100-watt light bulb and a mount with four rods. Then he established a contact with the Nazi embassy in Turkey. The Nazis gave him the code name of "Cicero" and supplied him with film. For the first group of photos the Nazis cheerfully paid Cicero's price of 20,000 pounds. They laid out this sum cheerfully because they paid it in counterfeit money that had been run off in the Sachsenhausen concentration camp.

Elyesa Bazna (Cicero), the master spy.

After the first deal, Bazna hid the money under the carpet in his room, spreading it out so that it wouldn't make lumps. As he took more photos, he added more counterfeit bills to his store.

In Germany the documents photographed by Cicero were extremely useful. Hitler examined them personally. From July 1943 until March 1944 Cicero continued to supply the Nazis with vital information.

By early 1944 the British realized there was a leak in their security. They installed an alarm system in the embassy. Bazna had to remove a fuse in order to get to the ambassador's safe. Finally he suspected that he was being tailed. Cicero smashed his Leica and its mounting and threw the pieces into a river. He put his money into a bank vault and retired from the espionage business.

HAJ AMIN EL-HUSSEINI (1894-1974). Arab leader; Grand Mufti of Jerusalem. In 1920, when the British established a protectorate in Jerusalem, the Arabs rioted against the increasing influx of Jews into Palestine. Haj Amin, then only 26, was arrested for inciting to violence. Already a violent enemy of the Jews, Amin was tried and sentenced to five years' imprisonment. He escaped. A year later the British High Commissioner Sir Herbert Samuel granted him a full pardon. When Amin's half-brother, the Mufti of Jerusalem, died, Samuel appointed Amin, only 27, to succeed him. Amin appeared to be an innocuous and pliant youth, but he immediately took the title "Grand Mufti" and began a program of insurrection against the British. He incited his Moslem followers to massacre the Jews. The British tried to appease the Arabs but eventually they were forced to issue an order for the Grand Mufti's arrest. He escaped to Syria disguised as a beggar. He then established cordial relations with Mussolini and Hitler. In 1941 he met with Mussolini and offered to lead another anti-Semitic revolt in Palestine if the Fascists would subsidize him. From Italy he went to Germany and conferred with Hitler. Meanwhile, the British had posted a reward of 25,000 pounds for his capture.

A shadowy figure, always shy of publicity, the Grand Mufti was a staunch ally of the Nazis. He eventually established a headquarters in Lebanon as a focal point from which he directed terrorist operations against the Jews. Occasionally he turned up in Syria or Egypt. Although the Grand Mufti died on July 4, 1974 in Beirut, the P.L.O. continues to carry on his self-appointed task of harassing and killing Jews.

الهَيْئَةُ العَرَبِيَّةُ العُلْيَا
لِفِلَسْطِين

Arabic letterhead of the Grand Mufti: "Arab Higher Committee for Palestine"

Signed photograph of the Grand Mufti of Jerusalem

CLAUS VON STAUFFENBERG (1907-1944). Born into a family of distinguished military leaders, Claus was superbly endowed with a powerful physique and a brilliant mind. He toyed with a career in music or architecture, but finally entered the army in 1926 as a cavalry cadet. His engaging manners and adroit mind brought him rapid promotions, and in 1939 he became a staff officer in Hoepner's 6th Panzer Division. By 1940 Stauffenberg was fed up with Nazi brutality and Jewish persecution and joined an on-going conspiracy to kill Hitler.

On April 7, 1943, Stauffenberg's car drove into a mine field and the colonel was badly injured and temporarily blinded, losing his right hand, left eye, and two fingers of his left hand. It was during his convalescence that he came to the conclusion that he was Germany's man of destiny. Unlike most conspirators, he had personal access to the Fuehrer, who looked upon him as a dynamic and promising young officer.

After practicing with his three remaining fingers and a pair of tongs how to arm a time bomb, Stauffenberg was ready to be the chief instrument of a group of conspirators headed tacitly by Rommel and actively by Beck.

On July 11 and July 15, 1944, Stauffenberg passed up a chance to leave a fused briefcase in Hitler's presence because Himmler and Goering were not present, and he hoped to get all three with one bomb. On July 19, Stauffenberg was summoned by Hitler to attend a meeting of the OKW (High Command of the Armed Forces) at Rastenburg; and to this meeting, held on July 20, 1944, Stauffenberg carried a time bomb in a briefcase. As Hitler and his officers were studying a map, Stauffenberg placed the briefcase next to Hitler's leg and slipped out of the bomb shelter. A tremendous blast followed, and Stauffenberg, unaware that an officer had moved the briefcase to get a clearer view of the map, was convinced that the Fuehrer was dead.

Although in a state of shock, Hitler was only slightly injured. He dispelled the rumors of his death by an address to the German people over the air. In the confusion that followed, the plot was uncovered and many of the conspirators were arrested. Stauffenberg, with General Beck and a few others, was seized and shot on the evening of July 20. His last words were: "Long live our sacred Germany!"

Signature of Claus von Stauffenberg

Claus von Stauffenberg

Signature of von Stauffenberg after being wounded

473

Panzerarmee Afrika
Der Oberbefehlshaber

Afrika, den 6.5.1942

Lieber Moll!

Herzlichen Dank für Ihre Glückwünsche zur Beförderung und Auszeichnung. Ich habe mich sehr über Ihr Schreib gefreut und wünsche Ihnen auf Ihrem neuen Weg alles Gute.

Langsam kommt die Zeit heran, in der sich die Kräfte auch hier wohl wieder messen werden. Wir hoffen dabei einen weiteren Beitrag zum Endsieg zu leisten.

Ihre hochverehrte Frau Mutter und Ihre Schwester bitte ich zu grüssen.

Heil dem Führer!

Ihr

Authentic letter signed by Rommel, Africa, May 6, 1942. Signed in pencil, possibly because ink evaporated quickly in the fierce tropical sun. "We must soon test our strength again. We hope to do our share in the final victory."

(Dienstsiegel)

(Dienstgrad und Dienststellung)

Generalmajor und Divisonskommandeur

Award of the Iron Cross (First Class), signed with a forged or secretarial signature of Rommel. Notice how labored the fake signature is, with every letter of the name formed incorrectly. There are other similar forged presentations of the Iron Cross (First or Second Class) on the market, all bearing the fabricated signatures of celebrated Nazi soldiers.

HANS-JOACHIM MARSEILLE (1919-1942). Captain in the Luftwaffe. Born in Berlin-Charlottenburg on December 13, 1919, Marseille enlisted when only 18 in the Luftwaffe. Early in 1940, flying a Messerschmitt-109, he downed his first British Spitfire. Within a few months he had added another six British aircraft to his kills. Marseille was shot down four times during his first year as a pilot.

In April 1941 Marseille was transferred to the First Group, Fighter Wing 27, in North Africa. His aerial success continued. On June 3, 1942 he destroyed six enemy aircraft in only eleven minutes. By now Marseille was celebrated in the Luftwaffe for his prowess and courage. During three missions on September 1, 1942 he shot down 17 planes. He was awarded the Knight's Cross with Swords and Diamonds on September 2, 1942, one of only 27 heroes to receive the medal during the war. Only 28 days later, while returning from a mission, Marseille was forced to bail out of his aircraft when it developed engine trouble. The "Eagle of the Sky," who had 158 victories to his credit and was only 22 years old, struck the aircraft's tail as he jumped and was killed instantly. Marseille's "Diamonds" was never officially presented to him by the Fuehrer, who usually made such awards personally, but it is today on display in the Luftwaffe Museum at Uetersen, Germany.

Hans-Joachim Marseille

Handwritten note signed by Hans-Joachim Marseille

state visit to Germany in September 1937.
As you turn the pages of this deep-grained
leatherette-covered book, the minute-by-
minute accounting of this event makes you
an eyewitness to history.

144 pages
175 photographs   **$14.95**

BELT BUCKLES & BROCADES OF THE THIRD REICH
by LTC (Ret.) J. R. Angolia

This book presents in-depth text relating to
buckle identification, condition for wear,
belts and definitive information on
manufacturing and markings. Misconcep-
tions and gun-show myths are laid to rest as
you, the collector, absorb the text and pore
over the 460 detailed photos showing
buckle obverses and reverses, and the
ratities in this field being worn.

192 pages
460 photos/illustrations   **$15.95**

FOREIGN LEGIONS OF THE THIRD REICH
by D. Littlejohn

VOLUME I: This series is devoted to the
history, uniforms, flags, and insignia of the
foreign volunteers in Germany's military
and para-military forces during W.W. II. Its
coverage is expanded to the collaborating
political parties of occupied Europe as well.
This remarkable and comprehensive first
volume deals with Norway, Denmark, and
France.

200 pages
523 photos & illustrations
    (171 in full color)
Deluxe Binding   **$17.95**

VOLUME II: This highly detailed and heavily illustrated second volume com-
prehensively covers the history, uniforms, flags, and insignia of the
collaborationist political parties of occupied Belgium and Holland, as well as
the volunteer military units from Great Britain, Italy, Luxembourg, and Spain.

288 pages
806 photos & illustrations
    (41 in full color)
Deluxe Binding   **$17.95**

ROMMEL: A NARRATIVE & PIC-TORIAL HISTORY
by R. Law & C. Luther

The authors of this book have set the
greatest importance on describing the
events, as historically accurate as possible,
connected with Field Marshal Rommel and
his campaigns. To illustrate this un-
paralleled documentary on Germany's
most famous soldier, photographs were
gathered from archives and private collec-
tions around the world. Most significant are

the personal photos actually taken with Rommel's camera and never before published.

368 pages
283 photos & illustrations
Deluxe Binding   **$17.95**

ON THE FIELD OF HONOR: A HISTORY OF THE KNIGHT'S CROSS BEARERS
by LTC(Ret.) J. R. Angolia

VOLUME I: deals with the recipients of the Oakleaves with Swords and above. As an added bonus, a detailed history of the Iron Cross is included from its inception in 1813 to present. This was deemed necessary since the Iron Cross was the embodiment of the act of valor, has a close relationship with the Knight's Cross decoration, and was the very symbol of the German nation.

288 pages
249 photos
Deluxe Binding   **$17.95**

VOLUME II: covers the first 441 holders of the Oakleaves to the Knight's Cross with detailed text and 400 photographs. This work offers you everything you could ever want to know about the Oakleaves recipients, based on available documentation and personal interviews.

368 pages, 400 photos, Deluxe Binding   **$17.95**

AMERICA'S FIRST EAGLES
by Lt. Lucien H. Thayer

This official history of the U.S. Air Service (1917-1918) has been hidden from public view for 65 years. Written by the Air Service historian, this definitive document chronicles, in colorful detail, the units, personnel, and aircraft that fought in the skies of Western Europe.

360 pages
230 photos/illustrations
Deluxe Binding   **$19.95**

MILITARY PILOT AND AIRCREW BADGES OF THE WORLD, Vol. 1
by Don Chalif

Over 25 years of research has gone into this history and evolution of international air forces and their badges from 1870-Present. This first volume covers, with descriptive text and photos, the European countries of: Albania, Austria, Belgium, Bulgaria, Croatia, Czechoslovakia, Denmark, Estonia, Finland, France, Germany, East Germany, Great Britain, Greece, and Hungary.

224 pages
559 photos/illustrations
Large 8½" x 11" format
Deluxe Binding   **$24.95**

CLOTH INSIGNIA OF THE SS
by LTC (Ret.) J. R. Angolia

This in-depth reference illustrates, under one cover, the cloth insignia of all SS branches. Combined with descriptive text on the major units and their sub-units, over 1200 photos/illustrations have been carefully entwined to show the numerous varieties of SS cloth insignia, plus period photos of them being worn. This major undertaking is virtually the only book you will ever need for a complete coverage of cloth insignia of the SS.

480 pages
1200 photos & illustrations
Deluxe Binding $24.95

Cloth Insignia of the SS
by
LTC (Ret.) JOHN R. ANGOLIA
Assisted by
SEAN COOK

P.W. Wegener, St. 85 (Mecklbg.)

Ernst Behrendt, Sturmf. 10, Bad...

Hermann Pakirat, Sturmf. 2, ...

Herm. Bender, Staf 87, ...

H. Pawlewski, Sturmf. 139, Danzig

H. Weber, Sturmf. 22, Nor D. Danzig

Fritz Hansel, Sturmf. 13, Berlin

Georg Polaczek, Sturmf. 6, Oels i/Schles.

Kurt Schönwitz, Sturmbannf. Cottbus.

Hans Döring, Scharführer ... 91, Dortmund

Erwin Hörmann, Nf. 72, ...

Hans Schauchinn, Ludwig, Hubert, 48, Berlin Steglitz

Arnold Lenzen, Scharführer St. 16, Aachen

Wilh. Lauschner, Sturmf. 12, Stettin

... Pauza, Sturmf. 7, Liegnitz Schlesien

Heinrich Hümmstein, Sturmbann V/83, Kassel

Konrad Meslener, Sturmf. 73, ...

Wilhelm Krüger, Trupp. 26/I./3, Groß-Berlin

Wilhelm Büschoß, St. 18, V, Schlesien, Hans G...

Reinhold Morren, Nf. 93, W. Elberfeld

Rudolf ..., Sturmf. 5, Linz, Österreich

... Peter, Sturmführer 74, Österreich